T0198729

Other Books
By
Loralee Dubeau

There's a Whole in the Sky

The Honey Pit: Finding the Grandmother's Way

LANGUAGE OF THE SACRED

LORALEE DUBEAU

BALBOA.PRESS

A DIVISION OF HAY HOUSE

Balboa Press books may be ordered through booksellers or by contacting:

Balboa Press
A Division of Hay House
1663 Liberty Drive
Bloomington, IN 47403
www.balboapress.com
844-682-1282

Because of the dynamic nature of the Internet, any web addresses or links contained in this book may have changed since publication and may no longer be valid. The views expressed in this work are solely those of the author and do not necessarily reflect the views of the publisher, and the publisher hereby disclaims any responsibility for them.

The author of this book does not dispense medical advice or prescribe the use of any technique as a form of treatment for physical, emotional, or medical problems without the advice of a physician, either directly or indirectly. The intent of the author is only to offer information of a general nature to help you in your quest for emotional and spiritual well-being. In the event you use any of the information in this book for yourself, which is your constitutional right, the author and the publisher assume no responsibility for your actions.

Any people depicted in stock imagery provided by Getty Images are models, and such images are being used for illustrative purposes only. Certain stock imagery © Getty Images.

Print information available on the last page.

ISBN: 979-8-7652-3945-2 (sc)
ISBN: 979-8-7652-3944-5 (e)

Library of Congress Control Number: 2023904990

Balboa Press rev. date: 03/20/2023

CONTENTS

Part 2: Trust and Truth

DEDICATION

For Mom and Dad

ACKNOWLEDGEMENTS

To Spirit, whose insight and direction has supported my life and the human I continue to become.

To my husband Paul Samuels, whose love and support has never wavered and who reminds me I am loved every day. Thank you for the front cover photograph. I love you.

To my parents Raymond and Theresa Dubeau, whose love for each other and family have instilled the values and foundation to become a good human being.

To my editor Samantha Plourd, whose expertise during the editing process was a valuable resource.

To the elders living and deceased, spirit ancestors and animal helpers for aiding in my growth and healing.

To my boy Shy and his company during the many hours of writing and editing of this book.

To all family, friends, relatives and relations who have shared this incredible journey I call my life.

To Balboa Press, thanks to the cover design and publishing team.

TERMS USED IN THIS BOOK

It is helpful to have a list of terms I use frequently throughout the book. They are spelled several ways by different people. Since the Lakota language was oral, many interpretations may be found in books. I have done my best in the way I was taught. I have given a brief description for the reader, but its meaning is more than I can describe in a few words. Each Lakota elder explained it a little different. I have also written an English pronunciation as best as I can to make it easier for the reader. It is not my language; therefore it may be flawed and I do not have any entitlement to it. I am using the terms as I was taught and therefore humbly use them in respect to the elders, to honor them and their sacrifices to keep these ceremonies alive.

For easier reading, I will use shorter versions or English words when I refer to them. The *chanunpa* refers to the *Chanunpa Wakan*. The *sun dance* refers to the *Wiwanyag Wacipi*. The *vision quest* refers to the *Hanbleceya*. The *purification lodge* or *lodge* refers to the *Inipi*. English words do not fully encompass the exact meaning of the ceremonies, but may give enough of a visual for the reader to understand.

Chanunpa Wakan - Chun noon pa Wah kun - A ceremony of smoking and praying. Sacred instrument used to smoke and pray, made of two pieces with one being of wood. A sacred moving energy.

Cante Juha - Chun tay Yuh hah - The container of the heart. A leather or animal fur pelt bag to hold the Chanunpa Wakan.

Inipi - Ee nee pee - A ceremony to pray, purify, cleanse and sweat in a lodge built with saplings. Brings back the sacred breath of life to live again.

Inyan - Een yahn - The sacred stones used in Inipi ceremony.

Ishna Ta Awi Ca Lowan - Ish na Tah Ah wee Cha Lo wan - A girl's coming of age ceremony which is done after her first menses.

Hanbleceya - Hahn blay chay yah - To cry and pray for a vision, a vision quest ceremony, a sacred rite of passage.

Mni - Mi nee - The sacred water used in ceremonies.

Mitakuye Oyasin - Mee talk oo yay Oy yaw sin - All my relations are interconnected.

Pilamayelo - Pee la ma yay low - Thank you and gratitude.

Wakinyan - Wa kin yahn - The mysterious bird of power that creates thunder and lightning - thunder beings.

Wiwanyag Wacipi - Wee wahn yahg Wah chee pee - A ceremony to pray, dance, fast from food and water, while staring at the sun, known as the sun dance.

PREFACE

I published my second book, *The Honey Pit: Finding the Grandmother's Way* in 2015. A month before it went to press, I was exhausted from writing and editing. I was ready to promote the book, and get back to lecturing, teaching classes, spiritual consulting, and my ongoing ceremonial life. While praying with the chanunpa, the words, "Language of the Sacred" revealed itself to me, and I knew it was going to be the title of my next book.

The Chanunpa Wakan or chanunpa, is an instrument with which one centers themselves, prays and then lights and smokes it. A special mix of tobacco and herbs is made especially for this purpose, however, none of the ingredients are hallucinogenic. The ceremony may be done alone or in a group setting.

A week after the book's release, my beloved cat companion of nineteen years passed. He was my baby boy and a source of unconditional love. As I held him for the last time, I sang a sacred song given to me on one of my several Hanbleceyas to help with crossing into the spirit world. A Hanbleceya is a ceremony in which one fasts from food and water for up to four days and cries for a vision. For this particular vision, I was sequestered all alone outside in nature on a high hill.

This song speaks of rest and going to sleep. I sang songs to him every day of his life as I rocked him on my lap.

I believe the crossing song gave him comfort. Upon taking his last breath I promised I would find him when I crossed and I was grateful for his companionship. His passing allowed me to review my life and grieve, not only for him but for parts of my life I had thought I had resolved. Every layer of healing goes deeper as wounds are identified. All my life I have been aware of a calling. I have worked hard to learn who I am and, many times, who I am not. Doing so has given me many healings, experiences, and knowledge for helping others, especially through the ceremonies I have been trained in and given permission to conduct. But more importantly, the Great Spirit, or *Spirit* as I refer to it as, has guided me.

I began the second writing of this book my third, in 2017 after the Wiwanyag Wacipi (sun dance) ceremony I was called in vision to attend.

I started this book and stopped three times over the years, thinking I understood the title and what Spirit wanted from me. Each time I wrote for a couple of months and then stopped. Each time I knew it was not right. I did not know I had more experiences to go through before I would understand what was being asked of me.

Before my vision from Spirit, I had no intention of writing another book. I could never have realized what this book would entail. I wrote now knowing it would be a memoire, non-fiction, instead of hiding my experiences in a lead fictional character. It is my personal story seen through my eyes and understandings.

Although the other two books I have written, *There's a*

Whole in the Sky and *The Honey Pit: Finding the Grandmother's Way,* had many of my personal experiences, I was allowed to play with timelines and add creativity to the story for better flow, interest, appeal, and teachings I wanted to share. It also allowed me to write about experiences in my life that were hard to share and relive, under the disguise of fiction.

This book is written with honesty based on my recalled memories, journaled experiences and possibly flawed understandings as a human being.

For privacy purposes I am not using the real names of people still living or dead for it is impossible to get all the permissions needed for the book to be published. Also, because the book is about *my* experiences, my perceptions, and my journey.

It is now 2022, seven years after my second book was published. As I begin the fourth round of the book, I have deleted all I had previously written. I am beginning again. I understand now what Spirit has asked of me and what the title *Language of the Sacred* means.

Why this title? Why this subject? I hope you will understand its purpose by the end of the book.

To begin understanding the purpose of the book, it is first important to understand the title itself. What is *sacred*? How does one define it in their life? Is it divine? Is it inspiration? Is it religious? Is it holy? Is it considered blessed or sanctified? The Merriam-Webster dictionary defines the word *sacred* as "set apart for service or worship, devoted exclusively to one service or use and worthy of reverence."

Next, define the word *language*. Is it a system of words? Or perhaps it is "the system of symbols and signs that communicate information" as the Merriam-Webster dictionary suggests? Is language merely communication in the form of verbal expression? Or is it a means to be understood deeply within the mind and heart?

I follow the guidance I am given. It is what I have done most of my life. At times, it has caused me great difficulty in my relationships, sometimes disappointing people whom I loved. Each time I followed the guidance, I would take a step closer to fulfilling my soul's calling. When I followed my spiritual path of growth, I often walked alone.

Spirit has prodded me to share my personal journey and experiences. I adapted at a very young age. I thought to get along in this world I needed to hide myself, my gifts, my experiences, insights and understandings of the energetic worlds. Over the last thirty years and with some resistance, I opened my heart and shared my self-knowledge and experience of the spirit world and cosmos to only a few close friends, spiritual communities, clients and people taking my classes. My two novels reveal many of those experiences, leaving the reader to decide what is true and what is not.

This book is written as my truth. The journaled experiences, visions, insights, and understandings are filtered through my perception and teachings from Spirit (Great Spirit/God/ Source) and elders of many backgrounds and culture. Not every person will experience the event the same way as I have.

It is a compilation of my experiences I willingly share. I might be ridiculed but I know it's true. You have the right to believe my experiences or not. I have no power over your belief. It is for only you to decide. These are my experiences over periods of my life. I am not special, better or lesser than anyone else. But I am now vulnerable enough to share them. I share this with all people regardless of age, gender, race, ethnicity, culture, religion, or belief, and I speak for no one but myself.

Although my life has been and continues to be surrounded and enlightened by nature and the world of spirits, I have come to understand that sharing ideas and thoughts, even if they are not agreed upon by others, is needed. It has allowed me to expand, empower, and embrace my true self. By taking the mask off, I am allowing everyone to see me, vulnerable and yet authentic.

My hope for you, as the reader, is to share my story and reveal my humanness. Maybe it will guide you to reflect on your own personal understanding of the *Language of the Sacred* and where it will lead you.

Part One
Hiding and Seeking

CHAPTER 1

Background

I was raised Catholic and was taught *not* to be seen or heard and not to draw attention to myself, especially because I was a girl. I became afraid of my body and felt unsafe with the unwanted attention it could bring to me as a young pubescent. By the time I was in high school, it proved to be true. I was sexually assaulted, grabbed in my breasts, pinched on my behind and fondled sexually under my dress without my permission. The world was not safe for my body and I had proof from my experiences. I told no one since I was trained not to use my voice.

At the age of eight, after having nightly dreams of friendly Indians and rituals which I did not understand, I was told by my maternal grandmother and great grandmother that my great grandfather was of a distant Blackfoot heritage and was a healer of blood, water and fire, a secret that was kept hidden in our family for many years for concern of discrimination and fear. He was taught by his mother how to heal. Although no paper proof of his heritage could be found.

Then when I was a preteen, my father was having excessive hair loss, and it was then I discovered of my paternal

1

grandmother's ability to heal through prayer. From what I was told by my parents she was able to petition her prayers to heal hair loss, blood and fire. Through her prayers I believe my father's hair loss subsided. As far as I know she did not pass this teaching on to anyone in the family. I saw her praying many times, but she spoke those prayers only in French. Both sides of my lineage has had a deep connection to a prayerful way and connection to Spirit.

When I embarked on my first vision quest ceremony at nineteen on the west coast, the native elder and medicine man confirmed in the Inipi (purification) ceremony, indeed I had ancestors of the red nation.

An Inipi ceremony is a cleansing and purification for the mind and body.

It is done inside a darkened dome shaped lodge where stones are heated in a fire and placed inside the lodge while sacred water (mni) is placed upon them to create steam. Through the steam, prayers, and songs, the purification takes place. When one leaves the lodge, one is thought to be renewed and reborn.

As a child, prayer, or talking to what I was taught was God, was my safe place. It was my peace and comfort. The first prayer my mother taught me was, "Now I Lay Me Down to Sleep" which I can still remember vividly from the age of four. But at night when I was alone, I preferred my way of talking to God. I would talk in my own voice in my head praying for good things, and people I had in my life and thanking God for all of it. When I prayed, I prayed in pictures. I would see the faces of my family and the objects I was grateful for in my head. It was very emotional. I did not speak out loud because when it was time to go to bed, I had to be quiet for fear of a spanking or scolding from my parents. It was not that I did not pray out loud before bedtime, but it seemed I had a lot more prayers than I had time allotted to me to go to sleep.

When I entered first grade in a Catholic school, I sensed people's feeling but I did not have words for it at the time. I remember I was in the schoolyard, and a boy in my class was being bullied by several other boys in my first-grade class. As I observed I could feel his fear and anxiety. My body began to shake and tremble. It was if I wanted to run away and hide myself from what he was feeling. As my body trembled, I became nauseous. The fear turned to anger. I had to do something to relieve my pain and his. I ran over to the boys and pushed them all out of the way and stood in front of the boy being bullied. I rose my fists and in a quivering voice said, "Leave him alone or you'll get some of this," as I raised both fists towards them. I was not a violent child, nor had I ever been in a fist fight. The sensations I was feeling were so great that I went into fight or flight mode. Later that bullied boy became a good friend of mine for twenty years until he moved out of state and we lost touch.

As I grew older, I understood what I felt was energy and vibration. It was overwhelming to my nervous system but eventually I adapted.

I followed the rituals of Catholicism: the mass, rosary, penance, communion, confirmation, and memorized prayers and attended novenas with duty and reverence. But I questioned a lot of things the priest and nuns in the church did or changed. Not that I was disagreeing but I wanted to better understand. Most questions I asked were answered with, "Because I said so and you don't question the church." This answer left me with more questions. I looked forward to night time when I could go to bed and pray my way.

I developed my own prayer system, or so I thought. It was not to heal anyone or anything but to become closer to God. I would breathe in and out slowly to relax until I became somewhat sleepy in the stillness. It was then I could feel and hear my heartbeat. Then I would begin my prayer. My head's voice would ask for help for people I thought may be in need and then I would envision their faces and visualize what I had asked for. I could feel the love radiating from my heart to the picture of the person, which was an emotional connection. I would often end up tearful holding so much love and gratitude in my heart.

I would end my prayer time with a thank you for my family and all I had in my life, like food, water, shoes, clothes, a place to live and a place to sleep. Sometimes it would take me just as long for the thank you as it did for the asking.

But one night when I was eight, something changed. When I relaxed and breathed and opened my heart to pray in my pictured thoughts, I felt myself drifting. It was as if I was lifted out of my body and brought to the location of where this person was. I was seeing this person in real time. He was sitting at a table on some type of farm or pasture, in a place I had never been before.

I had been told by my mother earlier in the day that this man had died, so my prayer was that God would take care of him and help his family, but what I had seen was that he was okay. He was alive and well. Feeling a sense of relief, I thanked God for the comfort, and as I did, I felt myself being pulled back to my bed in my darkened room. My eyes were open the whole time, so I knew it was not a dream. It felt real. But what did it mean? Was he in heaven with God and everything was fine? Did heaven look like a big farm and pasture? I finished my prayers and went to sleep puzzled.

The vision became a little clearer the next day as I learned the man was not dead. It was a rumor from tabloids, so what I had seen was true. He was alive and on his land in the country where he lived with his family.

The man I prayed for that night was Paul McCartney. I was a big Beatles fan since I was a toddler, and Paul, of course, was my favorite singer. Even as young as I was, I wanted to give comfort, peace, and blessings to everyone, even a celebrity. It was who I was inside. Feeling everyone's pain, anger, and sadness would help me to become a compassionate caring person in the future.

I still work with prayer that way today. But I have added a few more steps to create deeper meaning and connection for me.

I made it through eight years of Catholic school and two more years of training to complete the sacrament of Confirmation, which is a renewal of your baptismal vows that were made for you by your godparents. They spoke for you when you were too young to speak to accept the Catholic faith. I received the sacrament with a group, but to be truthful, I never recited the words myself. It no longer resonated in my heart. I had seen too much beating, punishment, and acceptance of sexual exploitation I did not understand and it felt wrong.

Unknown to me, I guess I was searching for a better

understanding of people, religion and myself. In high school, I met an older girl who followed Buddhism and another girl whom practiced Hinduism. Being curious, I picked their brains with questions. I learned yoga poses, their religious practices and the names of their deities. At the time, I was not searching for the best or the right path. I was trying to understand the world.

I wanted to learn about other cultures, beliefs, and customs, and how they were similar to the one I was taught. I can't really say why, I just wanted to understand the world and humankind. It was a calling, a bridging of some sort as I reflect now. Everything I was learning and trying, I kept to myself.

At the age of sixteen, my curiosity led me to a local pow wow (Native American social gathering and dance) sponsored by the Nipmuc tribe. I went with a friend after our summer job on a Saturday afternoon. We both went thinking it might be fun to try different foods and see native crafts being made.

When the drum began immediately at noon and the singers began singing, I was utterly amazed. I could feel the earth rumble beneath my feet. The vibration of the earth, breathing in and expanding out with me was a real connection to my very being. I had experienced this before as a child, when I was outside whether it was in the sun, wind, thunderstorm or rain. I could feel and see the energy but I did not completely understand it. Trying to explain it to others when I was young was futile. It was frustrating/concerning/confusing that no one could understand, so I stopped sharing my experiences all together.

Here at the pow wow, the song, the drum and the prayer was stronger. It was a prayer as it made me feel the same way as talking to God. As I got older, I did not need to recite a memorized prayer, I talked in my own voice. That was a real feeling of connection. It was something mysterious, sacred and loving that vibrated to my core. What I experienced at this pow wow was a feeling of home. It felt like I had been here before and that it made sense to be here.

My friend was not as enthused as I was and wanted to leave. She found herself bored after consuming her buffalo burger and bought a beaded necklace to commemorate the experience. I wanted to stay to continue to explore this new feeling of connection, but she was my ride. As we were about to leave, a woman in her sixties noticed me bouncing to the beat of the drum and approached.

"Hello. Are you enjoying yourself?" She asked.

I nodded.

My friend answered, "We are just about to leave."

"Oh. I have something to show you," she winked and pointed to me. "Where do you live?"

"Webster," I answered.

"Don't worry I will find someone to give you a ride home."

"But I have to be home by six o'clock," I replied.

"The pow wow closes at five o'clock and then it starts again tomorrow. I will make sure you get home on time," she confirmed.

After consulting with me briefly, I told my friend that I wanted to stay, so she left and I was free to experience my first pow wow. The elder woman was of the Micmac tribe and came to the pow wow from New Hampshire. She brought me over to her booth and showed me the dreamcatchers she was making to sell. They were made of sweet grass. They were different from what I had seen in other booths that day. Other booths made them with a willow branch, which is customary for dreamcatchers. She sat there as I watched her and she prayed and sang in her language as she completed each of them.

Is this what she wanted to show me? I thought silently.

"No, this is not. Let's go over to the wooded area," she replied.

I hesitated briefly as I realized I did not ask her out loud, yet she heard what I was thinking.

"You think you're the only one that can hear thoughts?" She winked again.

"Spirit told me who you are and that you have dream medicine along with several others. But it will take time and many years to understand and come to them all. For now, I have to start you off by doing a naming ceremony. Let's begin."

She grabbed a deer skin bag filled with what I would learn later was tobacco, sage, cedar, sweet grass, a large shell and wooden matches.

"Sit here," she demanded.

I sat to her left on the grass. She sat with her knees bent to the side and I followed her lead.

She pulled a bowl and stem out of the long leather bag and smoked, or *smudged*, everything including myself with the sage.

"To cleanse and purify," she explained.

She said everything in English and then in her language as she offered tobacco to each of the seven cardinal directions. She then placed it in the connected bowl and stem. She spoke her intention of asking the spirit ancestors to give me a name to start my journey on this path that I came here for, and so they could work directly and more closely with me.

As I watched her light the bowl and smoke, she offered the smoke to each direction and blessed me with the smoke. It felt familiar as I remembered my dreams of seeing this ritual as a child. Then she offered it to me to smoke. I did not know what to do as I did not smoke. Growing up in my household, I was forbidden to smoke.

She must have sensed my hesitation and advised me that it was sacred. She showed me how to hold it, how to inhale in my mouth, not my lungs, and to how to make a prayer and blow the smoke out towards the sky.

I did as she instructed.

I felt warm inside. It felt right and for a moment I felt I was home on the earth. Everything was connected and I belonged to something bigger than my human self.

I handed it back to her and then she finished the smoke. We sat in silence for what seemed like a long time. Then she spoke.

"The spirits have named you, Little Raven Spirit Dreamer, aho."

She disconnected the bowl and stem and smudged everything again before she placed it back in the deer skin bag. She explained that the full name was never to be shared with anyone. Only a piece of it could be shared. I decided if I was ever to share it, I would use "Little Raven."

After the ceremony was completed, she stood up and said, "Let's get you home."

I tried to ask her how I could get in touch with her again but she told me there was no need. She did what Spirit asked and now that I was connected, Spirit would continue to guide me.

Throughout my life I have learned about many cultures, religions, customs and healing traditions that were put in my path. Traveling to places and meeting different people over the years has helped me acquire techniques and understandings similar to and different than my beliefs. I also received healings from many elders who have helped me move forward in life, always growing and learning. I came into this world with a curiosity for understanding how things are similar and how beliefs and understandings are different in order to get along in this world. To this day that has never changed.

I am no expert in all the teachings, traditions, healings, and experiences I have received nor do I claim to be. But the ones I use and practice, I have developed a deep understanding through the communication of ancestor spirits, and Spirit.

Today, I understand why I learned and experienced the teachings of Huna, Reiki, Hinduism, Buddhism, Limpia, Peyote, San Pedro Cactus, Andean, Toltec, Lakota, Cherokee, Navaho, Hopi, Yavapai, Blackfeet, Penobscot, Seneca, Protestant, Episcopal, Lutheran, Star ceremonies, Santeria, Pagan and many other religions and practices. All have their place and right to be practiced. Just because it may not be the one I follow, I believe if it helps people to connect to a higher power of goodness, and helps their ancestors work in their life to fulfill them, and brings no harm to anyone then that makes me happy for them. Years later I realized I needed to understand many beliefs, traditions, rituals and customs so I could relate and communicate with people, to be of service to Spirit and assist people with the communication of and to the world of the unseen.

CHAPTER 2

When the Dead Appear

At eighteen, I began to work two jobs for what would become most of my working life. I saved money to travel and to experience other ways of living and culture. I took training from reputable people and experts. I spent the beginning part of my life exploring and finding myself.

By twenty-eight, I had moved out of my parent's home to live by myself. I was responsible for only myself and my little adopted kitten. I loved it. Now I could practice meditation and yoga, burn incense, light candles, travel and take classes without the scrutinizing.

I made my little apartment my oasis of tranquility. It is where I began to take clients doing reiki, energy work, and intuitive readings. The readings became a place where people who had died would come to talk to my clients. Although not in my control, many times they would just show up to give a client a message. It became clear that this was part of how I would help others.

There have been times over the years that a dead spirit would appear before I even had a client reading booked. This is the story of one of those times.

I was alone by myself relaxing, meditating and clearing my energy centers when I heard a small cry. I opened my eyes because I thought it was my young cat caught up in some mischief. There in front of me was a vision of a baby, with the umbilical cord still attached. The difference between a spirit and a real living person is very subtle. The spirit, although looking as clear as a live body to me, has a light mist or glow around it. The energy vibration is a much faster sensation because there is no matter to contain it.

As I looked down upon this infant, it became apparent that it was not born among the living, either yet or ever. I allowed the pictures to float into my mind to get clarity. The picture I understood was that it was still in the womb, but struggling, as if its life force was being cut off. It felt stressed. I was feeling stressed too, though I could not see anything physically wrong. I felt tension around me. I made a prayer for it and asked what I could do.

I heard a faint voice in my mind, *"Tell her when you meet her."* I nodded in return.

The spirit infant was no longer present. I didn't know when, how or why but I had learned that it would give its message at some point and that I had to remember it.

Within the week, I was asked by a family member if I could do a reading for one of her friends, and I agreed.

The minute she entered my space, the infant with its umbilical cord appeared. This time its life force was weaker. As she sat down and before I began the reading, I told her that I had a message for her. I could see she was very pregnant and I had to relay the message.

"Before I begin, I need to tell you something and please

listen closely. Your baby is under a lot of stress. You need to go to the doctor. Your stress is affecting the baby. It is not good for it."

She began to cry and told me her story of how she was in conflict with her family for months and that it was getting worse.

Once again, I urged her to see a doctor. I told her that I could see the baby was under duress. The spirit infant left and then I continued. I imparted some techniques of relaxation to help her and completed her reading. I again reminded her to immediately see a doctor. At the end of the reading, she asked if the child was a boy or girl. I could not answer her. I did not see the child living through the stress. Imparting this idea would not be helpful. I kept it to myself. But advised going to a doctor to be checked right away.

To end the story, the woman did not go to see the doctor right away. A month after the reading and shortly before her due date she found out she would be delivering a stillborn baby. Could she have helped by heeding the warning and using destressing techniques I gave her? I will never know for I do not possess the power to give life or death. I only try to guide and help. She did, however, eventually have another child.

Sometimes deceased spirits have a sense of humor. What I have learned and experienced over the years is that there are many levels of communications with the dead spirits. Some communicate very well, some come through walls or doors, some show pictures and even communicate in a telepathic voice to my mind, and some explain symbolically with a feeling or sensation to my body. But the only thing I am ever sure of is they show up when *they* want. Over the years I have learned to ask them to return when the person was in my presence to deliver the message, to which they obliged after I promised I would help.

Here's an example. My husband was at work one afternoon and I was in the silence of quiet time. I heard a knock at my front door. At the time I lived on a hill over two hundred feet from the road. Who would climb the hill to get to my front porch? I went to the door and opened it. There in spirit form stood a stocky man.

Knowing he was a spirit I said, "You know you could have come in through the wall. You're a ghost. You know you are dead right?"

That's my nature, to the point. No wasting time with words. It takes too much energy for me to talk. With that, he nodded. He was holding his chest tightly. He didn't really know how to communicate. He did not use telepathy, nor did he send me pictures or sensations.

"Okay, come on in." He floated into the house. I closed the door and asked how I could help. Again, he did not respond. I could sense this was going to take time.

"What is your name?" I asked. No reply.

"You know you can spell it in your mind and then I can receive it?"

I could see him pondering.

"Can you nod your head if I ask you questions?" He nodded.

"Are you here to give a message to someone?" He nodded.

"Is it someone I know right now?" He shook his head.

"Is it a client?" He shrugged. I guess he was confused.

"Can you spell your name in your mind or think of a picture that sounds like the name?" I waited.

Then he showed me a picture of a bird's egg. It was blueish in color.

"Is it a bird or egg? Does it sound like that?" He shrugged.

What the hell, I'm playing charades with an entity not alive in this world. This will be an interesting dinner conversation with my husband I thought.

"Let's try again. Think of something else that it sounds like."

Then he thought of a particular bird, a robin. "Robin? Is your name Robin?" He shook his head.

"Rob?" I asked again. He shook his head.

"Bob, Bobby, Robby, Robert?" He nodded his head on Robert.

"Okay Robert, I am going to ask, why are clutching your chest? To me it means that you have a heartfelt message for someone very dear to you and that you died having issues with your heart. Is this correct?" He nodded.

"Now that you have found me, you know that you can find me again. I promise to help you give your message if you go now and come back when that person is in my presence. Okay?"

He nodded.

"This person you have a message for, is it your spouse?" He shook his head.

"Is it your daughter or a son?" He nodded on the word son.

"Robert? Come back when your son is with me. You can leave through the wall. You don't have to use the door." With that he was gone.

Four days later, I was leading a medicine wheel prayer circle on a friend's private property. There were a dozen regular faces and a couple of new invitees.

During the prayer circle, a gentleman entered the circle to make his prayer aloud. I was deep in prayer when I felt a familiar presence. I opened my eyes and saw Robert before me. This gentleman was his son. His son was praying to release the anger he held inside him. Through telepathy, I told Robert to wait until the circle was over. He did, but he stayed inside the circle with me the entire prayer circle.

After the circle gathering was complete, I quietly introduced myself to the man. When we were alone, I told him his father Robert had come to give him a message. I retold him of our first introduction and told him he had passed due to a heart ailment. The man just nodded and began to tear up.

"What does he have to say?" He asked.

I waited. Robert looked defeated. He began to use a form of sign language, a similar Native American version I had learned some years ago.

"He is sorry that he was not a good father. He drank too much and left your mother when you were young. He wants forgiveness."

His son softened and cried gently. "That is why I came to pray - to let go of my anger towards him."

After a few moments of tears he spoke, "I forgive you dad."

Robert smiled and left. That was the last I heard from Robert.

His son continued to come to the prayer circle for a couple of years and his anger for his father had definitely been released and he was happier.

CHAPTER 3

Right Place Right Time

The spirit world really opened up the more I prayed and sat in the silence. Living by myself gave me so much quiet time. I became more in tune with the flow of life and followed what I believed to be energy and instinct. But it was more than that. The unseen world had become open all day long. Not just with readings and energy work, but all the time. I could receive insights or inspirational hits as I called them, at any time. I could be in the middle of something or with someone and I would feel called to go somewhere or visit someone. It took me a long time to completely trust these insights. With each time I came to realize that I was sent or called by an unseen force, which I call Spirit. There are so many names for this force or being, but this is how I experience it. I believe there is no one way, custom, religion or tradition. When one comes to communicating and connecting to the power or force in a humble, calm way, all ways can come together. No one way is greater or lesser, better or worse. The methods may be different but whatever gets you centered as a human being and connected to the mysterious life force and spirit inside you, that's the way it will work for you.

The way I experience Great Spirit, Spirit or what some call God, is a flowing energy. It connects all things like a spider's web. It touches and moves within all things. It is a powerful force filled with unconditional love that lifts us from our darkest moments and challenges. I do not experience it as a spirit form of a man or elder sitting in the sky. For me it is unseen to human eyes but felt within. It lets me know I am connected and will be connected to all things forever even when I no longer have a body. It is a kind energy, not an angry or punishing one.

A lot of my challenges in my life are because of choices and decisions I made or actions I took, willingly or unwillingly, with or without awareness. Most of my challenges are due to personality flaws and wounded patterns. When I work on those and see the real truth, life becomes less difficult. Every human will experience hard times and unexpected grief. We are not punished. We need to learn and experience, sometimes by trial and error. We live life and get to choose how to live it or not live it. Sometimes choices are made for us and are not in our control, but how we respond and react will determine how our life will be.

I did not always treasure my gifts. I was afraid and often hid or ran away from them. But to be my authentic self, I have to use the unique talent that I have to be of service. That is why I am here.

Acceptance, prayer and quiet reflection a few times a day allows me to be in closer communication with Spirit and people. It brings peace and guidance to my life. I have learned to follow even the most subtle nudges. Here is one of those stories.

I was on my way home from visiting my parents, when in my mind I saw the face of a family friend who lived in the next town. I felt called to visit. I tried to talk myself out of it. I had laundry and many other chores to do when I got home. But the feeling would not go away.

The usual way home to my apartment would pass the very street this man lived on. I felt a pull in me the closer I came to the street.

I argued with myself in my head. What was I going to say when I showed up at his door? Was he even home? I couldn't show up without calling. All these excuses were rolling around in my mind. I was not paying attention and I hit the curb on the passenger side of the car. The car jumped over the curb and rolled onto the beginning of his street. Okay I thought, I will give in and visit him.

I parked outside his house and knocked on his side door several times, wondering what I was going to say. But the music coming from the inside of his house was very loud. I contemplated excuses such as needing to use the bathroom, I was in the neighborhood, or was just thinking of him, before considering the truth of my calling, that I needed to visit him. It's not like he didn't know of my gifts, because I had done a reading for him in the past.

When he opened the door, he was disheveled and crying. His eyes were swollen.

He looked surprised and called out my name. He gave me a big hug and didn't let me go. I could smell he had been drinking heavily.

"Can I come in?" I asked. He led me into the kitchen and he spoke before I could speak.

"I can't believe it. I can't believe you're here. I asked God to send me an angel to help me and it's you." He hugged me tight again.

I turned and looked down on the kitchen table and stiffened. A gun was pointing directly towards the door as if it had been waiting to be used.

Horrified, I asked, "Is that loaded? Why is it here and is it yours?"

He stammered, "It's mine, it's loaded, it's legal and I was going to kill myself. But when I heard a knock at the door, I put it down on the table."

I moved carefully to the other side of the table and asked him to unload it and put it away. He did. He locked it up. I asked if I could hold the key because I would feel safer. He agreed.

He proceeded to tell me his woes and personal reasons for wanting to leave the earth. I listened and asked him if I could use my hands to work on him with energy. I put my hands on his head and heart and sent him love. He relaxed enough and fell asleep. I threw out the rest of the liquor and dumped the empty bottles in the trash. I stayed with him until midnight then went home. I also took the key to his gun lock box with me.

The next morning, I called to check on him and he was doing better. We had a discussion about his drinking and getting rid of his gun. I asked him if he would ever try to hurt himself again.

He chuckled when he answered me.

"I asked God for an angel and he sent me one. I was saved last night. I said if there was a purpose to my life then send me an angel to stop my pain. I know now that there is a God and I am loved. You are my angel."

It was a happy ending and I was glad I was there for him. We did keep in touch for many years afterwards.

Another experience of following the inner guidance comes to mind. My husband and I were getting ready to go shopping for a few necessities. He has always been a person who takes his time and putters around; so much that he makes me late and off schedule. If you ask him, he says I leave too early and allow too much time to get to a location. I don't like to be late to an event. I think being late is disrespectful.

On this day it was just shopping, no grand event. We could have left anytime but I wanted to follow my schedule. I usually coax him to get a move on. However, on this day, he was ready and I was dragging my feet. I had this sense of doom within me. I kept feeling we needed to wait a little bit. There was no rush or hurry. I wanted to leave but sensed I was being held back for some reason. I knew enough to follow my instinct. We waited another half an hour. I wondered if someone I knew would be calling me for help.

We got in the car and drove down our country road, made a left-hand turn and crossed a small intersection. Up ahead we could see traffic backed up on the other side of the intersection. People were gathered chatting outside of their cars. A few policemen were telling cars to turn around and take another route. The road up ahead was closed. When the policeman approached our vehicle, he explained there had been a fatal accident about 30 minutes ago. They were still investigating and trying to clear the two vehicles. The life flight helicopter had just left the scene.

The doom feeling left me. I felt assured that my hesitation to leave had saved us from the accident. That could have been us. Grateful, I began silent prayers for the dead and the ones fighting to survive. In the end, my last prayer was of gratitude for our lives.

Following my instinct, inspiration or guidance, whatever one might call it, has become the way I live. It might not always make sense to those around me but I have had enough confirmations to give it credibility.

I am not suggesting that I will always be saved from harm or death. No one escapes when our time is done. But I am of the mindset to pay attention to the signs, feelings and insights that come to me through the unseen world.

CHAPTER 4

Unpredictability

After almost twenty years of traveling and walking the ceremonial path, I was given permission to mentor others needing guidance and healing. This happened after becoming a singer in the purification ceremony and becoming a chanunpa carrier/follower.

Spirit sent students to me. If they asked in a humble, correct way, I could consider the mentorship, but only if Spirit gave permission.

The guidance from Spirit comes through my prayer. I pray with the chanunpa and ask for signs of confirmation. Sometimes I ask for a specific sign, and sometimes I ask for a vision in prayer. My answer usually comes in a vision within four days.

I have learned through experience that once you agree to mentor, you take on teaching, giving guidance and providing protection. Although it seems easy, it is not. The responsibility is hard. I experience their emotional and mental states personally, and will know when my prayers and ceremony are needed to protect them.

Not every person that asks to be mentored is accepted.

These experiences are hard. I have had to turn away at least a dozen people, both men and women, because I was not the right person to help them.

The mentorship can last a short time or for several years. It depends upon what the person needs to learn, heal, and what path they choose. Some do not need to be in ceremony but need to learn methods to find their path. Others were with me anywhere between four and seven years.

I have only trained one person to conduct the ceremony of the purification lodge in all my years. It was confirmed by Spirit when I was praying with the chanunpa.

When I agree to mentor a student there must be an agreement between myself and the mentee. They always have to tell me the truth, support me when I conduct classes or ceremony, and follow the guidance that Spirit provided them to the best of their ability. The final agreement was that when the time came that they no longer wanted to be mentored, or I knew they no longer needed assistance, they would disconnect from me in the right way with a good completion in a chanunpa ceremony.

This is vital to the agreement for me. When I accept someone to mentor, I am putting my time and energy into their future. I am feeding Spirit with my prayers on their behalf for guidance and protection all the time, until they feel ready to do it on their own.

Once accepted, I will conduct a chanunpa ceremony with my new student and connect them to myself and my heart. When they leave or are completed with me to find another teacher or path, I need to conduct another ceremony with the chanunpa to disconnect them from me. I will no longer be responsible or feel their energy. It is a delicate balance, but one that must be agreed upon.

I have learned many things through the student/ teacher relationship. Every one of them, although different in personality, needs help with something I have learned, experienced, and healed within myself. One cannot be of service to others if you cannot relate and have the knowledge and experience.

Some of them tested my patience and others tested my boundaries of sleep, time, and energy. But all of them received my unconditional love and loyalty no matter what struggles they brought upon themselves or life brought to them.

I would like to share two of my experiences of being connected to a mentee/student with the chanunpa.

My husband's brother and sister-in-law were visiting us from Canada. They were staying with us for a week. My husband took them on daily excursions. On one of the days, we decided to go to the local lake to have a picnic and sit under the pine trees to read, relax, and converse in nature.

After lunch we were chatting and my mind became a blur. I could not concentrate. I had this fear in the pit of my stomach. I closed my eyes and took some deep breaths to center my mind and slow down my body's sensation. In my mind I could see the face of one of my students. I knew that she was traveling out of the country. I could feel that she feared for her life. I could hear her prayers for help.

I opened my eyes and said to my husband, "I have got to go home now."

He looked confused. I repeated, "Now," firmly and loud. His brother and wife looked at me like I was a crazy person.

We packed up quickly. As I was running to the car, I spoke over my shoulder, "I have got to get to the chanunpa now. She is in trouble."

Thank goodness we were close to home. When we returned home, I quickly retrieved the Buffalo Chanunpa and made my way on our land to where our purification lodge was built.

I sat in the sacred space and began the ceremony. The deeper I became in prayer and the more I centered myself, I could see that she was hiding inside a building in fear. By the time I completed the ceremony over an hour later, I could feel the threat had passed and her energy was calm. I wrote the day and time on a piece of paper so that I could discuss this with her when she returned home from her trip.

We shared our experiences, when she returned home. It was exactly as I had seen on that same day. She was running from a large pack of wild monkeys. They were out of control chasing people. She got inside and waited until they disbanded. She did confirm she was scared and prayed for help.

She was grateful I stopped what I was doing to help her. She also learned the student/teacher connection was real and perhaps why a proper disconnection would be important when she was no longer a student.

The second experience is similar. It provides more confirmation that time and place have no boundaries when connected to a student by the chanunpa.

A student had traveled cross country to one of the reservations. I gave her the contact information of a native woman I had met years before, and who lived on the reservation. She was someone who was trustworthy and who could get my student around safely. It is proper to get permission to enter a reservation.

My student made her connection and the native woman graciously took her into her home while she visited. I prayed for her each day. On this day as I was praying, I became nauseous and had pains in my stomach. I barely completed the ceremony before having to vomit. For the next hour what came out of me was gray bile. I vomited four times the next hour. I was weak and light headed.

I knew I had not eaten anything different the day before, nor had I eaten that day for I was called to fast through an inspiration I received from praying that morning. My husband worried that I had picked up a virus, but I hadn't gone anywhere for the last couple of days.

I went back to sit and smoke the chanunpa again to get some clarity through prayer. During the smoking I was transported to the reservation and I could see my student was at a ceremony or dance. I could see that her energy looked unstable. But what was revealed to me in vision was that she had ingested something and a man with a medicine different than my protection was trying to lure her sexually.

When I understood this, I had to figure out which of my spirit helpers or animal spirit helpers to call upon to help with the release.

A spirit helper for me has usually come to visit when I was fasting and praying on a vision quest, a purification lodge or praying with a newly gifted chanunpa. It may be a feminine or masculine spirit. Sometimes they appear as a little blue light and speak to my mind. Others times they appear as a ghostly face or body of a human or a ghostly body of an animal. If it appears as human, they will have a name but it could take months to build a relationship with them before it is revealed to me. If it is the spirit of an animal no name is needed. The relationship is built through the qualities that a living animal possesses, which has taken me many years of observance to learn. This connection takes years of time, energy and focus and permission from Spirit.

On a vision quest, if a living animal appears to you during your fast, it is important to pay close attention to their behavior for it could be an animal having a message or wanting to work with you for your healing and protect you. Most of my human spirits and animal/bird/insect helpers have come through a vision quest. I work with nine human spirits and nine animal/bird/insect helpers, and seven plant helpers that protect and assist me. I also have three star-being protectors that have been with me since I was a child. This is only my personal experience. Many people will go on a vision quest and never receive a spirit name or spirit helper/protector. It is not a usual experience for everyone. I believe it happened for me because it was offered to me to further my healing, to understand healing and to learn how to help others.

As I prayed for my student, my helper came forward and I asked it to take care of the situation. I watched as it traveled, entered the situation and pulled his connection and medicine out of her. After a few minutes I could see it was removed and that she would feel better.

I did not say which medicine or helper I used for it because it is what I have been gifted and have built a deep personal relationship with through fasting and sacrificing in ceremony. Working effectively with different medicines can take years.

Not everyone can or should try to find or work with medicine, or are gifted the permission. Maybe one day Spirit will send me someone to receive my teachings. Until then, medicine in the wrong hands could be harmful in the worst case or useless in the best case.

Let me digress here from experience. Medicine is that which brings balance and harmony. It is a knowledge and wisdom. When one is out of balance physically, mentally, emotionally and almost always spiritually, ailments, issues, problems, struggles of all kind can happen. Most people only notice when they are out of balance physically. For healing to truly take place it has to happen in the spirit first. Then the rest can follow in the body. The spirit's heaviness will be released and perhaps the body can release the issue. Medicine wisdom can be herbs that are prayed and sung over and nurtured in a particular way, or it can be animal spirit that counteracts to provide protective support. In some cases, it can be an ancestor spirit that has lived on the earth previously or one who has never had a human body. Medicine happens with intention. It can be used to hurt or help. It is dependent on the intention of the person sending and the connection and knowledge they have to the medicine, helpers and Spirit. Spirit is the healer. There is a difference between healing and curing. Every person has the ability to accept healing. Healing is a shift of energy and consciousness in a person. Not everyone is cured on a physical level. I can assist through prayer, love and my knowledge of medicine but only Spirit has the power to cure. The person who wishes to receive a healing must also take part in their own healing. Their will and surrender to receive is important to complete the process.

I have found in my experience that the ones who want to work and know medicine are not the ones who should or can do it. It has to be a calling, one that comes from the confirmation of elders who work with medicine and work with unseen spirit world, and identified only by Spirit itself. You do not choose it. It chooses you. You do not control it, or have power with it. It is not from you, but comes through you.

To explain what happened with this student, she confirmed the same exact date as my experience and that she felt a little off at this ceremony which was called a public dance. Prior to the dance she was given a small portion of snake venom to drink. The dance was a snake dance. The snake dancer was the husband of the woman she was staying with. He told her that it was okay to ingest a small amount of snake venom for the ceremony. Her energy was unstable and this coincided with my vomiting, prayer ceremony and calling my helper medicine in for her. She felt better a few hours later.

What she learned that day was not to ingest or partake in anything that she was not trained in or taught, especially being connected to me. I vomited to release the poison that she ingested, the energy connection of the man and was alerted that she needed help. This man had a sexual intention. He worked with snake medicine in a negative way to gain power over her to create a connection. It was not to kill her but charm her to gain access to her body and energy. However, he had to go through me to do it which caused me to experience the sickness much worse than she did. She confirmed to me that he didn't come around much after the dance or the rest of the time she was there and wondered why, but she soon understood after hearing my side of the story.

CHAPTER 5

Service

Not all of my experiences came through ceremony or client readings or energy work. They happened on ordinary days, vacations for example. I had become accustomed to both symbolic and intuitive messages from the unseen world. They could happen quickly and intensely. You cannot shake them or walk away from them. You are pestered until you act on them. I do not consider myself a psychic. I do not like the word. I prefer a mystic or an empath. One who works with the mystery of the unseen. Over the years, I have learned to listen to the messages and see them confirmed.

While I was on vacation alone on a cruise in the Caribbean, a planned sight-seeing day was changed in an instant. I had met another woman passenger the previous night and we both decided to take an island excursion to the beach. We planned a day of sunbathing, lunch, and shopping. She was a few years younger than I, but I was excited to spend the day with her. We left the ship to catch a van that took us to the beach.

We had barely set our towels down on the shimmering sand, when we were approached by two men from the island asking if we would like to go parasailing. In an instant, I sensed a dark energy. There was a dark cloud around them and the hair on the back of my neck was alerted as I shivered. I was not sure if it was because they had evil intentions or doom surrounding them. I did not want to engage further.

My new acquaintance however had other ideas. She was excited and wanted to go with them. I tried to deter her as I pulled her aside.

"We don't know them and I have a bad feeling about them."

A bad feeling is how I usually labeled my insights. It was hard to explain to others, especially to new people I just met that my bad feeling was a message of sorts. However, though I was nearing thirty, I had enough experience with them to know I needed to follow what many people would label as hunches.

Here I was on the beach in the Caribbean with a troubling insight. The men kept enticing her. She would not listen to me. They explained they had a boat near the shore for parasailing and we could have the first appointment at noon.

I explained, "We can't take the appointment for noon because we have already paid for our lunch reservations."

The men assured her it was safe and it would be the experience of her life. I must note that I do not go into someone's energy field without permission, but I had to quickly assess what this darkness was about. I asked her to take a short walk away from the men. She agreed and explained all the reasons why she wanted to parasail. I walked in silence taking deep breaths to center myself and see if any guidance would come - perhaps a visionary picture, a sensation, or a knowing of clarity. I did not have the time to sit alone and meditate. This would be a walking prayer.

The picture that came to mind was that the men were not skilled. They were trying to earn a living. They were not evil but the energy was doom. An accident was going to happen to them today. As I allowed the picture to expand, I also saw the person who was sailing in the sky would be hurt. This was clear enough to me. I did not go further to look for death because that is beyond the boundary of their energy field. I only wanted clarity on my feelings.

I looked at the younger woman, wondering how I could explain this to her. I did not want to scare her or reveal my eccentricity but I trusted the information.

"I know you want to go and try this new experience, but I have a bad feeling and I am not usually wrong. We are in this port for two days. If you want to come back tomorrow, I will come with you to parasail. For today let's just take in the beach and sunshine as we planned."

I just needed to stop her for this moment. This relaxing beach day was anything but relaxing. My body sensations were through the roof. My nervous system went on high alert. My stomach started to get upset and my head was filled with an intensity to act.

She pondered my words and finally agreed.

"Okay. But tomorrow?" She asked.

I nodded.

The men were on to the next group of girls. You may wonder why I did not go over to them and intervene. The sensations and visionary pictures had passed. I have learned up to that time not to intervene in another's energy field or interfere with a life's lesson unless I am requested to do so in service. The requests come from outside of me to within me, which I believe is Spirit. My connection and devotion of meditation and daily prayer throughout my day helps keep the line of communication open. I know it is outside of me and not my own mind's fear of distrust because it comes from out of the blue. The sensations are more intense and persistent. It won't let go of me until I begin to follow and act. I have learned this through trial and error over the years.

We took a walk along the shore until it was time for lunch at the hotel on the beach. The lunch would be served on the patio facing the water's edge and where the parasailing boat was docked. We both were sitting across from each other looking over one shoulder, so we both could see the shore. We ordered our lunch and drinks and heard the engine of the boat start. A small red-haired girl was connected to the apparatus and sailing harness. I found it odd that she did not have some type of water ski on her feet. How does it work when she comes down in the water? Does she just drop? I had never seen parasailing so I was at a loss for what to expect. We both watched as the boat took off quickly and two men on the beach held her sail open and she ran as fast as she could towards the water's edge. She was pulled quickly and lifted jerkily. The boat seemed to move too fast but what did I know. The boat hit a wave and bounced out of control, shooting her in the air. Then it happened. The boat skipped on top of the wave and flipped over and the girl came crashing to the water. Everyone screamed. Some men ran into the water and staff in the hotel called the ambulance.

We both looked at each other horrified. My new acquaintance looked at me, wide eyed and pale.

"That could have been me. That could have been me." She said in shock.

"But it wasn't. Let's say a prayer and keep good thoughts for all of them," I said changing her focus.

We watched in silence the commotion of the men pulling the bodies to shore. The red-haired girl was limp and both her legs looked crooked. We could not eat our lunch. In the next two hours after the medical team arrived, we heard that both the girl's legs were severely broken and that one of the men in the boat had died of blunt head trauma.

Once the chaos on the beach was over, we moved to another part to sun bathe until the excursion van came to bring us back to the ship. But we were anything but relaxed.

She was speechless for rest of the day. Her only question was, "How did you know?"

I could not answer her. I kept insisting to her it was a gut feeling. I could not go into too much detail. Most people did not understand or believe me, though I've tried to explain. I learned at a very young age not to speak of it because it made others uncomfortable.

For example, in my early twenties, I was planning to spend a night at a friend's house and I received a premonition about my brother. I was always worried about my siblings, especially when I received a premonition about them. I saw my brother getting into a car accident that night.

This time I pushed the thought away and went ahead with my plans. My friend and I went out for dinner and to a dance club near Providence for the evening. It was after midnight when I got a sudden urge to leave. I felt my brother was in an accident. I saw him hit a small tree flying through the front windshield. I also saw a passenger but I could not determine who it was. I told my friend I did not feel well and I wanted to drive back to her home in Connecticut. Thankfully she obliged, but I did not tell her why.

When we got back to her house, I wanted to call home to check on my brother. She talked me out of it for many reasons, especially because it was too late to disturb my parents and family. I did not sleep that night. I prayed all night for my brother. As soon as sunrise came, I was out the door. When I got home my brother was sleeping in his bedroom. Perhaps I was wrong. Then my mother told me that my brother was in an accident and almost totaled his car. He was lucky to be alive. She told me the story of what he told her happened. It did not match what I had seen. When my brother woke up, I privately told him what I had seen and he confirmed the information I got was true. He had not revealed all the details to my parents. After that day, I always acted on my visions for others. Though I have no control over them, I would not dismiss them anymore.

Another time, when I was on a trip to Arizona, a newly befriended woman that attended a local medicine wheel prayer circle that I led for several years, took a tour with me to the canyons and sacred sites. I had been there before in the nineties a couple of times so I knew the landscape a bit. There were half a dozen of us in the van that picked us up in Sedona. The woman leading the tour was taking us to the second mesa on the Hopi reservation to meet a Hopi woman who would be our tour guide. She had permission to enter the reservation and had a friendship with the Hopi woman. It would be a while until we got there.

We chatted with the driver who provided us with some local facts about Hopi customs. As we were driving, I kept feeling and visioning a spider. I had been learning, observing and having experiences with different tribes of native peoples since I graduated high school. A spider has symbolic meanings that may be different from nation to nation. I was paying attention. Spider to some tribes is a grandmother who creates and to others it is a trickster and one who brings chaos.

The feeling was getting stronger. I felt a creepy sensation up the back of my neck. My nervous system was on high alert. I began to perspire. It was hot but the van had air conditioning. I wanted to get out of the van quickly. None of the others seemed to be bothered.

I asked the driver when the next stop would be. She said she could stop in another fifteen minutes.

I silently closed my eyes and made a prayer to ask for clarity. I took long slow breaths, clearing and emptying my mind to allow only blackness.

I saw a black spider with a red dot on its back. It was crawling forward. I was not afraid of spiders or snakes. It was not my fear but I felt there was a danger. Then I saw the spider being crushed.

That was all. I learned as a child to have reverence for all life and not cause intentional harm to anything. It was always my mind set even before carrying the chanunpa and leading ceremony.

When the van finally stopped for a rest break, I approached the driver who said she worked with native elders and asked her if she carried spider medicine. Maybe she worked with spider energy.

"No," she replied. "I have never been given any medicine or been on a vision quest. I do not work with medicine. Why?"

"Does the Hopi woman or her clan work with the spider?" I asked looking for some confirmation.

"No, I don't believe so. She is of the butterfly clan and her husband is a snake dancer."

"Why?" She asked again.

"I am a visionary person. I am picking up on a spider with a red dot on its back. I feel it crawling around me. It is a strong sensation. Like a warning, I can't explain it better than that," I answered.

"Do you feel it now?"

"No, not now but when I was in the van."

"Well, we are only about a half hour away from the reservation. Maybe you could share this with the Hopi elder when we arrive and ask her."

"Okay." I nodded.

I was not looking forward to getting back in the van. But I did. I continued to pray all the way to our destination. The sensations were still intense but prayers for safety and clarity were my focus.

Once we arrived, the Hopi elder came out to greet us. She was not as old as I thought she would be, maybe in her forties. Before I could approach her, the group was taking their back packs out of the back of the van when someone screamed. On the top of a light colored back pack was a large spider. Someone yelled, "Black widow. Watch out."

The Hopi woman got a broom, swept it on to the ground,

said a quick prayer and crushed it under her shoe. I was speechless.

The driver said, "Oh my God, you knew. You felt it. That's a powerful vision."

The driver proceeded to tell the Hopi woman about my feelings, vision, and sensations. Now I was embarrassed. I did not want any attention.

The Hopi woman warned us to watch for snakes around the land. Her husband was a snake dancer like many of the men in the area and you had to be careful because there were always some around. I asked her why she killed the spider. I thought we lived with and respected all creatures. She looked at me tenderly and then her energy changed.

"I pray with cornmeal every morning and every night, for all the dangerous creatures to stay away from this house and respect my boundaries: spider, scorpions, and poisonous snakes, all of them. I warn them and their ancestors. I have to protect the children and my family. If they come close then they will go back to the creator. This way they can tell their relatives they cannot enter here. That spider could have killed a young child with one bite."

It was a good lesson for me to use in later years on a fire ant situation on my first support of the sun dance. I prayed for them to stay away from my tent. I placed a boundary of limestone powder and tobacco and never had one the entire week cross into my tent, while other campers had issues.

The Hopi woman took an interest in me, and at the end of the day we exchanged addresses and agreed to write. She did not have a phone. Before I left, she told me that we were sisters and I could come back anytime to visit with or without my students. She knew way before me that I would take students in the future. Within two months, I was approached by four people to become students of which I would only accept two.

I kept in touch with her for a few years, long enough to send her one of my students to her for a vison quest. This was before I had a place or permission to conduct the ceremony.

Our connection faded gradually over the years. She was a powerful visionary in her own right.

Any day and anytime can be quiet and uneventful or plans have to change quickly because I am filled with unseen messages and the urge to act. I have accepted this calling and have agreed to be of service to Spirit who will direct me to the people to assist.

I was told by Spirit long ago when I was in ceremony with the chanunpa that my service, devotion and commitment was only to Spirit, not to a teacher but Spirit only. I learned many things from all kinds of elders: initiations, songs, teachings, ceremonies and eventually permission to run ceremony, but I was never connected to teacher in the traditional way. I always offered tobacco and gifts for healings in gratitude, but I made it clear it was for gratitude, never to become a student. For Spirit has always and will always guide me through my life. I had asked why I could not become a student and have a human teacher on my third vision quest.

What was shown to me in a vision and what I heard in a voice outside of myself over my left shoulder was, "*Human teachers have egos and can misunderstand what are Spirit's words and what are their own words of guidance. Sometimes they get lost in having a little power. They forget the power comes through them, so they can give poor guidance. You have communication and a direct line. It is clear for you. I will guide you. As for people, you cannot service all people. Some humans need to make their own choices and learn lessons to grow and that is why you must ask for guidance before you try to help. You will be shown when and how if it is needed."*

I have accepted that Spirit will guide me. It comes from devoting much alone time to the silence and long hours of daily prayer. It feeds my soul and my prayers feed Spirit. At times the message is clear. At other times I need to pause to receive more clarity, sometimes for several days.

That is why I knew at a very young age I did not or would not have children. I had the responsibility to help with my younger siblings at a young age and yet never felt a maternal need or desire to have children. I received the reason why I did not desire children on my first vision quest at age nineteen.

CHAPTER 6

First Vision Quest

I met a Lakota elder in Boston at a conference and holistic fair when I was eighteen. He was going to lecture about Native American, or what he called, Indian culture. The elder spoke of the earth and our connection, and that he was writing a book with another person's help as he was not educated in writing English. His presence was humorous and he smiled a lot. He made a few jokes about life in general, and in my opinion, he seemed authentic and genuine.

I had recently purchased a car and now had the freedom and the ability to make my initial steps into the vast world. He began to tell stories of his life growing up and how they led him to where he was now in his life. He was in his fifties but the energy body that I sensed had more life force.

The lecture was supposed to last one hour and although the organizers tried to tell him that other speakers were scheduled, he continued on. His English could be understood but sometimes had to use his own language when he didn't have an English translation. He continued on for almost three hours, singing songs and speaking about the Inipi (purification lodge) ceremony and the Chanunpa Wakan (the sacred instrument used in a prayer ceremony). It was the first time I heard those words spoken in the Lakota language.

He revealed that he was being called by the spirit world and what he called Wankan Tanka, a term used for something sacred but for which there is no real word to explain it in the English language.

He spoke about why he needed to reach out and offer these experiences to non-Indians. He said that humans needed to be cleaned up and connected to the earth and all of its creatures. There needed to be a bridge of understanding. Many of his tribe were not happy with this sharing and committed violent acts against him over the years. But his connection and commitment held strong to his last breath nearly twenty-five years later. His partial description of the purification ceremony had me remembering some of my dreams as a child - being with Indian people, now called Native American and witnessing and experiencing a ritual in a darkened place.

The elder had a few people around him who took care of him, who I later learned were his warriors (protectors) and his students.

At the end of the lecture there was no time for questions or to approach him. They scurried him out and another lecturer was ushered in.

I followed the elder out of the room but he was surrounded by his warriors and a sea of people.

I went to the area where merchants were selling food. I bought a vegan sprout pita with hummus. It was a shock to my taste buds as I was raised on pasta and chicken. I also bought a couple of books that seemed interesting, but still I had the Lakota man on my mind.

There had been another lecture I was interested in, so I entered the elevator to make my way to the correct floor. Several people got on and off until I was finally alone in the elevator, with another floor to reach my destination. When the door finally opened, the Lakota man and his group entered the elevator. To my surprise, the door closed and I found myself in the elevator with him on my way to the next floor.

With courage I spoke to the man, "I enjoyed your lecture very much, thank you. I have so many questions. Perhaps we will meet again."

He nodded and smiled. He said something in his language to one of the men. The man scribbled something down and tore the tiny strip of paper off. As we all made our way out of the elevator I lagged behind. I didn't want to invade his space. They moved ahead and then the man who scribbled on the paper gave me an address and phone number.

"This is my number. Grandfather wants you to keep in touch. The spirits said that you are okay and you could be updated where he would be traveling."

I replied, "Thank you."

Over the years, I did follow him to several places on the east coast and west coast and was even allowed to experience ceremonies of vision quest, the purification lodge, the chanunpa and impromptu healings. I helped build the frames of the lodges and learned how to make his altar and the sacred foods for ceremony and anything that was needed.

In one of his purification ceremonies in New York, he announced that several of us were to do a vision quest. He gave us instructions on how to prepare, pray, and fast. He explained with the help of his students the how, why, and the importance of the ceremony.

The *why* is usually a question, "Who am I." This should be the focus he instructed for a first vision quest. If you don't know who you are, why you're here, and what to do, then how can you be of service on earth?

I prepared in secret by fasting every week and praying daily for a year before the ceremony would happen. I went to the local lake to sit in the wooded area by the shore to pray, fast, and make my prayer ties (pinches of tobacco placed and wrapped in small colors of cloth). I tied them to a string, wrapped them around a piece of cardboard so as not to tangle them and kept them safe in my car. When the time came, I did not feel comfortable explaining to my parents what I was doing because they were both not open to other religions or beliefs.

I planned a trip to Florida with a friend after the vision quest out West. We would be flying separately and I would meet her there. I did not lie about my trip but omitted the part of my first four days out West for the ceremony. I would go to vision quest for the first four days and then on to Disney World in Florida to meet her.

When I arrived out West, I would be in the first group to be placed on the high hill in the wilderness. The elder gave a few instructions while his students filled in the rest. He asked us if we were prepared to die which concerned me as I was trying to learn how to live, not die. No one knew where I was or what I was doing.

I was scared. He explained that we had to be ready to die

in this body to get an answer or vision about our question. Not everyone gets an answer or message. If you prepared well and prayed in a humble way, stayed awake and paid attention to everything that happened around you, you may get a message that he would interpret for you.

Now I was in a dilemma. I thought I was really prepared but I was scared that no one knew where I was. I gave a phone number with my parent's names and said, "If anything happens to me, call them."

That was the best I could do. I hoped -- no I prayed -- that I would make it through the ceremony.

Once we were purified in the lodge, we were each taken to a separate secluded space. I did not carry a chanunpa at the time, so I was loaned one by the Lakota man. He cleaned it in a sacred way and said he used it for those who did not carry one as of yet. It would be cleaned again when I completed the ceremony. He did not allow one to go through ceremony without one, for it was a protector and what you pray with during the time. He filled it with tobacco for me while he prayed in his language.

My space was surrounded by the colorful prayer ties that had I worked on for many hours. As I was left alone for the next twenty-four hours or what would really be thirty-four hours, I experienced an overwhelming strangling fear. Fear whipped up into so much anxiety that I almost lost my breath. My mind raced. Out in an open space, under the heat of the sun and what would be the darkness of night. I was given a can and a stick to make noise if I needed to scare a bear or mountain lion away.

Who did I think I was? What was I thinking? Wait isn't

that the question I was supposed to be asking? Who am I? Since it was my first ceremony, I would only be in ceremony for one day and night. Others will do two, three or four. Some medicine men and leaders have done much longer vision quests, I was told.

I stood with the chanunpa in both hands and prayed to each of the directions over and over asking my question and expressing gratitude for my life. I had learned a few purification lodge songs and sung them over and over as well. When sunset came, four ravens came to visit and flew to the ground outside my altar. They walked around in front of me. They each made sounds at different times. It was not a cawing sound like what was familiar. I sang a gratitude song back. This went on for few minutes and then they flew off.

At night I could hear howling noises. Not sure if it was coyote or a wolf or perhaps something else. My face and arms were sunburned. I began to get a chill on and off through the night. I heard whispers in the night from the West. I stood and prayed aloud again. The whispers got louder until a voice became clear.

"You are called by your ancestors to follow in their footsteps. You have gifts to access if you want them. You will learn for many years but Spirit is your only teacher. Your raven helpers of the earth world came today. Listen to them. You will sacrifice much if you commit to these ways but you will be guided. Just follow."

I was shown a vison in my mind of myself conducting ceremonies - ones that I believed I had no business doing or wanting. I rejected the vision and put it far away from me.

I heard different separate voices with each sentence. Or at least that is what I understood. It seemed to be coming from

outside of myself and the altar. A group of spirits I could not see.
Then a shift of cool air came and gave me a chill. I could see I
would be walking this path alone for some time and having no
children. The vision did not make me sad, for I felt alone in
my life every day except when I prayed and sat in silence. That
is when I truly felt alive, connected to things I could see, sense
the unseen and feel things that many others I knew could not
understand. Then the voices faded.

Perhaps that is why I was drawn to the Lakota man. He
could see and knew much more than I could or understand.
I prayed for him in that moment on the hill for his health,
happiness, and my gratitude.

The rest of the evening was the same - standing, praying
and singing. Sit, listen, and observe. Then repeat. Sunrise
came and went. The sun was now high above me again. I
could feel the sweat pouring down my neck and the salt of
it burning me where the sun rays had scorched me the day
before. I wondered if I had been forgotten. Then I realized
maybe they had taken another quester down before me so I
continued to pray. I was not feeling hungry at all but the thirst
had begun. I prayed for all beings that were suffering from
hunger and thirst. Their pain was my pain. My suffering
seemed small after those prayers.

A short while later, one of the warriors came for me. He
cut my prayers ties to my altar and led me down the hill in
silence. I was ushered into the darkened lodge and the Lakota
man began the closing of the ceremony to clean me up and
release me from vision and ceremony. I was asked to tell in
detail everything that I noticed or all that happened. This is
what he called, *talking out*. It was the way Spirit could talk

to him and explain the symbolism of anything that was said or happened.

I relayed the part of the four ravens and the different voices they used and the whispered spirit voices I heard and what they said. He sat and listened and took a moment to listen to Spirit or his helpers.

Then he replied, "The raven is your helper. When you see four of them pay attention. They protect you. Honor and greet them. The whispers are your ancestors. They are Indians from long ago calling you to learn their way. Listen to them, know them. They'll teach you to know who you are. You will sacrifice having children for your path is to serve Spirit."

I am glad to have met and traveled to be with this Lakota man. I would be in many ceremonies with him over the next twenty-three years.

Before his passing in early 2004, I had found another community closer to home in 1998 until 2000. I was able to be in ceremony with him twice before the last time in western Massachusetts in the autumn of 2002. I had learned, experienced and traveled to work with him and it was hard to believe that it had been twenty-three years since I met him. At our last meeting together, he imparted more wisdom to me. He told me that a chanunpa was coming to me and tatanka (buffalo) would bring it. Confirming the vision experience I had with him in the purification ceremony. He then proceeded to give me more chanunpa teachings. Some I had heard many times over the years and some new that felt specifically from Spirit to me through his words.

I had already been a carrier/follower of two chanunpas, gifted to me two years prior and within six months of each other. I told him about this. He said this new one was made just for me.

He laughed and continued on saying, "Spirit must have plans for you. One who follows three chanunpas is one who is called to work with medicine and spirit helpers."

Seven months later, I would be told the same thing in a purification ceremony conducted by an elder of another community I joined.

CHAPTER 7

Unfolding Vision

I had met the new elder a year before the last time I sat with the Lakota elder. He met one of my new students and they talked about me. I am not sure exactly what they discussed but he commented he would like to meet me. It took a couple of weeks of emails before he and his wife and I met for coffee. They both peppered me with questions and asked about my journey thus far. I mentioned that I had been in a couple of lodge communities over the years. They asked about my experiences in ceremony. It was difficult at first for me to speak about my experiences as I still kept them humbly hidden.

At the end of our meeting, he invited me to attend his next lodge ceremony. He had a small group of people in his community. He and his wife were genuine people and I was honored to be invited.

Although I was invited, I did not expect to actually be allowed to participate in ceremony. Usually, a new person to community helps with ceremonial chores. One would gather firewood, stones, cook for the feast or clean up after ceremony.

The day before, I called his wife to ask what to bring

for food and how to honor his protocol. Each elder, leader, medicine person has a slightly different version of the right way to run the ceremony. Although similar in nature, some have songs, altars, teachings and protocols that the community abides by. I had always been in communities with twenty-five or more participants. The lodge size and frames were large enough to hold two rows of people.

Every leader has their own direct line to their helpers and to Spirit. Ceremonies are changing and fluid energy. For example, the number of tobacco filled prayer ties and colored cloth swatches to put them in could be different. The songs sung could include personal ones the leaders obtained through a vision quest. Some leaders smoke the chanunpa at the end of the ceremony inside the lodge. Some smoke it outside and others may smoke it in the middle or beginning of ceremony. I humbly respect each leader's way or teachings. It is their intent, connection, and respect of Spirit that is most important. Also, the number of stones to heat in the fire may change from ceremony to ceremony. I have been in a sixty hand-sized stone ceremony with seven rounds for a young girl's healing and a one large boulder ceremony for a woman's lodge. I learned to follow the protocol of each leader. I learned this new leader's ceremony teachings led back to the lineage of a Lakota medicine man

His wife told me what to bring for food, what to wear for ceremony, what colors of cloth to use and the amount of prayer ties that would be made once the fire and ceremony started. I was surprised that I would be allowed to participate and was even a little nervous making sure I was humble and staying in the background as an observer. That was my way since I was a child of bringing less attention to myself. I just wanted to keep my head down and pray.

I met the community and was embraced in the ceremony for the most part, though I could feel that not everyone was comfortable with a stranger. I followed the group's lead and offered to help in any way to have the ceremony go smoothly.

As I said, this ceremony was slightly different. Only a few songs were sung but the beauty of this was that everyone in the small group got to speak their prayers.

It was a smaller space, with only one row around to hold us. The ceremony was a more intimate experience for me. The elder led us impeccably through the ceremony. His authenticity and love for his community, Spirit and his helpers were clearly present during the ceremony. After the lodge and the feast were complete, he announced the date of the next ceremony would be in two weeks. He nodded to me and I nodded in return. This was his subtle invitation to join the community. There would be ceremony twice a month.

Months later, another chanunpa was gifted to me. It came from a woman who owned a buffalo farm. I had met her in her small shop of native crafts and bison meat. She shared some of the personal issues that she was struggling with. I offered to come back with the chanunpa for her to pray with. She was helped in that ceremony and in return she gifted me a larger chanunpa.

I asked the elder in the new community if he would bless the chanunpa in the lodge to connect me to it. I gifted him tobacco. He agreed. We did the ceremony with just the two of us. He was surprised I had been in ceremony all these years and was just now gifted one.

When I replied it was not my first one, he asked me to explain.

"This is the third one that I have been gifted."

I relayed the stories of how they all were gifted to me.

"Please do not mention this to the community. If a person is allowed to carry and pray with a chanunpa, usually it is only one. Sometimes one can start off with a social one for learning but three is rarely carried. A medicine person might carry that many to serve the people in ceremony, but this is highly unusual."

Once again, the working with medicine topic was in my face.

Keeping this secret was easy for me to do. I was good at keeping secrets. I was thinking I am nobody of importance so he didn't have to worry about me revealing the secret. I was just trying to live and follow my connection with Spirit and the spirit world and wherever and to whom it might lead me. That is all I wanted. That is what felt comfortable. No explanation to others and no conflict.

It was a little over a year, when the elder approached me and told me that it was time for me to start conducting purification lodge ceremonies. He would train me and grant me the permission to conduct them for the community. It was only then I told him of my first vision quest years ago with the Lakota elder. I explained that I had seen myself conducting this ceremony but I did not share the other ceremonies I had seen in that vision.

"Good, then my spirit helper's words are confirmed."

"But who am I to conduct this ceremony? I can't follow

the vision unless I am trained and given correct permission." I argued.

"Spirit has given you permission and through my guidance and Spirit's protection, I will train you," he replied.

That was the end of my resistance. The elder spoke the words of Spirit and offered me to accept the path of conducting ceremony. It was not of my choosing or asking. It was guided. I trained alternating and conducting ceremony with him and as a participant every two weeks. Though I had been in many other Lakota ceremonies, I honored and conducted them his way.

In May before he was to leave for the summer, he called me and asked if I would come and have a lodge ceremony alone with him. He had added that his spirit guides were pestering him to do this before he left for the summer. His schedule was very full but he asked if I could meet him the following week after I got out of work. He also asked if I had any idea why the spirits might want this to happen.

The only thing I could think of is that I was gifted another bowl that matched the last of the four stems I had made. The stem is the wooden part of the chanunpa that connects to the bowl. It is where the tobacco once lit can be smoked through its opening. I made this stem before I came to his community.

In a dream, I was shown four stems and what shape of stems to make. My father had all the tools to help me create them and under his careful eye, he allowed me to use his woodworking tools. I smudged (fanned sage smoke) myself, the room, the tools and the wood before beginning. I prayed and sang sacred songs under my breath the entire time. Eventually they were completed. When I was done, I knew to whom three would be gifted. When the time presented itself, they were passed on. The fourth did not find a home right away. The fourth was called to be made in an odd shape. More of a square elongated shape, but very plain.

I was gifted this personally made bowl by my best friend who said she was called to make me a bowl but did not know why. It was the second one that she was called to make. She gifted it to me four months before I conducted my first lodge ceremony. I knew immediately that the last of the fourth stems had a home if it fit the bowl's connection, and it did.

When the elder asked me if I knew why the spirits wanted the ceremony, the new chanunpa came to my mind. It had not yet been blessed or connected to me. I relayed the story to him and he agreed for me to bring it to the ceremony. He would bless it and connect it to me.

I arrived on time and began to build the sacred fire alone. The elder came out to check on me and gave me one wooden match. He said I only had this one match to light the fire. Then he left. I was shocked. I had never only used one match to light other sacred fires, but I trusted there was a reason or purpose. I made many prayers of gratitude over the wood, the leaves, the stones (inyan) and for the reason we were called together. Then I made a prayer over the lone match to call upon the wakinyan (thunderbird nation) to light this sacred fire for Spirit's purpose. I struck the match and lit fire in the west direction. I prayed a long time watching as the fire caught in the West, then the North, then the East and eventually the South - until the smoke was rising through the center of the top hole of the specifically laid wood. The elder appeared an hour after the fire started.

"Hey, how'd you get that fire started?" He asked in surprise.

"With the match," I replied.

"You started it with only the one match and not with a long lighter?" He asked again.

"Just the match, you didn't give me a lighter. You said light it with the match," I answered confused.

"I was just kidding. How did you do that?" He looked surprised.

"I prayed really hard." I answered.

He laughed. I laughed. That day I came to realize his sense of humor. It would be the most endearing and helpful trait that helped me grow and heal in the seven years I spent in his community.

When the time came for the ceremony to begin, he called for a certain number of stones to be brought into the lodge. Since there would only be the two of us, he called for double the usual number of stones. Once inside, we were in complete darkness except for the glowing of the stones. He began his calling song for the spirits and his helpers and proceeded to pray and pour the mni (sacred water) over the hot stone pit. The steam and heat was intense. There are *four doors* or four times the flaps to the lodge door are opened to end a round of prayer. We went through two rounds before he asked for the flap to the door to be opened. Then I passed the rest of the hot stones inside to him. Again, it was double the typical amount.

He announced this round he would bless the chanunpa that was strung above to the roof over the stone pit inside the lodge. The steam would clean and bless it.

I hunkered down as he began to pray and ask for a blessing for the power of this chanunpa and for me as its carrier/ follower. The steam was so hot I felt as if my face was melting away.

I was rising out of my body, not intentionally, but it just happened. I went above and rose outside of the lodge into a blackness of stars. There I met a friend that I grew up with. In reality she was dying of cancer in the hospital. In that moment I knew she had left her body but she needed help finding her way. A vision of the chanunpa that was in the lodge being blessed rose and met my spirited hands and I knew I needed to pray. I understood that the chanunpa being blessed in the lodge was to be used, to guide people home when they leave the earth. She left me and moved on after my prayers for her.

Quickly I slammed back into my body in the steamy heat.

The elder was still in prayer and singing when I returned. After a few minutes, I was fully back in my body. I noticed that his voice and tone had changed. It sounded deeper and with authority. He was talking as a third person in the lodge through the elder's voice.

He said his name and that he was the spirit helper of the elder. He said he called us together. He proceeded to say the elder was to help me and teach me what he knows. He said I am a woman who works with medicine and would become the successor to his lineage.

He said I was the elder's teacher in a past life and that now he is the human guide to help me to fulfill my commitment to Spirit in this life. If I was willing to accept this role I would have to sacrifice much. He said I had been training for this all my life.

The voice of the helper spirit spoke indirectly, "She can speak and hear the spirits clearly and directly. She will help many people."

Then his voice spoke to me personally.

"You have been called to the path of medicine. You must willingly accept his help. You will prepare for a two-day vision quest, aho."

Then the voice that came from the elder left the lodge. The third round completed and the elder called for the door flap to be opened. His limp body crawled on all fours out of the lodge exhausted. He wobbled over to a chair, and with his head in his hands. I stayed inside the lodge and laid my exhausted body down too. That was one hot, intense round and there was still one more to go through to complete the ceremony. He sat talking to himself in the chair for about ten minutes. When he became silent, I reminded him that we had one more round to go through. He gathered himself and entered the lodge again.

He looked at me and said one thing. "I had no idea, darling. Guess I need to get to know you better."

The last round was a little cooler and faster. We both completed our prayers and then smoked his chanunpa to complete the ceremony. I untied the chanunpa that had been blessed and wrapped it in its bundle. Before we went to change out of our wet clothes, we sat by the smoldering coals and we discussed what we both experienced. He asked me to remind him exactly of what his spirit teacher had said and what I had heard. He said it made sense that I was being called to the medicine path, with the fourth chanunpa.

LORALEE DUBEAU

But then he added, "My spirit teacher said you have been training your whole life."

'Yes, that is what I heard too," I replied as I started to cry. "But I'm not that person. I know nothing. This is nothing that I want. I am nobody. I don't know anything about medicine. I just pray."

"Spirit has chosen you a long time ago. I don't know what I can teach or how I can help you. But I am willing to share all I do know and help you in any way. All I ask is for your love and that you pray on it before you accept. If you are to be my successor then I need to get to know you better."

I agreed I would pray. The elder's teacher came from a line of medicine men teachers. Although the elder did not believe he had any medicine knowledge, that is just what a medicine person would say. As I grew to know him through the years, I knew this man was special.

My confirmation came two weeks later when I was praying. I was to accept any help he could give me. I learned and confirmed seven years later, his help was about giving me permission to lead chanunpa and purification ceremonies. He also eventually trained me and gave me permission to conduct vision quests. He allowed me to lead his community, teach them sacred songs and share my experiences and lessons from years with many elders. He opened the door for me to be me and reveal myself - my gifts, running ceremony, crossing dead spirits from land and the blessing of land. These were all things that Spirit had directed me to do. These new experiences of conducting ceremony with permission would give me the confidence to lead and eventually be open to leading my own community.

Since I was a young girl, I was given responsibility for others. When I was old enough to work, I was promoted and given responsibility in every job I had. I led and trained others and become a supervisor. It was what was given to me, but I never felt comfortable in the forefront. I did not want to draw attention to myself. This would continue for most of my life. People would often ask me questions and somehow, I would have the knowledge of what to say and help.

Eventually, I shared some of my life experiences and what I had learned with him and the others in his community. The seven years flew by quickly. I had many experiences in those years. It seemed the spirit world and I would begin to have an even deeper connection - where I could no longer sustain a regular job for my living. I needed to be available for spiritual consults and ceremony. The career I had worked hard to establish for twenty years for my financial security was vanishing before my eyes, once I accepted the path of ceremony and medicine.

CHAPTER 8

Man of Importance

I was involved with three types of work: technical, working with clients, and conducting ceremony. It was beginning to take a toll on me. The spirit world was asking more of me and leading me to teach holistic classes of many spiritual genres I had learned.

As I began to lead ceremony for the elder's community, it was becoming more obvious that the medicine path and ceremony was a calling from Spirit I could not deny. It needed to be my life's commitment.

Within five months of my commitment to accept learning from Spirit about medicine and begin conducting ceremony with the counsel of the elder, a man of importance entered the picture. Unknown to me at the time my heart had to open up to a partner. My previous relationships were mostly short-lived, including a bad marriage.

The previous failed marriage of three months and previous relationships did not last after I shared my visions and experiences. I became reluctant to share all of myself in relationships because I was met with fear and ridicule. Some of them, to be fair, did not last because I was not willing to share and reveal my connection to the spirit world.

At a sun dance ceremony, I shared my struggle with an elder who was in her third year of commitment to the ceremony. She was guided by Spirit to commit to the sun dance to pray for her granddaughter, who had been diagnosed with breast cancer. I also committed to support her and the dance for the next several years in the ceremony and the vision quests she needed to complete before each ceremony.

I met her while undergoing a weekend initiation vision quest ceremony into a women's society in Texas. The community I had belonged to for the prior three years in western Massachusetts was affiliated with the society. The year before there were many preparations I needed to complete for the ceremony. In the society, the elder granny and her sister would become my mentors and beloved friends.

At this year's sun dance, I shared all of my struggles leading a career in tech and the calling of Spirit. I was deeply immersed in leading ceremony on weekends, teaching workshops, and helping clients with energy work, flower essence consults, and readings. I was overwhelmed.

Both grannies in their profound wisdom offered the same advice I received from them two years prior at sun dance when I struggled and prayed for my next steps to help people.

"Take it to the tree," they both replied.

I took prayers to the sacred cottonwood tree twice before in previous sun dance ceremonies and my life had brought huge changes. I ended a relationship, a job, got a new job, left a community, joined a new spiritual community and was given permission and training to lead ceremonies. Was I ready for more? Did I really want or could accept what was about to transpire?

"Take the prayer to the tree," they repeated again.

To explain from my own experience what *taking it to the tree* entails, a supporter is allowed inside the *mystery circle* (the place where the dancers pray, fast, dance and stare at the sun) during break times when the dancers are resting. They are allowed to go inside the sacred circle and pray holding a chanunpa. During their focused intention of prayer for help or guidance, a small piece or pieces of flesh are cut from their arms by a leader, elder, chief, or medicine man.

I focused my eyes on the sacred cottonwood tree that was erected in the middle of the circle. It was covered with both small and large colorful prayer robes and ties filled with tobacco prayers. The slight breeze gently and barely swayed the tree's top branches. It was the most breathtaking and deeply moving experience I had personally ever had.

My prayer was to ask for help on how I could follow the call from Spirit on the path of medicine and ceremony, and continue to financially support myself. One doesn't charge for ceremony and my client work money was used to support and help native communities. I have always been a hard worker, responsible and independent, since I began my first part-time job at fourteen. I supported myself for many years alone.

As an offering to the person taking the flesh, a package of tobacco is given, as well as small red square pieces of cloth into which the flesh pieces are placed and then tied on the tree's trunk. I gifted what I thought was two small red cloth squares to the leader and began my silent prayer.

"Four pieces," he announced to me.

I was confused. I thought I had provided two, but the pieces had stuck together and there were four in all. I was being shown that I needed more time and more of an offering for this prayer. Our body is the only thing that we truly own that we can offer, so I give my flesh and a small offering of my life's blood to Spirit. I received no vision or answer to my prayer that day.

After the prayer was completed and flesh taken, the tobacco was offered as a gratitude to the leader. I told the grannies about my experience of the four instead of two flesh offerings, and they chuckled.

"It must be a big prayer and change that is coming for you. Pay attention," they directed. And as always, they would be correct.

Four months later, I was teaching my first class at a new adult education program and in walks a man in a suit who, in my judgement, was out of place. I thought he was in the wrong class and politely told him so.

My personal judgement was incorrect. He was exactly where he intended to be. I began the class and throughout the three-week session I felt a strong connection to this man. Overwhelming, yet I was not interested in a relationship with anyone. I had enough on my plate to deal with and not enough time for anything else. When the class ended, we were both called by Spirit to exchange contact information. Neither of us new why, but we felt a strong connection towards each other.

When I look back, it was not physical attraction or lust. It was the kindness and calm he emitted. It was his energy vibration.

He was living alone and going through his third divorce. He had four children ranging from high school to college. There were enough red flags for me to stay far away from him. When he called me for the first time, I had been talking on the phone with my best friend until my phone lost battery power and died. My best friend and I both knew that if my phone battery died, our conversation was completed until the next time.

Five minutes after the phone had died the phone rang. I was surprised because it did not have enough time to charge.

I picked up the receiver and heard a voice, "Hi Loralee, it's Paul from your class."

I was shocked, excited and nervous all at once.

"Hi Paul, my mobile wall phone battery is low so I might get disconnected from you. If it happens you can call me back in a few hours," I explained.

Call it synchronicity or Spirit led, but we talked for two hours on a phone that had a dead battery five minutes prior. We had our first date two weeks later, due to conflicting schedules.

I was called to bring one of the four chanunpas with me when we had our third date. Why, I did not know. They are a source of protection and like a child needing attention - to be smoked, cared for and honored. I had learned to trust if I felt an urge or vision to follow, and that day I did.

Paul was aware of my being involved with clients, ceremony, and my full-time technical job. In the first two dates I had been completely honest and vulnerable to share my experiences and what I was led to do for people. I am sure it was a lot for him to take in, but he never wavered, asking me many questions to understand and know me better.

When I met him at his apartment, I told him that I was called to bring the chanunpa with me and asked if I could put it somewhere so that it would be safe. He agreed without batting an eye. I placed it on the bureau in his bedroom. He just accepted and respected what I was called to do.

On this third date, he made me dinner and nonchalantly shared that he had been dating another woman for the last several months, but that it was not serious. She dated other men too. I was confused and surprisingly hurt. In any other case, I would have stormed out and said good-bye and ended it by never seeing him again. Why would he date me if he was dating someone else for months?

Instead, holding back tears I asked him, "What the hell is wrong with you? If you are sleeping with her and she is sleeping with other men, all of the energies are getting mixed up and drained. Does she like it that way? Do you?"

I was angry. What kind of man was he really? Had I read his energy wrong?

He looked shocked at my reaction and replied, "She doesn't want to get serious with anyone and I'm okay with that."

"How is this okay with you? Don't you think you're good enough to have someone that wants to be with just you? Don't you love yourself enough to believe that you deserve that? I am out of here. I am not dating a person who is tied in energy to all those people, serious or not."

It was shocking to me, that I was taking the time to communicate my feelings to someone I just started dating.

To even bother with this conversation was out of character for me.

He pleaded with me to stay. I told him I was only interested in dating one person at a time and that I was not expecting anything from him. I just deserved honesty and a willingness to get to know each other without distractions of dating other people. Being ten years older than me, I thought that he would be over that phase.

He again pleaded for me not to leave and told me he was not serious with the other woman.

Then I heard the call of the chanunpa asking to be smoked. Seriously, right now? Was this the reason it called to come with me.

"I have to smoke the chanunpa and pray," I told him.

He asked, "What do you need me to do?"

Bluntly I said, "Stay out of the way."

He went into his bathroom and closed the door. I opened the bundle and sat in the middle of his living room floor and began my prayer ceremony. In my experiences, answers, guidance and visions may come at any time, during prayer, during smoking or during the silence at the end. This is how it usually happens for me.

At the end of the ceremony, I waited in silence. My prayer was for an understanding of why I was feeling so hurt or even cared about this man. Should I continue dating him? A vision came.

I was standing at the sacred tree five months ago offering my flesh and praying with the chanunpa. Asking for help and how I can follow the call from Spirit to the path of medicine and ceremony and continue to support myself. Then another vison came, I was standing with Paul being married in a traditional ceremony with the chanunpa. The vision would advance one more time. We were opening our home and land (which by the way happened three years later) to build a community of the very ceremonies I was beginning to conduct. Then the vision ended.

My mind said, no way, no thank you. He has no experience in ceremony. He won't understand. He is a white-collar worker. Every excuse I conducted in my mind was not to believe. Fear had a hold on me. I told myself, I don't even know if I really like him. But my heart said something else. There was a pull, a connection to him and with the serious prayer and commitment to Spirit I had already made, things were in motion.

Early on, I learned from leaders of prayer, do not pray or ask for something that you truly do not need because you will get it. Not exactly how you expect it but you will get it. In my experience, a prayer is a thought and with intention of the heart (love) when it is spoken aloud, for example in a ceremony or ritual, it has already taken place. It's as if you know, believe and are grateful for it already happening in the unseen world and will wait for its physical manifestation. But what about things you ask for that never seem to happen or get answered? In my experience, they are answered. Sometimes we ask for something that is not needed, but we can't see it at the time. Or not given guidance or answers that need no answers, because you already knew but were not ready to accept. Or you ask for help for someone else. That is a tricky one. Wants are different from needs. Needs are a necessity and happen in the present moment. Wants come from our egos, to be collected in the future that cannot be seen in this present moment. We are not to interfere with the growth or learning of another person's journey. If a person is helped that is good. If not, it may be because they need growth or a life lesson first.

What I have learned in the path of medicine is to pray and visualize the best for them, not what I think (ego) is best for them. I can send my prayers and pictured thoughts with unconditional love and let the unseen world of spirits, Spirit, and my spirit animal helpers to work on their behalf. My intentional thought and love is pure that way. This pureness sends good frequencies into the ethers to balance each situation. Each adult person is responsible for their choices and growth. If I am asked to help, I always pray and ask for permission from Spirit to help on their behalf.

I have learned the hard way. Many people do not really want the help to change. They are not ready for it or it is not their journey in this life to learn. They take no responsibility to help themselves. Much effort, time and prayer went into help for ones I was not to or could not help. Not because they were not worthy but because I was not the one to help them. Just the same as a refusal to take on a student that was not led by Spirit. If I had agreed it would have not led them to the right teacher or spiritual journey they needed to live.

When the ceremony was completed, Paul opened the door and peeked out from the bathroom.

"Can I come out now? Are you done?" He asked.

If he only knew then what he knows now almost twenty years later, it is never done. My life will always be led by Spirit and prayer. I chuckle now remembering the sheepish serious look on his face. He allowed me to kick him out of *his* living room and be sequestered in his bathroom so that I could pray for guidance. I can say for certain today, he is exactly the answer to what I prayed for that day long ago. Not exactly what I thought it would look like or to my comfort level, but what I needed.

He sat in front of me on the floor and took my hands into his and spoke.

"I have decided I am done with her. I won't see her again. I want to see where dating you will go. I am serious about this. I am not looking for another marriage, to be honest, since I am just getting out of my last one but I want to get to know you better. I am in awe of you."

I did not tell him of my vision that day. But I did confirm that as long as he ended the other relationship, I would agree to date him. He had one final meeting with her to exchange personal items left behind and then the relationship was over.

My vison of that day completed. We married in a traditional ceremony with the chanunpa within two years and a year later we bought a home with land, built a purification lodge, and had a small community for chanunpa, purification lodges, and vision quests ceremonies.

My husband is a man of importance. He does not always understand the workings of the unseen but he understands and accepts me and the service I am called to do in this life. From our first date, I was truthful about my experiences, who I was and who I was not. I learned from my past relationships, that my gifts, experiences, and purpose were not going away and keeping them hidden would not build a strong partnership. I would have to be open and honest. I shared it all with him before we married. I wanted to make sure he would not be blindsided. If he was going to end the relationship because he could not handle the peculiarities of my life and what *our* life would be, let him do it sooner than later. I did not want to waste my energy and time.

In the beginning there were events that I am sure were frightening at times. He might have been disappointed when our plans abruptly changed and I could not attend different events and functions with him, because I was guided in service to others.

But as hard as I try to help him understand, even to this day, he sometimes cannot. Trying to explain why, how and when to anyone, is complicated when they have not had the experience themselves. I am not special or abnormal. It is just the way things work for me. I devote my time to a practice of prayer - morning and night to be ready to serve.

With almost twenty years together, he has been my cheerleader and supporter. His support allowed me to pursue the sacred work while he worked to financially support both us and his ex-wife and children. Before we married, he encouraged me to leave my tech job. I would earn no income from classes and client readings compared to my full-time job since they were given to charities. He knew it was important for me to be available to the spirit world.

Leaving my career was hard. As I said before, I was independent. I paid my own bills and supported myself. I did not depend on anyone. It was tough to trust him. It took several years of our marriage. We had one difficult year in which his pay was cut in half after we bought our home and land. But because he was loyal to his company, he would not leave his position to look for another one. We barely squeaked by. He continued to pay the support agreement for his ex-wife and children. He is a man of integrity, responsible, hardworking, kind, calm and loving. Most of all, he believed in me and whatever I shared with him. That is what I needed most. To be trusted and believed with what I see, hear, feel and know, without doubt, was the greatest gift he gave and still gives me.

I am sure there have been times in his own mind that he might have questioned certain events, but there was always some type of confirmation or validation that would happen, that came from outside of my insights that would put to rest any suspicion he could have. In his quiet, calm manner, he became my champion. One that I never knew I needed or wanted in my life. Spirit has blessed me many times in my life, but he is my most profound blessing.

CHAPTER 9

Land Spirits

The first time I assisted in the blessing of a home and land was with the elder who trained me in ceremony. Over time, he had become more keenly aware of my abilities and my connection to the unseen. He was asked by a friend to bless the land of one of their relatives. They were having trouble with a lot of accidents and odd things happening in and around the home. He agreed. The elder, his wife, and I would have to travel to a place on Cape Cod. This was before meeting and dating my husband.

Since I was a seer of the unseen world and could communicate effectively, the elder thought I could be of assistance. The family allowed us to pray and smudge (fan the smoke of burning sage). We opened several windows to allow any dense energy to dissipate. His wife kept the family busy chatting while we did our work. This must have felt odd and strange to them but they allowed us to continue.

I felt no entity or spirit within the home. There were some dense spots in the bedrooms that released immediately. We exited the home and went to bless the land in the backyard. The minute I walked outside, I felt ill. My chest and heart had a stabbing pain and my mind was having fearful thoughts. The land felt dead.

"The problem is outside. It's the land," I told the elder.

We continued to smudge the perimeter of the front and backyard. I placed a tobacco prayer in each of the corners of the directions.

I asked the elder if we could sit on the ground and have a ceremony with his chanunpa. He agreed and got the same information from the spirits. While he was filling the bowl, I felt the earth shake beneath me, as if an earthquake was happening.

I asked if he felt it too. He said he did not feel it but did know something was happening. When he began offering the smoke to the directions, a group of native spirits appeared before my eyes.

In silhouette form, many women, children and old men were moaning. It was deafening. They began to walk across the yard right to left as a group. I made a silent prayer for them. They looked my way. I could see them and they could see me. They stopped. When it was my turn to smoke, I blew smoke their way. I prayed for them to be released from the earth. Through pictures in my mind, one of the spirit women showed me a village that was massacred. Their blood covered this land. She showed me the entire past scene as if it were yesterday. I handed the chanunpa back to the elder to finish the ceremony and I sang a forgiveness song and then a healing song out loud. This is what I was called to do. Over the years I have learned many songs from different elders. Some were used for ceremony and others were prayer songs. In that moment the two songs came into my head, one after the other and I sang them. I did not intentionally choose the songs.

They just came into my head and I sang them. The group of spirits moved on walking towards the South, and disappeared into the ethers.

The elder could feel it happening but asked what I had seen. I relayed the image.

"Interesting," he commented. "What were the songs you sang?"

It was only then that I identified the songs. "It was a forgiveness song and a healing song."

He nodded and said, "Let me tell the family what has happened and break things gently to them."

I could understand that they looked very frightened to begin with, but the elder had a calm and light hearted way of communication. I, although very compassionate, could be a little serious and too blunt.

The family was grateful and provided us with a wonderful meal before we left. It is important to understand that this took most of the day. Dealing with the unseen world takes the time that is needed. They just don't leave right away. It takes time, energy, encouragement and a compassionate open heart. Dealing with dead spirits through vision can take an hour or hours. Although it seems quick when I write about it, it is not.

In the previous chapter, I mentioned many times that there are confirmations afterwards. Two weeks later, the family contacted the elder and explained that both home and land had returned to normal. Through investigation with the town hall and historian, they learned that there was a massacre of a village of native people on and around the area of that piece of land, although I don't remember the exact tribe now. I wondered if the surrounding neighbors would contact the elder for more clearing, but it never came to pass.

I do not need confirmation for myself to believe. But there are times when the people you are helping need it. It is hard for some to wrap their mind around something they cannot see.

I have done many clearings and blessings throughout the years. Most of them have been alone or with my husband assisting me. It is intense and arduous work. There are times when the spirits of the dead do not cooperate right away, leaving me to open my bag of medicine, songs, rattles, drum or prayers.

One that comes to mind is the time a woman who had attended one of my classes contacted me.

She told me that every time she walked on the land behind her backyard, she got a strange feeling and her dog was hesitant to walk in that area. She asked if I could come and take a look. I knew nothing about her land but I prayed on the matter, to see if I could help her in this case.

Most of the time, there is a physical sensation that happens in my body when I get confirmation. However, I also get a visionary picture or hear a yes or a no for an answer in my left ear. If nothing happens, then I wait four days and ask again. If still nothing, then I do not help.

In this case, the physical sensation came right away. I was shown also that I would have to smoke and pray with the Medicine Chanunpa on the land. I made plans to visit the land on the weekend.

Once I arrived, her land felt content and fine but when she led me to the area behind the home, I felt queasiness in my stomach and darkness over the ground, like a veil covering my eyes. I confirmed that she was correct and asked her to stay in her home until I completed the work.

My husband assists by bringing things back and forth to me, like a gopher. It is so that I can save my energy for the spirits or clearing. When I am done working with disassociated spirits, I feel like I have run a marathon. My physical and mental energy is taxed and I need to rest. My husband helps with the earthly details so that I can stay in communication with the unseen world. He helps keep me grounded and tethered to the world of the living. His heart connection and silent prayers while I am doing the work, help hold that balance for me.

What I did not understand in the early years, was that working with medicine requires balancing both the seen and unseen worlds. It is good to have someone to be tethered to, to keep you here and doing the work. This allows me to do more. The grounded one handles the mundane tasks so that the other can be open. I am not saying that to work with medicine one has to have a partner or assistance, but this is how and what Spirit wanted for me personally.

I stood at the border of her property and offered a tobacco prayer, fanning the sage smoke toward the direction of the wooded land ahead of me to the North and West. A blessing song to honor the land came into my head and I sang it with my rattle over and over.

After a while, several native women appeared in spirit form weeping. Since they were coming from land the woman did not own, I did not cross the boundary. I stood at its edge and I waited as they made their way through the woods to me. Some spirits move in less than a second and others who carry sadness tread slowly.

In prayer, out loud I asked, "Aho grandmothers, how can I assist?"

I proceeded to sing a song that honored grandmothers and elder women. Once again, this song came to mind but it was not of my choosing. When I finished singing, they proceeded to place pictures in my mind to communicate. They were looking for their children. They were lost. They needed to find them.

In my mind I could see the faces of the boys aged about ten to fourteen in a group, going into the woods to hunt with bows and arrows. That was all they could show me. I nodded to them.

I asked Paul to bring me the bundle for the Medicine Chanunpa and sat down on the ground and proceeded to prepare for ceremony. I understood why this bundle was shown to me to bring for this case. It needed much medicine to help all of the boys and their mothers. It would be a big task.

I sang an opening song to begin the ceremony and proceeded to fill the bowl with the sacred mixture of tobacco. I continued a long time with spoken prayers and then emptied my mind. Another song came to mind. It was a deer song. A song I learned from the elder who trained me in ceremony. I sang it over and over.

Several spirit deer appeared and gathered around me. I smoked and allowed it to drift. The spirit deer were around me and the spirit mothers were on my left side as I smoked. One by one, the boys appeared with their bows looking for their hunt of deer. It was not my intention to lure them with the deer spirits. It was just the song that came.

79

I have no control over what happens. I just listen to Spirit and follow what is needed. That is why it is important to make sure I can help in the first place. If I do the work out of my needs or wants, nothing will happen. The power of Spirit communicates through me and with my human body. I conduct the ritual by following Spirit's lead. That is why it is important for me to empty my mind and heart before I begin.

One by one the boys sat down and laid down their bows as the deer disappeared. They sat in a circle with me and watched as I completed the ceremony. In my mind I asked what happened to them.

In pictures quickly passing through my mind, they each told their story. They were hunting and they heard several loud noises and then they were laying on the ground no longer hunting.

They did not know they were dead. They had been wandering in the woods a long time. In my mind I communicated they were all shot and killed and that their mothers were here waiting for them. All but one of the boys reunited with their mothers quickly and then disappeared.

The oldest boy of the group would not leave with his mother. I could see guilt in his heart and I could feel shame in my own emotions. He felt responsible for what happened to them. His mother tried to coax him and called to him but he would not budge. I picked up the drum and began to drum a slow and steady heartbeat rhythm. The drumming was soothing and hypnotic. I could see he was relaxing and the guilt feelings were clearing and melting away. After several minutes he finally stood and went to embrace his mother and I stopped drumming. Then they too disappeared.

I packed up with my husband's help and went inside the

house. I relayed what information I felt was important and appropriate to the woman.

She offered us some tea, a snack, tobacco and a small gift. I chatted for a few minutes to ground myself back into my body.

The woman called me again, a few weeks later. Everything was good in that area when she walked with her dog. She did confirm the area and adjoining towns were known to inhabit tribal villages. If the area had a village, then the abutting land definitely could have been used for hunting.

Not all land and home blessings that I conduct are to release spirits. Some are just to clear the energy of previous dwellers in an apartment, condo, or home and bless them for the new occupants. I have found it is always good not only to physically clean a new place to live but to cleanse the dense energy that can be left behind.

CHAPTER 10

First Sun Dance

Wiwanyag Wacipi is what it is called in the Lakota language. In the English language it is referred to as praying, dancing and staring at the sun or the sun dance. Just like the Inipi in English may be called purification lodge or a lodge, and the Chanunpa Wakan or chanunpa can be noted as a sacred instrument to smoke and pray for ceremony.

To me, these are more than a dance in the sun, a place that you cleanse and purify, or an instrument to smoke. Ceremony has a life force. Many sacred things happen during ceremony. The purification lodge is a structure built outside where ceremony takes place. The people inside the lodge are the group or mass of people participating. I found it to be similar to the church and mass I experienced as a Catholic. The church is a building and the mass is considered a group of people participating in a ritual of prayer. But what happens during the ritual gathering for many that are devoted is much more than a group of people, a ritual, and a building. When participating, it has meaning and perspective, one that can't be explained in words.

I have learned many words and phrases to use in prayers

and songs. But it is not my language. What I have learned is from being in and around ceremonies and elders for many years. I use the Lakota terms in and around ceremony out of respect to those who have given me the privilege of learning and experiencing their sacred ways. I do not speak for them or any tribal culture. I only share my personal experiences and understanding of how to pronounce their words - which can both be flawed.

As I have written previously, I was invited to sponsor an elder in her commitment to the sun dance ceremony. This story is about my first experience. Many ceremonies are closed to outsiders who must be invited and given permission by someone within the community to attend.

This was not my first trip to Texas, but my first time to a sun dance. I was called to bring along the Child's Chanunpa (I will explain in another chapter). I was not sure if it was appropriate but it was clear to me that it needed to come. Three times as I went through security to connecting flights, it was removed from my carry-on before boarding the plane. I was stressed as it was handled roughly by people who had no understanding of the care needed. On one of those times, it was handled by a woman. I asked her if she was on her menses and she glared at me without answering.

When a woman is flowing on her menses, she does not touch sacred objects or participate in ceremony because she is in her own ceremony in her body. The blood flows down in her body to the earth and ceremony prayers with the chanunpa go upwards towards the sky. The two directions do not mix in ceremony because of a different focus.

By the time I arrived at the land, to say I was stressed was putting it mildly. I told the granny I came to support and she suggested I take the matter to one of the chiefs, with tobacco in hand as an offering. She had asked his wife if she and I could meet with him to ask a question. That is the customary protocol of respect.

The chief's wife approved. Once we were in his teepee, I explained that I was called to bring the chanunpa and of my experience worrying about it being handled, especially by an unknown woman. I was worried that he might be upset that I chose to bring it to the ceremony in the first place.

He thought about it for a few minutes in silence and then he spoke.

"It is good that you brought it with you. It shows that you know of its power and connection to you. You are learning to take care of it properly. Spirit has shown me the people who handled it needed a blessing from it. You helped bring them each a blessing whether they knew it or not."

He then explained how to clean it and the contents before I smoked it again. He said that the woman was not on her menses when she handled the bundle. Spirit must have spoken to him to confirm she was not on her menses which was a relief to me. It seemed to confirm my calling to bring it to bless the people who handled it - or so I thought.

After cleaning the bundle and contents at about midnight the first night, I began the ceremony alone. I prayed for all the dancers that would be dancing in the ceremony, especially granny. Everything went fine and once I completed; I was able to nap for two hours before starting support chores for the next day. Not much sleep happens in the week of sun dance ceremony as the energy is too high. I would learn to power nap at night to get through it all.

After the third completed day of ceremony, my support chores were finished at ten o'clock at night, and I went to my tent. The wind began to pick up. I went outside of my tent and the air felt different. I did not know why or how but I was alarmed. I went to another elder's tent and told her that I was concerned. She asked around the camp and people thought a storm might be coming in. I told her that I felt danger and we needed to take shelter. She had a van parked half a mile away from the camp area and we gathered up half a dozen children in our camp to go to her van. I went back to my tent to retrieve my purse and the chanunpa bundle, but I felt the bundle did not want to leave. It was resistant.

Trying to get out of the tent I tripped and fell and the bundle dropped. I picked it up again and felt a sick and dizzy feeling. Then finally at last I saw picture in my mind of the bundle sitting in the middle of the tent floor all by itself. Trusting it would be okay, I left it in the tent. It was one of the hardest things to follow but I did.

I told the elder what I had done and that I was so worried about leaving it. She assured me that it did indeed seem to her like it was Spirit led. We turned on the radio in the van and in the distance, we heard a siren. The radio confirmed a tornado was sighted in the area.

I wanted to run back to my tent, but the granny insisted to let it be. In the darkness the wind howled, shook the van and pelted us with heavy rain and hail, on and off for a couple of hours. We prayed together out loud to Spirit for the safety of everyone here on the land, in the ceremony, and that the ceremony could be completed. Granny turned on the radio to keep track of any news of the tornado. We must have been exhausted because it had been two hours since we dozed off and the sky was in its early stages of brightening. We woke the children and made our way up the dirt road to the camp. Everything was flattened - tents, teepees. Everything was wet and soggy. It would take all day to clean up. The camp kitchen was a mess. Things were blown all around and trash was muddy. People in the camps had all run to their vehicles for shelter. It was a mess, but we were all alive. The car radios said the tornado had taken a turn and hit only a few miles away, sparing us while severe damage was done elsewhere. Lives were lost down the road.

As we entered our camp and walked through the mess of flattened tents and chief's teepees, we saw that only one was one standing. Yes, it was the tent that I was staying in - where I left the chanunpa inside.

Everyone noticed and commented on it being the only tent in our camp that survived. They all asked whose tent that it was. I did not comment for fear of drawing any attention to myself.

The lesson I understood that day was to listen when the chanunpa speaks to me and follow it. It was that simple. It was a test of trust. There would be many more tests in the future.

CHAPTER 11

Catcher of Songs

It took me years to realize I was a catcher of songs, a term used in native people's circles. A song is a prayer. At least it is to me. A song has intent and the melody has a vibration of bringing or sending energy with a fast or slow tempo. It affects the mind, emotions, body, and the spirit within us. It brings or releases emotions, making us tender-hearted or excited to stand up and dance.

I loved music and dancing as a child and I still do to this day. Learning ceremony songs was of course a strong interest to me. I had a good memory and could pick up both the melody and words pretty quickly. I traveled after high school and experienced many cultures. I was given many opportunities to hear and experience songs/chants used in prayer. I picked them up to repeat, but I felt to understand them I needed to learn their meanings, where they came from and how they were used.

Most of the prayer songs I sing in ceremony are not in English. As I learned, I asked the translation so I could know what I was saying. The translation is not exact for it is not my language, but I learned enough to know what they convey and are speaking to.

As time went on, I met many elders that passed on their songs. Some of them were passed on to them by their elders and others were personal ones given to them by Spirit on their vision quests. It is good to have the background and lineage of a song as it honors the elder and the song. There are many songs in my prayers. I pronounce them as best as I can to honor the language while honoring the memory of their melody. Whether in ceremony for a group or alone, they are prayers. Some songs are meant to be social prayer songs. Sometimes I sing alone, or with accompany of a rattle or a drum. Some of my own songs were given through vision quest ceremonies. It may come from a bird, animal, the sound of the wind or the song sung to me by a spirit ancestor.

Every one of the chanunpas I carry/follow has its own prayer song that came from a vision. One of the bundles has four prayer songs.

The songs I was given by elders was because they counted on me to use them to help others in the proper way while keeping their songs alive. The healing that I have gained through these songs is what I share every time I sing them.

I have sung some of them with students when they were in ceremony with me. The medicine ones, my personal ones and the chanunpas will be passed on to the right person or persons who have been sent to me by Spirit. Time will only tell if that is meant to be as I will not choose for myself.

The process sounds so easy but it is not. It usually happens when I am sequestered in prayer and fasting. I do not ask for song. It happens slowly over hours in prayer and when on a vision quest that can take up to four days. My sacrifice is given, but a song does not drop from the sky easily. I need to be quiet and still. Listening and opening my heart in prayer with gratitude and commitment to serve Spirit. Only then one may come for me to catch for praying.

Once it is caught, I have to practice it over and over alone, so that no one can hear. I need to practice day after day, and month after month so that I can understand its meaning and purpose.

To catch a song given by Spirit is both an honor and responsibility for it is sacred. In my final ceremony into the lineage to work on the medicine path, I was gifted a new name to use when I prayed alone. I have been initiated into several societies and indigenous cultures and healing traditions. All the initiations I have had are a preparation to accept the teachings. I use them in my life to grow as a human and spiritual being. It is far from glamorous and not for everyone.

Before I was trained and given permission to conduct a purification ceremony, I was given the opportunity to be the singer in the community in western Massachusetts I was praying with at the time. The lead singer was on her menses on the date assigned for ceremony. The leader then asked me to sing for him and the community, since I knew the songs and because I had been with them for two years. As nervous as I was, when I finally calmed down and centered myself, the songs came through me when he called for them. It was the first time I could not recognize a voice that was my own. It did not sound like me. It felt foreign as if I was being helped by an ancestral spirit grandmother. For a couple of months in a row, the woman continued to have her menses on the dates assigned for ceremony. Thus came my training to become a ceremony singer. To this day, the assistance from the grandmother spirit to sing has never left me. I am far from a good singer with my own voice, but when I sing the songs in prayer and get out of the way, the voice flows through me and the songs come alive. For this I am grateful and in awe.

CHAPTER 12

Songs for Our Relations

Since I was a young child, I was inquisitive and observant of the world around me. This was especially so when I had the chance to be in what little piece of nature there was in our small apartment's backyard, or at the lake and once a year at the ocean. Everything from ants, spiders, frogs, bugs, night crawlers, butterflies and of course birds. I loved to watch birds. They are delicate, fragile, resilient, beautiful and just truly amazing.

I loved to be outside, something that still holds true. This love has only broadened, as I began to travel. My internal compass, to not cause harm or intentional pain to anything or anyone has always been strong. Though I have not been perfect, I have tried my best.

I have an empathetic nature and can sense strong feelings and emotions as if they are my own, but I had to learn how to distinguish which were mine and which were others. That includes the winged, four legged, creepy crawlers and mammals. All of them are instinctual. Although they emit a vibration different from humans, they still feel suffering and fear. What they feel, I can feel. Here are a few of those experiences.

Seventeen years ago, I was driving home to our condo rental. Paul and I had moved in together after our engagement. Less than half a mile from the complex I traveled over a small bridge near a brook. There were no other vehicles behind me or driving towards me from the opposite direction. Close to the middle of the road where I was traveling, I recognized a medium sized box turtle. If I had continued, I would have killed it or someone else eventually would have. I stopped in the road, put my hazard lights on and proceeded to approach it. It had stopped moving and had withdrawn its head into its shell. Turtles do this to protect themselves from predators, however by stopping, drivers could run over them and kill them. I knew it was the time of year that eggs were laid, so perhaps this was a female. Immediately after checking both directions of traffic, I proceeded to carefully lift the turtle, and watched that it did not edge its head out of the shell to snap at me. I continued in the direction it had been moving to get it safely across in the grass on the other side of the road. I learned many years ago, that a turtle knows its direction. If you guide it off course and turn it around in an opposite direction, it will reverse its course to get back on track.

I was halfway to the other side of the road when I heard a loud horn. A screaming irritated man stopped and watched me carry the turtle across. I guess I was taking too long and was holding up his day.

He beeped the horn at me and yelled, "You f---ing nut. You're holding up traffic, you crazy bitch. Get out of the damn road."

His yelling and cursing caught me off guard and made me tear up. He gunned the gas pedal to pass me and screeched down the road. When I got to the other side, I placed the turtle softly in the grass. I crossed the road again to return to my car. By this time there were more honking cars behind me, with drivers screaming at me. I pulled over the bridge shaking and parked on the side of the road to compose myself. I sobbed for several minutes. I did not understand what I did wrong. When I got home, I took a deep breath and prayed, thanking Spirit that the turtle was put in my path to stop the traffic and keep it safe.

In another experience, Paul and I and decided to visit the Ecotarium. I had never been there before, and we both thought it would be nice to spend time walking outside. Indoor exhibits were primarily geared to families with young children. Outside exhibits had environments for injured birds and a polar bear.

We left to arrive exactly when they opened to avoid the biggest crowds. As we entered the walkway outside, there was a pair of owls. I greeted them and we watched them for a few minutes. I have had an affinity for owls since I was a teenager. I collected sculptures from flea markets and yard sales for many years. When I was twenty-one, a friend's brother had found a great horned owl with an injured wing. He kept it in a cage for a short while until it could fly better and then released it. While it was healing, he offered to let me see it, which I excitedly accepted. I put on an elbow length leather glove. He gave me a raw piece of chicken to hold in the fingers of the glove while I held my arm outstretched.

"Don't move and hold the chicken tight. Let it fly to you."

He opened the cage, and I concentrated on not flinching. The bird flew shouldered height and landed on my arm. It attacked the chicken in my glove. The owl was much heavier than I expected. It was a thrilling experiencing to be so close to something that majestic, but make no mistake, it was a predator.

After visiting with the owls, we moved on to the next large open area where two bald eagles were sitting on opposite heavy branches. It was a caged area and the sign said neither could fly enough to be released. They were male and female. They were beautiful but I sensed sadness in them. The sign read that although the female had laid eggs over the years, they had not hatched. Maybe this is what I was feeling, their longing for a hatchling, or perhaps they had forgotten they were eagles - powerful, majestic and revered.

There is a spotted eagle song that I had learned from a Lakota elder years ago, and the song came to mind. I looked around and Paul and I were alone. I began to sing the prayer softly and quietly. They both cocked their head and tilted it toward us as if to hear me better. I went closer to the cage and sang louder. They both jumped down to the ground. I began to increase the volume and sing at a faster pace. They began to hop around on the ground in time with the beat of the song. They danced around each other. They began to shrill and sing with their own voice. In that moment I felt a connection to them.

Then I heard a child's voice, "Look, Daddy, the birds are dancing."

I ended the song and turned around. There were a dozen

parents and children behind me. Embarrassed, I moved on to the next exhibit.

"I can't believe that happened? What were you singing?" Paul asked.

"It's the spotted eagle song. I just wish there had not been a crowd behind me. I hate drawing attention to myself." Again, it was the theme that would run throughout my life.

Another story that comes to mind happened in early October of 2018. I was on my usual four mile walk down the country road on which we lived.

On this morning, a large black bear jumped over a stone wall and stopped about seven feet in front of me. The bear was facing me directly. We both were surprised. My heart began to race. I slowly took a step backwards to show I was not a threat. I took a breath to center myself and slow my fear. As I did, I could feel the anxiety of the bear diminish as well.

I took another step backwards and in a soft voice said, "It is okay, brother. I am not going to hurt you. I know you are just hunting for food and traveling. I too am traveling. Forgive me for being in your path and scaring you."

The bear song that I had learned over thirty years ago came into my head and I began to chant it. I sang slowly in a soft voice. During the song, my mind was sending honoring thoughts to the bear. My thoughts were of how we were related and how I was just here to honor him or her. I sensed that it was a male but I could not be completely sure. I continued the prayer song, and it went from standing on all four paws to bending forward as if to bow, with only his hind legs standing. It inched forward, taking a few steps like a crawl. I was relaxed and the bear was relaxed. I felt our connection in our gaze. I sang the song of four verses, four times. When I sang it before, it was always at a faster pace. Today it was much slower. When I completed the song, it stood back up on all four paws, jumped back over the stone wall where it came from and ran off into the woods.

My heart began to race again. One, because of the gift of its presence and our connection, and second, I just came face to face with a black bear! I continued my walk filled with tears. I began to sing a gratitude song under my breath. I had an experience and I was blessed.

A few days later, I called an elder granny and shared my experience with her. She listened carefully as she has done many times. She shared her thoughts on the matter.

"I know Spirit speaks with you directly, but this is what I am getting from Spirit for you. The bear bowed to you because you made a connection and honored him with a prayer song. It also was honoring you on your medicine path. The bear gives healing power. You have learned many songs and prayers over the years to help others. You caught some from Spirit and the spirits of animals. The bear was honoring you and all your hard work on this path. It has seen you, truly seen you."

I took her wisdom and accepted her view on the matter, for she has healing gifts which I have witnessed many times.

CHAPTER 13

Spirits of Animals

The world of unseen ancestors, both human or those who have not been incarnated, have communicated with me since childhood. It took me into my late twenties to better understand how to best help them and effectively communicate. Later, the world of animal spirits began to open communication. The beings that had passed and their dead bodies needed attention for their spirit to disengage from their bodies.

Some just need a prayer of tobacco. Some need a song, while others need their bodies honored by wrapping them and burying them in the earth. I don't get to decide which way to help their spirit disengage from their bodies. They communicate in pictures and feelings. I feel and see a short vision of what they want by connecting to their body and unseen spirit.

When this happens, I feel a pulling sensation and follow it to a particular place. There I will find a body. When I find it, I then slow down my breath and empty my mind of all thought. I focus on its body, look at its detail and I open my heart to stillness. I listen and pay attention to whatever I see, feel, or hear in a vision. It usually happens very quickly. Then as best as I can, I accommodate both the spirit and body.

The very first time it happened was when I was driving down a back road into Connecticut. I received a shiver up my spine in the middle of summer. I knew from previous experiences it was a sign to pay attention. Less than a half a mile around the corner, there was a dead cat on the side of the road. I noticed there was a large farmhouse and barn up a long driveway. As I drove past the body, I felt sadness.

It was then I heard in my left ear, *"Come back and take me home."*

I slowed my car down and the voice and the pull in my stomach got stronger. I had to go back.

When I began to learn the path of native people, I began to travel with what is considered the four sacred herbs of tobacco, sage, sweet grass, and cedar as well as with a shell, lighter, and wooden matches for impromptu praying. As time passed, more dead animals called to me and appeared in my path, requiring other essential items to be added to the list.

I returned to the cat. It was a beautiful orange and white tabby. Its presence felt young, like it was a couple of years old. I stood over it and offered it a prayer of tobacco for its spirit to be released and for the earth to claim its body. Thinking that was all I needed to do, I began to walk away. The pull and discomfort in my chest made me turn around and look down upon it.

I began to see in vision a young girl crying and missing the cat. Then I saw myself bringing the dead cat up the long driveway and placing it on the land near its front door where it could be found.

Fear came over me. What if they think I hit and killed the cat with my car? I may be getting myself in a heap of trouble if I follow this direction. Doubt entered my mind for only a few moments and then the fear passed and I was calm again. I had nothing to place the cat in, like a blanket or garbage bag so I laid it in the rear of my hatchback. I drove up the hill and as I approached, a woman came out of the house to meet me.

Oh no. I thought I could leave it and take off. But this was not meant to be. I exited my car.

"Hello. I found a dead cat on the side of the road at the bottom of the hill. I wondered if you know who it belongs to. I just couldn't leave it there, especially if it was a young child's pet. I am sorry to bother you, but could you help?" I opened my hatchback and her eyes misted.

"Yes, it is my daughter's cat. Can you help me bring it to the barn?"

I once again lifted and cradled the limp body and placed it in the entrance of the barn. I felt as if it was a funeral procession bringing the body home. I remembered the voice I heard in the car, *"Take me home."* The woman explained that it was an indoor and outdoor cat. Her daughter would be getting out of school soon and she was glad her daughter did not find it herself at the bottom of the driveway.

She thanked me for being a kind person. I left and traveled on to my destination in Connecticut.

Another story happened twenty years later, during an outside medicine wheel prayer circle that I conducted. The dozen people that usually attended would often ask permission to bring a friend. On this occasion the gracious property owner invited someone she knew, who in turn brought her daughter.

I try to greet and touch base with everyone before the prayer circle begins. This circle is conducted in a particular way and with particular chants/songs taught to me by an elder and later his student and tribal chief who gave me permission to conduct this ceremony after he had passed.

Everything was going in the usual order until I came to make prayers in the west direction. Instead of singing the correct song, I began to sing a horse song.

By the time I realized I was singing the wrong song, a horse in spirit form came and stood in the West facing me. I completed the song and made a prayer out loud for the horse spirit that had entered the circle. I thanked him for his presence and for giving us this honor. I asked him to return to the place where he came from, and then he vanished.

I proceeded to sing the traditional song for the West and continued on until the gathering had completed. As everyone greeted each other to share their experiences with each other, the woman and her daughter approached me teary eyed.

They explained that her daughter's horse had died recently and that they, especially the daughter, struggled with his death. I hugged them and told them what had occurred in more detail.

"The song came first. Then the horse came galloping from the West and stood at the gate of the circle. It looked strong and stood tall. When the song was finished and my prayer was complete, it turned around and galloped back toward the place it came from and then disappeared."

They both commented they were both standing outside

the circle near the west direction. I do not pay attention to where people stand in the circle when I am in prayer. When I am in communication with Spirit or the unseen, all outside physical vision disappears and I am in the present moment. Their confirmation to me as to where they were standing in the circle sent a chill up my spine and gave me goose bumps. Over the years, this was a confirmation sign that I learned to embrace.

The last experience I will share happened three years ago as of this writing. I had been gifted an eighth chanunpa and began to build its bundle and learn about its use and teachings, which I will discuss in more detail later in the book.

I was on the highway driving to my parent's apartment in Connecticut. Once again, as in many times before, I received a chill up my spine. I paid attention and made sure I was fully present by taking deep slow breaths. I did not know what to expect. The car in front of me passed something in the breakdown lane, and a wing flapped up in the air. Dark and light fluff blew in the gust of wind created by the car in front of me. I quickly passed by it, thinking it might have been a goose.

As I passed, I felt the pulling sensation in my stomach and the call in my left ear to, *"Come and get me."*

Oh no. I don't have time today I told myself. I am expected at my parents. The feeling would not let me go until I exited at the next off ramp. I found myself following the voice in my ear in almost a dream-like state. I don't remember anything after exiting the ramp. I found myself back on the highway and approaching where I had been almost twenty minutes before. I saw the wing flap up once again and I slowed down to a stop in the wide breakdown lane. I got my bag of items out of my trunk and proceeded towards it.

Did it need its spirit released? Did it need to be moved further into the grass to allow other animals to feast on it? Did it need me to bury it? All these questions rushed through my mind. When I got closer, I stiffened as I identified the bird. It was a barred owl.

A side note: although I had an affinity for owls since I was a teenager, I did not believe I had its medicine to handle. Different tribes and customs have different beliefs and teachings. I was taught the owl can bring sickness and a warning of death and rebirth either actually or energetically. To handle a dead owl or feather could bring sickness to oneself or family. My teaching was that one usually had to receive a vision or calling for permission to handle or use its medicine. Over the years there had been several times I had been gifted owl feathers, fans, and wings. I have even found a dead owl, years ago, that called me to bury it.

Each time they found their way to me, I cleared them with sage and cedar smoke, wrapped them in red cloth and hid them away in the basement separately, in a box immersed and covered with cedar leaf and sage. Then I cleared myself before entering my home or engaging with people. I eventually passed all of them to a heyoka (backwards, sacred clown) medicine person who attended the sun dance ceremony years before. Owl was definitely his medicine, so he was very happy to receive them. I gave him all the owl medicine I had to this point.

Once again, this dead owl called for my assistance. I stood

over it and made a prayer for its spirit to be released. I emptied my mind and opened my heart to pay attention.

My mind could see me taking it home, singing to it and burying it in my yard, where I had buried many birds and animals since living and having ceremony on the land. The vision was clear. It wanted to be buried next to the other owl that was on the property.

On my travels over the years, I learned to carry protective gloves, bags, tarps and cheap blankets just in case I am called to help dead animals. Not every dead animal will call to me. Not every one of them needs to be buried. I only follow to assist them when that pulling sensation happens in my heart or belly.

I traveled on with the owl in the back of my trunk and carefully smudged myself before I went in to visit my parents. After an hour visit, I returned home before my husband came home from work. I took the owl and laid it on the picnic table in the backyard and again smudged myself and everything for the burial with sage smoke.

I smudged and started the ritual of prayer. I laid the soft feathered bird on the red cloth and made prayers for its spirit and body.

In the stillness and vision, I saw it offering a piece of each of its wings. Only the front tips, not the entire wing. Then I saw me cutting the small bones. Then the vision passed.

On no, I don't want any more feathers, I thought. I gifted away all I had been given in the past. Then I accepted, for maybe they were to be gifted to someone else. Since I could not refuse its offer and blessing for someone else, I followed what the owl had shown me. I do not want to take any piece of an animal's body when I bury it. I will only take a part of the animal if I am shown in a vision by the animal. It is an offering and serves as an exchange of gratitude in honoring its spirit and body with a burial.

I know the vision is correct and it's not my ego wanting to take a feather or wing, because I am shown what to do, where to take it from and it comes out or off the body very easily and gently. If one has to struggle to pull a feather or take its part, then it is not meant for you. It is as simple as that.

Once I completed the prayers and the wrapping for burial, I offered tobacco to the earth and dug a hole in the ground. I knew exactly where it wanted to be buried from my vision. I picked up the owl with both hands to walk it over to the front yard but was stopped in my tracks.

I heard the bird's spirit begin to sing. The chant's melody repeated over and over and I was taken in a vison and shown that I needed to bring it to my chest, coddle it and rock back and forth. I chanted with it in melody. Then a couple of words came to add to the melody, and I continued to sing it until it became part of my memory. I rocked the bundle like soothing an infant and welcoming it into the world, my world. It felt alive though I knew, in reality, it was deceased. I cried silently as I sang. Then I heard the voice in my left ear, "This is the last time you will be offered my medicine. Do not give me away."

I understood. Memories came flooding in. The first time I received an owl feather was at a zoo when I was a teenager. It was the first time I had been to a zoo. I went with my cousin and her parents. I visited with a great horned owl. I was in awe of its size and beauty. In my mind I was telling it how beautiful it was. I was in such admiration. It had been injured and now lived at the zoo. As I finished my thought, the large bird flapped its wings and a large fluff floated out of the cage and stuck to the front of my shirt on my chest.

I also remembered the time after a lodge ceremony, I was to spend an overnight alone in the darkened lodge with a newly gifted chanunpa that had just been blessed in that ceremony.

A spirit owl came in a vision that morphed into an elder woman spirit. She claimed to be my ancestor. She sang to me until I dozed off into a deep sleep. I will explain more in another chapter.

After that zoo experience is when I began to collect owl figurines. I kept the fluff and brought it home with me that day, keeping it for many years until it too was a part of the box that I shipped to the heyoka.

After the vision ended, I understood I was called to its medicine long before I knew anything about the path I would come to walk. It was offering itself to me one last time. It chose me. I did not choose it but now I had to make a choice. Would I accept?

I understood the song was a medicine song being gifted from the owl's spirit for me to use in the future. It did not come to me on a vision quest, but it came from a vision.

It seemed I misunderstood that if medicine was to come to me, it would only come to me on a vision quest. This was a new teaching for me. The vision I was now experiencing helped me to accept its final offering. How I would use the partial wings and song would be revealed weeks later.

For now, I accepted it. I dug the hole and placed the bundle in the earth alongside its kin. Then I covered the hole with the soil I had removed. It was a process that took over two hours. As I walked to the front porch, my husband's vehicle was coming up the driveway.

He smiled and said, "Hi honey. How was your day? What's for dinner?"

I laughed. "It's been one of those days, you know the kind."

He had accepted that my day was not always going to be in the earth realm and never complained.

He laughed too and said, "Takeout then?" A phrase to this day we use more than I would like to admit.

CHAPTER 14

Crossings of the Spirit

Having a glimpse into an unseen world at a young age was a challenge. I understood what I could see would not be seen or believed by people close to me. I was concerned I would be labeled mentally ill or a liar striving for attention.

I was ashamed of seeing, hearing, and feeling premonitions in a world I could not fully understand back then, so I chose to be quiet, accepted and become like everyone else. I decided I would not share my experiences with anyone. It was a way of shutting down that world, but it never completely shut down. It just gave me a rest from time to time. Not every moment or day had experiences, but it felt more often than not.

I felt most comfortable being with old people, like my grandmothers, great grandmother, great grandfather and grandfather, though I was not really sure why. I felt very comfortable observing and listening to them. Their energy felt familiar and comforting to me when I was among them.

It has always been this way in my life. I was a child that was filled with empathy and compassion. I have learned over the years that I wanted to be around them, because *they,* being the elders, were closer to home - the unseen world and Spirit.

You can call it heaven, the Milky Way, paradise, the kingdom, Great Mystery or the spirit world, places that are unseen to earthly eyes. It is a place we may fear or a place of great faith and comfort. The Great Mystery is a place where all is created and to where all that is created will return.

As years passed and I became an adult, little by little, I came out of my shell. Traveling helped to open the door. Meeting people of different ideas, places, lifestyles, customs, and stories helped shape my inquisitive mind. I thought in the first twenty years out of high school, I would find my home - a physical place that I belonged and felt comfortable. I had made many friends in my travels, especially with older people whom I honored by calling them an elder. Not all of them would I have considered to be old. But they were older than I, had more life experience, and within that, contained much wisdom.

By the time I was forty, I finally realized there was no physical state or town I needed and that my home was within me. It was wherever I took it. The center of who I am was my comfort. Living my life, the way I was guided. Using my gifts and sharing them with people was the home within me.

It is a vulnerable place, so I proceeded at a slow pace. I moved out from under my parents and started living alone at twenty-eight. Being born into what is considered today, a large family, I craved to be alone. The night was my only refuge for a quiet place. As a teenager, when I was permitted and my parents were home and chores were completed, I walked and spent time at the local lake to replenish.

When I began living alone, it allowed more time to travel and be independent. Having my space open to do readings and energy sessions helped me take a fuller step into the world. I then began teaching adult education classes at night. Opportunities began to come to me. I did not have to search them out. I still was working a day job in the tech field in those days building a career to support myself - or so I thought.

The unseen world became more prevalent in my life. The more I was available to teach and serve clients, the more the unseen world was harder to close. It was blissful and I was in a state of a flow that felt correct and comfortable. But to be led, you have to be open to pay attention to your surrounding world of reality. I cannot live in the unseen spirit world all the time, but I can touch it for others when Spirit agrees.

In the last twenty-two years of my life, I have continued to devote myself to the unseen world through prayer. I pray and have good thoughts with everything I do. To me, a prayer is just a good thought, a wishful blessing for everyone and every situation. It is not only in ritual or ceremony. It is a simple good and hopeful thought of love and energy sent out into the world for anyone in need.

There is no separation to the flow of the divine within me or around me. It has always been this way, only I have learned how to work with it better. I still have to be present, grounded in love but I also must be open to the work, whenever and wherever I am guided, or it presents itself.

Make no mistake, I have had to sacrifice. I spent time learning and traveling. I gave up a job and a career that would have given me financial stability. I left people I loved that were not emotionally supportive. I gave energy to help others and not had children. Working in service to help others was a sacrifice of both my time, finance and energy.

Some people have courage to do this every day in their jobs of service, even if it costs them their life, fulfilling their call or purpose drives them, real heroes. I am no hero. My service does not bring rewards of fame or fortune. My true service comes from the heart. Seeing a need in the world and offering to help.

I could never pay my living expenses with class or client fees as they are donated to charities or with ceremony for which there is no charge. It was not a business but a service. I learned I could not service all people, all the time because I would deplete my human self.

The reward for me is seeing darkness lift, comfort from pain and having the opportunity to help others heal and move forward. The inner peace it brings to me is the reward, that perhaps it has made a small difference in someone's life and in the world.

The more I worked with the unseen world, the more people would find me through word of mouth. It took many years to open my private world and build relationships with those of like and unlike minds.

The spirit world in my experience cannot be controlled. I can open myself to it when needed but I cannot force any spirit to come forward. They have completed their human life and they can choose to come forward as needed. Working with them is on their time, which can be quick or take hours depending on the spiritual level they have attained on earth.

I have been called many times to help someone cross from one dimension to another. Their bodies can be tethered by unfinished communication with loved ones, fear of the unknown and in many cases, fear of leaving relatives in emotional pain. Other times I am asked to do a ceremony after someone has died as a memorial, or to make certain their spirit has left and is not hanging around. I would like to share some of these experiences.

I was married to my husband for a few months, and I was no longer working a tech job. I was teaching classes, helping clients, conducting ceremony with students, and balancing our home filled my life.

The condo we shared was a lovely place. It had been a little over a year since we moved in together. The owner approached us and explained that he would be putting it on the market. We were shocked. His asking price felt too high for something with no land.

This put pressure on us to move but it also helped us move forward in setting down roots. Paul knew from the beginning of my being called by Spirit to the ceremony life and building a community on our land. I trusted Spirit would take care of it when it was time, but this was too soon even for me.

I continued to conduct ceremony and support the elder's community but we both knew it would not be forever. My husband began to search the housing market and did the financials of what we could afford. After I left a good paying job less than a year ago, we thought we had more time to save. We went to the bank to see if we could be approved for a mortgage.

With the numbers in hand, my husband began our search. For the next month nothing felt right. The properties were not conducive to building a small ceremony place. I was feeling stressed and rushed. We had until September to move out.

Not long after, a close friend of mine asked if I would do a ceremony for her partner's relative. She had passed and there was some turmoil in the family. She asked me to make sure her spirit had completely crossed over to the spirit world. I agreed to ask permission from Spirit and if accepted, she would gift tobacco to me out of respect. This is tradition.

I prayed with the chanunpa to receive a confirmation for permission.

Interestingly enough, the woman's spirit came through to me. I asked her to return when I conducted the ceremony but she refused. It seemed I had to help her right now. I sensed through the pictures she sent to me that her health had been failing. Her husband had passed before her. Her emotions were very sad. The issues in her family caused her great pain. It took everything she had to leave her pained body.

Now she stayed hovering in between worlds, attached to them. I consoled her by singing a song of healing and offered to pray for her family now and moving forward. I prayed for her husband or close relative to come close and guide her home.

Please understand I did not call him. I only offered a prayer on her behalf.

It seemed to soothe her. I sang another song for her spirit to dance, and to lighten and release her hold to the situation. Once again it seemed to calm her. After what I would later realize was an hour, a male spirit came forward from an opening of light and she turned and followed. Their energy was compatible. I understood it was her husband.

Once her spirit was gone, I continued to pray for her

family by singing a forgiveness song. I sang it for a long time until I felt the shiver up my spine and I felt it was complete.

I relayed what I had experienced to my close friend whom asked for the ceremony and said, to my knowledge, it was complete. She came and delivered the tobacco and a thoughtful personal gift for me.

Later, at the beginning of May, my husband found a house of interest and wanted us to view it. I refused because we had planned to go to a local pow wow, a tribal social dance. He was disappointed but our house expeditions had been so taxing that I just wanted to relax and enjoy the day.

As we drove to the pow wow, I heard a voice in my left ear, *"Turn around. Go back and see the house."* After the third time of hearing the voice, my body felt the familiar shiver up my spine.

"Paul, we have to go back to see the house. It's important."

"What about the pow wow?" He asked.

"We'll go later." I answered.

He turned the vehicle around and found the address of the house on the GPS. The moment that I saw it, I felt home. As luck would have it, there was an open house that day. We parked at the bottom of the driveway. I felt compelled to offer a prayer with tobacco to honor the land.

There were two other families browsing the house as well. I walked outside on the land for about twenty minutes while my husband took a tour of the inside.

Eventually the real estate agent asked my husband, "Will your wife be coming inside?"

My husband called to me and motioned me to come inside the house. I was deep in thought and it took several minutes for me to acknowledge him. I entered the kitchen through the glass siding door on the back deck.

It was then I exhaled and sighed, "This is my home."

We toured the rest of the house but that was not necessary for me. I did not care about the inside. This was it, the place for ceremony, community and to plant roots.

Prior to moving, during a call from the close friend that had asked for the ceremony for her partner's relative, I shared that we would be moving and purchased a house with land. She was excited for us, and of course, asked where it was. She and her partner lived in the same town and wondered if we would be neighbors.

She seemed to know where it was but said she would ask her partner specifically. A couple of days later she called me back to tell me all about the history of the land which used to be a farm. She gave a lot of detail and then she said something unexpected. The house was the same house of the woman I crossed over for her partner. Her partner was absolutely sure. Within three months, we were living in the home and on the land.

In my heart, I know we were guided. The woman whom I crossed into the spirit world guided us to her former home. It was a wonderful place to live and have ceremony. I am grateful for the many wonderful years we had there.

For those that have shared ceremony with me over the years, there is a spiritual bond. There are times I am called upon to help, even if they no longer are in ceremony with me. They know they can call upon me.

I received a phone call from a man whom I call a spiritual brother. His father was taken to the hospital and was in between worlds. He was going to have to make the decision for the hospital to let him pass.

He asked me to pray for him to give him guidance on how to help his father. He wanted to make the right choice, but his emotions were overwhelming. I agreed to see if I had the right to gather insight. When calls like his come in for help, I drop everything I am doing and cancel any personal plans I may have had. It is my commitment and service to Spirit.

Immediately, I sat with the Medicine Chanunpa. I know which chanunpa to pray with because they call to me and let me know.

As I began to fill the bowl, a clear vision of a man lying in bed came to me. I did not go searching for him. It happened without effort. It confirmed I had permission to conduct ceremony on his behalf. When I said his name aloud, his spirit lifted up from his chest. It was halfway in and halfway out. He began to communicate with me with pictures. He was ready to leave his body, but he was waiting. He showed me that his son needed to tie up loose ends emotionally. He did not want to leave until his son got to communicate all he needed before he passed and then he could let him go. I was not privy to what needed to be said but just that it was important. He had been hanging on to life for a couple of days. Decisions had to be made for him and the son was not ready. I completed the ceremony by communicating to him what his spirit should look for when he did pass, to make the transition easier to let go of his family.

I called the son back and relayed the message that I understood. He accepted the guidance but did not know what he had left to say. I told him to just sit with him and speak whatever came from his heart and most importantly, to tell his father it was okay for him to leave his body and as his son, he would be alright.

A couple of hours later, the son called me back to say, he did as Spirit suggested, and his father passed on his own not long after from what I remember. He did not have to make the choice to end his life.

There are many experiences similar to this and there are others that do not involve a ceremony with the chanunpa. I often pray in the presence of a sick or dying person in a setting that cannot allow smoke or ceremony, like a hospital. I can open myself to prayer at any time with sincere intention.

There was a woman for whom I had done several spiritual readings for over the years. She called me one day.

"Can you do a reading for me today?" She asked.

I asked "Why does it have to be today?"

I do not usually take clients on the same day of the booking, but I sensed she was tense and needed help.

"My daughter has been in an accident and she is in bad shape."

I knew immediately she needed prayers, not a reading.

"Where is she?" I asked.

She proceeded to disclose which hospital she was in, and we made plans to meet her together. I grabbed my bottle of blessing water and hurried off. At the time, I lived alone and was able to change my dinner and movie plans with a group of friends.

Once we arrived at the hospital, we made our way to intensive care. The woman advised the nurse that I was a relative and asked permission for me to see her. The woman was in tears. Her daughter was in her early twenties. She was not a child but was far too young to be lifeless and hooked up to a machine. She was in a coma and on life support. It was a head injury, and they were not sure if there was any brain activity. Tests still needed to be done. I asked her mother if I could have some time alone with her and she agreed.

I held her hand in mine and called her name four times in a soft tone. I made a prayer and proceeded to sing four songs softly under my breath. The first song was about the sun. I received it on my three-day vision quest. My intention was to ask Spirit for strength and vitality on her behalf. The second song was a prayer of healing to ask Spirit for whatever healing was necessary for her, body, mind, and spirit. The third song was a prayer to ask Spirit to help her to either return to her body or to return home to the spirit world - whatever she chose. The final song was an honoring song. A prayer to honor her life and all she had accomplished.

When I completed the songs, I sprinkled the blessing water below her heart and above her belly. I have found that many spirits lift out of their bodies in this place first and it is also the energy center of the life force in the body. It would help her to return to her body or move on peacefully.

I sat in silence with her. Pictures came into a vision. She did not want to leave her body, and she wanted to live, but she was tired. I could feel her weak body and her sadness. To my human eye, she seemed young and athletic. Her only injury seemed to be in her brain. It did not make any sense, but she emitted such fatigue in her energy field.

I squeezed her hand and told her that it was all up to her now.

I returned to her waiting mother. She went in to be with

her daughter for another hour as I sat in prayer in the waiting room. When the woman returned to me, she was in tears. I hugged her to give her comfort.

"Did you sense anything?" She asked.

The hard part is to know how much to share, and how much to withhold because I didn't want to cause more suffering.

"I sang prayers over her, and I understood she was very tired and depleted. I told her that it was her choice to choose to fight to come back. But I got she was very tired even though she had no other injuries besides her brain," I replied.

The woman began to cry again. "She has had severe depression for the last seven years. It has been such a struggle for her and our family."

I nodded in return. Nothing else was needed from me. It was between Spirit and the young woman. The doctor's test proved there was no brain activity and the mother had to make a choice. I continued my daily prayers for the girl at home for the next week. What I sensed was that there would be no turning back for her and she would not return to her body. Before her mother had to make a choice to put her in a convalescent home or taken off life support, the young woman left on her own because her heart gave out.

There have been many times in my life when spirits needing help appear out of the blue. Many came through during client readings and others in ordinary circumstances, like going to a restaurant, staying at a motel, or at any random place.

On one occasion, it happened at a theatre during a play. There were spirits that had died in a fire that asked for help.

Later on, it was confirmed to me that many years ago, several people died in a fire in that exact theatre. It was hard to imagine they were hanging around all that time.

Not all spirits need or ask for my assistance. I have seen that many people carry heavy grief and unintentionally keep their loved ones connected to the earth plane. There are times I need to act in the moment and other times I just continue on as if I do not see them.

Departed spirits ask for my help often. I can see and sense them clearly. There have been times I have crossed over a wandering spirit without anyone around me noticing. I connect to the spirit telepathically and ask if there is a message or something they need to express before I send them home. It can happen very quickly, or it can take hours. The quick times go easily unnoticed.

Ceremony with a chanunpa was not always necessary to release spirits, especially in the early days before one was gifted to me.

I would like to share two more of my experiences that happened on ordinary days.

I had been teaching classes on the Japanese healing art of Reiki for over ten years at the time. This class, a first level beginner's class, had six attendees. It is where the history and hand positions are taught and then the class practices the hand positions on each other. Throughout the class there are four individual initiations. This is where the channel is opened, and the transmission of the energy passes from teacher to student.

During the first initiation of one of the women, a male figure entered my space. He was a young man who was connected to her. He communicated very easily in pictures and thoughts telepathically. He wanted to give this woman a message. There were still a couple of hours of class time left, so I asked him to wait until the class was over and I would relay his message to the woman. He disappeared immediately.

When the class ended and people were exiting, I asked the woman if I could have a moment alone with her. She agreed.

I proceeded to wait for several minutes, opening myself up and holding space for the young man to re-enter. On cue he entered. His thoughts were clear but coming at a rapid pace. He was truly upset.

"She has to let me go." He repeated over and over.

"There is a young man here who came hours ago when I was giving you your first initiation. He says you need to let him go."

Her eyes widened.

He communicated again.

"She needs to release my ashes. It has been too long."

His thoughts and pictures communicated that he had passed a few years ago and his spirit was restless.

"He has been gone a while and his spirit is restless. He wants you to let him go." I spoke again.

The woman began to cry. "I miss him. It was so sudden. It is so hard."

The young man's energy softened. "I know Mom, but I am stuck here."

I relayed the message and explained that our mind and emotions can hold our loved ones here.

"If you let him go, you can still hold your memories in

your heart. He will always be a part of you because he is now a part of everything in the universe. That is where our spirit will return."

I hugged her. She relayed all her feelings and how he passed until her tears dried. She agreed that she would release his ashes. I gave her guidance on how to complete this.

The young man was still waiting to relay one more message. "I love you, Mom. I am okay and stop wearing my pants."

I relayed the message word for word. Her eyes and mouth opened in shock. She was wearing a pair of his corduroy pants on this day. She said she felt closer to him when she wore his clothes.

"I guess you better release his clothes too," I added.

"I miss you and love you too," she replied to him. Then just as quick as he appeared, he disappeared.

The next experience happened when I was traveling with a group of spiritual women in Mexico. The tour leader had planned a trip that would involve ceremony, working with an elder healer and visiting tourist sights off the beaten path. There were a dozen or so of us, not including the two translators.

After a women's ceremony the tour leader conducted at night, I made my way to the quaint hotel room I was sharing with a woman I had just met on this trip. We both settled into our beds for the night and I became very restless. I could not fall asleep. I have found when this happened, going outside, breathing in the night air, and looking at the stars usually settles my mind.

Before I could do this, two spirits floated in through the ceiling - a dark skinned man and an eight or nine-year-old with blood on their faces and hands. I could see only their upper bodies. They did not know where they were. They were confused and scared. The man was holding the boy's hand.

Neither of them could relay pictures or thoughts to me. I would be on my own. I communicated to them where they were, the town, the hotel and in my room obviously, I also relayed that they had somehow died.

Still, they were bewildered and scared. I made prayers and sent energy of love beaming from my heart to hold the space for them. I also prayed quietly that if there were any relatives that could come and help them, I would hold that space for them to come through. It took over two hours of holding that space. The memories of their life on earth flowed through their spirit in a rewind which I only got a glimpse of. They did not fully understand that their bodies were dead and what happened to them. It was four o'clock in the morning before a spirit relative appeared from the tunnel of light beckoning them. Her presence was older, maybe a grandmother. They smiled and turned to follow her through the opening of light and disappeared.

I drifted off to sleep for a few hours.

I didn't know who they were as they could not communicate well enough, other than they were father and son. The impact of what happened to them was quick.

The next morning, I had a confirmation. I was sharing my night's experience with one of my friends on the trip, when another woman overheard the conversation.

"Did you hear what happened last night? A small plane crashed at the local airport a few miles away. A couple of children and adults died."

A tingle up my spine was my confirmation. Two in the crash needed help and somehow found their way to me through Spirit. I was glad that I was able to help them, and I silently made prayers for the others that died in the crash.

CHAPTER 15

Healing

Through the many skills I have learned and my own personal healing experiences, I have found this to be true: healing does not happen first in the body, healing may never happen in the body, healing happens in the spirit of the human first. A dying person filled with cancer can be healed in their spirit and mind but not necessarily cured in the body. Again, I remind you healing and curing are two different things.

If one carries sadness, guilt, shame, anger, fear, grief, or cannot forgive, it creates an imbalance in the thoughts and emotions which get stuck in the body creating imbalance and illness. Yes, we all age and the human body is not supposed to last forever. As the saying goes; no one gets out of here alive. Our body, like all of nature, is made to die, but the spirit is eternal. The life force of energy that is connected to the unseen divine in all things is where true healing takes place.

I know this because I see the spirits of those that have passed on. They are eternal. While they do not have real bodies, they do appear to me in a sheer ghost-like appearance because I can relate to them in this form.

Each person is responsible for their own healing and balance of mind, body, and spirit. One cannot heal if one does not accept responsibility. No skill, technique, prayer, song, or ceremony will work if one does not assist in their own healing.

There are times one may need assistance from someone. Everyone at some point can use some help and guidance. One must be willing to surrender to the struggle, suffering, habits, beliefs, and dense emotions the spirit life force carries to transform and heal.

When this change is acted upon, life becomes balanced and smoother. When the spirit is not connected to the divine life force and we are not living the human life of meaning, relationship, and purpose, we can become lost.

True healing takes place in the spirit. Ceremony, in my experience, heals all forms of pain. It clears and cleans issues that are no longer needed. It is like filling a suitcase of all the pains I carry, setting it down to be transformed and then opening the suitcase after the ceremony and finding it is empty and is ready to be filled with only what I need to live a fulfilling life. Prayer in ceremony helps me to connect to the divine and let go of my pain. Ceremony has enhanced my life. It has helped the people I have prayed for who are willing to shift their energy and receive the divine.

Do you ever wonder why some people heal from illness and others die? No person is better than another. No one is being punished. We punish ourselves with what we think and how we live and treat our body. I know I don't always treat my body right, get enough sleep, or eat the best food. But still, I have a strong spirit. Until my body dies, I will continue the healing work for my spirit to stay aligned with my true self and purpose.

I took clients in person for many years. As time went on, I understood that I did not have to work with energy in person. I could connect to them wherever they were in the world. This helped the flow of the work to be quicker and more efficient. When a client is in person, they often take so much time speaking their story of pain that there is little time for me to help the energy.

In the early days, I had a woman come to me for energy work. She was referred by another client.

She did not know why, but she thought she could use energy work because she felt tired and unbalanced with her emotions. I immediately sensed she was filled with anxiety and deep-seated fear from childhood. She never felt safe. I started my work beginning at her head. Then I continued laying my hands back and forth from her stomach area to her head. Eventually I ended on her heart to end the session. During the session, I could feel cold spots (density) and warm spots (good flow). Sometimes I will see colors or images. At the end when I was over her heart, I saw, with my visionary eyes, a dark spot inside one of her breasts.

The woman fell asleep during the hour session. I had to wake her from a deep sleep. She said she felt very relaxed. When I see or feel something during a session, I am careful not to diagnose for I am not a doctor. What I see many times is lodged energy, not always in the physical, but lodged energy can eventually create a physical issue.

"That was wonderful. I feel so relaxed," she said.

"That's good, I'm glad that you feel so relaxed. While

I was doing the energy work, I felt and saw deeply rooted anxiety in your stomach and heart. That is why I kept going back and forth until I felt a small release. I feel it started in your childhood. You might want to explore your childhood to find out when it started. A feeling of experiencing that you were unsafe and this created the anxiety you feel in your body. I also felt a dense spot in your breast. I also laid my hands in the area, but it did not completely shift."

"Do I need to come back?" She asked.

"That is up to you. See how you feel and let me know. The density in the breast could be a message that you are not nurturing and taking time for yourself or issues with your mother or being a mother."

"You know, that breast has been a little sore."

"A way to take care of you might be to see a doctor or get a mammogram, just to address the soreness."

I knew the information I received was physical, but I did not speak it to scare her. A few weeks later she called to make another appointment and confirmed that they found a benign cyst on the test. She came for two more sessions. We discussed some tools she could use every day to improve her life.

Over the years with Spirits help I have used energy to help many small and large situations - helping to relieve relatives' pain when physically hurt, helping an accident victim I came upon from going into shock until an EMS arrived, and helping with migraines. But *I* have cured *no one*. Only Spirit has the power to do this. My smallest issue to help was for my husband.

It was such a simple thing, but he still talks about it to this day. We were just married and I had made a nice dinner for when he returned from work. I sat with him but I ate dinner much earlier as I could not wait until he came home from work. He ate his dinner and we chatted. I went off to pray on our deck. When I returned inside, my husband was having a bad case of hiccups. He said they had been going on for nearly an hour. He was exhausted. He could not get them to stop.

I had him sit on the couch beside me and told him to close his eyes and relax. I made a prayer of intention for his relief and placed my hand between his throat and heart, allowing the energy to disperse and balance. Within a minute the hiccups stopped.

You can decide if it had to with energy and prayer or with him relaxing. From time to time, he will again get a case of hiccups and his first words are, "Honey, can you do that thing for me?"

Understand that "I" do not do any healing. I am just a channel that I keep clean and open for the power, information, and guidance to pass through. If healing happens in the spirit, then the mind, and heart then the body can follow. I just hold a space of intention and love. I take no credit if help takes place or not.

I open and center myself through daily mediation and prayer to keep the channel clean. I connect myself in silence to the unseen mysterious power of the divine, which I call Spirit.

I use no alcohol, no recreational drugs to affect my mind. If I am to conduct a planned ceremony I may fast and refrain from sexual relations for four days. This is what Spirit has asked of me to show my commitment.

Abstaining is really not a big deal. I was never a drinker,

though I had my times in my early twenties. The only sacred herbs I have taken were in healing ceremonies, peyote, and a diluted form of San Pedro cactus. I do not need or use hallucinogenic substances to receive guidance.

Once I became a chanunpa carrier/follower, refraining from alcohol and drugs was my commitment to my path. I realized later why. I could be called upon to help at any time and in any place. I could not go into ceremony without a clear mind or under an influence if I used the chanunpa. It and the ceremony needed respect. I needed to be able to be available to use it for prayer.

Since healing of the spirit must happen first before anything else can take place, here is one example I can share.

Fifteen years ago, the sister of the close granny in Texas called me on the phone. She had become my spiritual sounding board - one with whom I have shared all my experiences over the years. She too has gifts and had become a trusted ally.

She has asked for prayer ceremonies for her friends, relatives, and herself over the years. This time she asked for prayers for her son who was struggling with depression. I said I would sit and pray for guidance.

During the ceremony, several men from nearly two hundred years of past generations appeared. These men were all carrying two black seeds - one in their ghost-like heads and the second in their sternum. Each of them pointed one at a time to their head and then to the area in their sternum.

They took me back in time to Native American persecution and slaughter. The pictures were gruesome and hard to witness. I understood they all carried the heavy energetic imprint that had been passed on to granny's son. The male Native American lineage was from granny's paternal side.

In my vison I saw a paper with the names of these men. I was to conduct four ceremonies with the chanunpa, speaking their names out loud. I understood I was given permission to do the work on their behalf. I needed as many names as the elder could go back and remember. The vision ended.

I immediately called the elder and explained what was needed.

"This makes sense to me. Dad struggled all his life. That is where our native heritage comes from in my family. I will send you every name as far back as I can go."

A week later the paper list arrived. I decided to conduct the ceremonies the next day after fasting from food and water. It was a beautiful sunny day outside. I took the sacred bundle and smudged myself and the bundle to clear the energy before I entered the lodge ceremonial area. I sat down on the north side, outside the lodge and prepared for the ceremony. It would not be the first time I smoked four ceremonies back-to-back. It does happen on rare occasions when it is needed.

During the first ceremony, several dozen men in spirit form appeared. I knew their names were not on the sheet of paper granny had sent me, for they were dressed in buckskin clothing. I prayed for them out loud.

"Aho grandfathers, I pray for you and the sickness of spirit that you carried. I honor you and ask the Great Spirit to clean your spirit from the atrocities and injustices you faced in your life."

I drew in a breath of smoke and pointed the stem of the chanunpa towards them, blowing the smoke up the stem to them, offering the blessing. I repeated this four times until the smoke was completed. I sang two healing songs aloud - an honoring song and then a closing song. One by one the small black seeds in them disappeared. Then as if on cue, one by one they turned away from me and disappeared.

I cleaned the bowl and stem and rejoined them in a sacred way to begin the next ceremony. The second ceremony began the same way.

Again, men stood before me in my vision. They appeared with leather moccasins, blue jeans, buckskin vests, and handmade cloth ribbon shirts. Some of them had a turban-like garment made of cloth wrapped around their head that held a single feather. Many of them held a small personal smoking pipe in their hands.

Each of them also, had the two black seeds inside them in the same place. Once again, I began my prayer.

"Aho grandfathers, I pray for you and the sickness of spirit that you carried. I honor you and ask the Great Spirit to clean your spirit from the atrocities and injustices that you faced in your life."

I read half of the list of the names on the paper out loud, to acknowledge them trusting most of them were named. Once again, I drew in a breath of smoke and pointed the stem of the chanunpa towards them, blowing the smoke up the stem to them, offering the blessing. I repeated this four times until the smoke was completed. I sang the same two healing songs out loud - an honoring song and then a closing song. Again, one by one the small black seeds in them cleared and they each turned away from me and disappeared.

Again, I cleaned the bowl and stem and rejoined them

in a sacred way to begin the third ceremony. The beautiful sunny day began to change and darken. Dark clouds drifted in, and the breeze increased. I covered the shell containing the burning sage and cedar with another shell. I did not want the lit sage to blow away and start a fire in the woods. There was no rain or wind in the forecast.

The third ceremony was slightly different.

The male spirits appeared while I was filling the chanunpa with tobacco. I was not ready to smoke yet. It was if they were ready and eager to be honored. They were dressed in jeans, and flannel shirts much like men of today. They too had the small black seeds of dense energy, but their seeds appeared larger and more visible.

The ceremony changed and the honoring song came first in my head, so I followed the song in my mind and sang it out loud to them prior to smoking. Next the two healing songs came to my mind, and I followed by singing them both as well. When I completed these songs, I spoke the prayer and the names of others on the list who had lived in the lineage more recently. I lit the chanunpa and began my smoke.

I drew in a breath of smoke and pointed the stem of the chanunpa towards them, blowing the smoke up the stem to them, offering the blessing. Instead of repeating four times, I needed to offer it to each of them individually, because one by one they stepped forward for the blessing. I hoped there would be enough tobacco in the bowl to smoke for each of them and for me to complete the ceremony. As the smoke was offered to them individually, the seeds disappeared quickly, and each spirit turned away and left until there was only one of them left.

The spirit moved towards me and nodded. I heard one word

in my left ear from him though I had never heard it before and did not know what it meant.

"Wado."

He turned away and left. I knew he was the granny's father because his mind kept sending me pictures of what she looked like when she was little, up until I could recognize her today. I sang the closing song, and the third ceremony was complete.

As tired as you think I might have been, Spirit holds me up when I am in ceremony. However, when I am done with the ceremony I am exhausted for hours. I need to rest my mind and body, and eat and drink something to ground myself.

I cleaned the bowl and stem for the final and fourth time and rejoined them in a sacred way. The clouds grew darker and the wind picked up tremendously. I did not know how long I had been in ceremony. Ceremony happens in the spirit realm and seems to go quickly but earth time can be several hours.

As I filled the chanunpa with tobacco I felt a sprinkle of rain on my cheek. I needed to complete this final ceremony, so in prayer I asked for pity from the thunder beings, who bring the rain and lightning to cleanse the earth and air.

"Aho, Wakinyan, who bring the rains to cleanse and heal. I ask for pity for this protected space to be free from storm so I can complete this ceremony of healing."

A crack of lightening ran across the sky was followed with a loud clap of thunder. This pattern continued through most of the ceremony with just a small mist on and off.

No spirits appeared as I smoked. The prayers were for the ones who were alive in granny's lineage - the one brother and her two sons and the grandsons. I spoke their names out loud and then asked that they too may be cleared of any heaviness from their spirits and head if it was what was best for them, especially her son that was having depression issues. I offered the smoke up the stem four times to offer the blessing.

I sang the same two healing songs as before when they entered my head. Then two songs of gratitude came, and I sang them with reverence. I smoked holding gratitude for the healing energy bestowed on them from my heart. When the last smoke was completed, I sang the closing song.

I cleaned the bowl and stem and closed the bundle. As soon as I did, the cloud that was hovering let loose and a downpour of heavy rain began to pelt the ground. I quickly ran into the house with the bundle and then returned outside alone for a quick minute to offer tobacco to the thunder beings for providing the window to complete the ceremony.

When I returned to the house, I had something to eat and drink and took a nap. I had been outside for more than six hours. I left a voice mail for my husband telling him to get us takeout for dinner. He was used to this when I had a day of working in the spirit realm. Not every day though. Most days I made him dinner or made it first thing in the morning after I greeted the sun in prayer. On Sundays I made several dishes for the week for us to reheat just in case. I never knew what to expect each day. Takeout meals became a less favorable choice for me but one he enjoyed.

After napping for a few hours, I awoke a few minutes before his bedtime. I relayed my day and experiences of the ceremony to him.

"Wow, sounds like a full day."

Never once since I have been with him, does he doubt my

experiences for he has witnessed many things with me himself. He does ask questions to better understand the spirit realm and has learned a little through his own personal experiences in ceremony.

In the beginning of our relationship, it was hard for him because he was fearful of what he could not see or understand. But he loved me and wanted to be with me, even when it might seem peculiar. I warned him from the beginning. I withheld nothing about myself and my experiences. Long gone are the days when he came home from work and asked, "What did you do all day?" As if I did nothing of importance and sat around all day.

He quickly learned to change the offensive question to, "How was your day, honey?" I chuckle when I think of it now. I admit I am not easy to live with. There are no routine days.

After a good night's sleep, I called the granny in Texas and related my experience with the ceremonies. She was grateful and said she would send tobacco, cedar, sweet grass, and sage in gratitude for the ceremony. She also gifted me a cante juha. It is a decorated leather bag to hold a chanunpa in a bundle. It belonged to her deceased sister who also worked in ceremony with medicine. Little did we both know at the time, it would be used for the next chanunpa I was gifted, a Women's Chanunpa.

The next time I spoke with the elder who I had been in community and training with for seven years, I asked him if he ever heard the word, "Wado."

He said that it was a Cherokee word and his understanding of the word meant, *Thank you.*

He had heard it many times and that is how it was used.

I recounted my experiences with the spirits and the last one saying "Wado," before he left.

"Sounds to me he was thanking you for doing the ceremony for his family and completing it in a good way."

Once again, a small confirmation of what came from the spirit world was true and separate from anything I could have known in my reptilian brain.

Healing, I have found through experience, happens in both the living *and* the deceased. Without this, there is no relief. In fact, the western ideology is that if it doesn't give immediate relief to the body, no healing has taken place. Not all healing needs to be in the physical body. Many times, the spirit only needs help to transform thoughts, beliefs, and emotions to create balance and ease suffering in the body.

Within four months, the Texas elder's son's depression lifted and he got his life back on track. He began a better relationship with his wife, sibling, and mother. Much of the depression lifted because I believe the ceremonies and Spirit cleared the lineage.

CHAPTER 16

Initiations

An initiation can be described as "a person who is undergoing or passed a phase, one who has been instructed in a field of principles or passed a test of self-reliance" as the Merriam-Webster dictionary states. In my experience all of these are true.

Not every person will or needs to enter into a society, ritual, or traditional ceremony. Certainly not every class of education or skill will have a formal initiation. I experience an initiation as a shift in consciousness, knowledge, and energy within me. Not all are completed in an elaborate ritual or ceremony.

We as humans have phases in our lives which are also forms of initiation. We pass from infant to toddler, school age to pubescent, teenager to adulthood, middle age to retirement age and into our golden years if we are lucky.

With most of these phases we become less reliant on others and gain more independence and freedom in our body, mind, and internal spirit. Every phase of life brings newness, a trial of learning and a passage into the next phase. It happens whether we like it or not. Challenging unexpected events, repetitive patterns and untrue beliefs can cause suffering and imbalance.

As a curious person and one who has always been self-reflective and comfortable in the silence, expanding my knowledge of how and why people think, feel, and act is always at the forefront in my life. Though I still am observant, most of my wisdom (how to use and disperse knowledge) has come from all types of experiences. My experiences are far from what most people will or need to experience an initiation.

My many initiations have helped me grow, learn, and promote the internal healing of my spirit. It is hard to imagine who I would be without having them.

There have been three traditional spiritual naming ceremonies. I never named myself. It always came from an elder. The last naming took place at fifty-two, after four traditional chanunpa ceremonies with the final ceremony being to pass on a successor lineage and began my deeper work in the medicine path.

I have been on eight vision quests so far, ceremonies ranging from one to four days of fasting and prayer. I trained in Huna (philosophy used by the kahuna healers) and Kai Loa (a form of light touch energy work, done by kahunas). Four initiations were of traditional Usui Reiki hands on healing. One initiation was for the White Buffalo Women's Society. Four initiations were for the Good Medicine Society and three initiations into the Andean tradition. Other trainings consisted of limpia (egg cleansing from the Yucatan), crystal skull mapping (Toltec), flower essences and crystal light balance sessions. And many other ceremonies I have participated in like peyote, San Pedro, moon ceremonies and not to mention other ceremonies of secret teachings. I still use and practice all the trainings to this day when they are needed.

Life phases like changing careers, getting married, getting divorced, remarrying, buying a house, selling a house, and downsizing your life are all considered to be a change into a new stage of life. At a workshop I took many years ago, the lecturer spoke of challenge, change, choice and commitment. She said the stages happen during the process of healing.

These initiations have improved my life and helped me see myself and the world with new understandings and perspective. No matter how hard and time consuming, it was worth it. It didn't happen overnight. I was guided to meet and find the people and travel to places without much effort. The synchronicity happens when you pay attention to the world around you and the world within you.

I would like to share an important experience of challenge, change, choice and commitment. After six years of training with the elder's community, I was given permission to build a ceremonial lodge and a community on our land. I continued to assist the elder twice a month at his lodge and conducted ceremony on our land once a month for the next year. At the end of the year, I disconnected from him and his community with a chanunpa ceremony. He is the blessing and catalyst who provided the opportunity to live my purpose. I love him dearly.

Four years later, I was primarily conducting all ceremonies from our home – chanunpa, purification, coming of age (Ishna Ta Awi Ca Lowan), vison quests, and naming. While sitting in ceremony alone with the Women's Chanunpa, I was offering smoke to the direction of the south.

A male spirit entered. I recognized him. He was a medicine man and the teacher of the elder who had trained me in ceremony.

I had met him for the first-time years ago when he was visiting with the elder. I later developed a personal relationship with him.

He was a vendor at pow wows and he traveled along the east coast for most of the year. He came to Connecticut every summer for several years. I would return each year to visit with him for the week and take in his thoughts, stories, and teachings. He was a funny man and a good storyteller. He was kind of rough around the edges but he made me laugh a lot.

The first time I met him, he said I needed to *grow tough skin* because although he knew conducting ceremony was Spirit's will for me, he knew it could be tough for a woman. I would need great commitment to overcome judgement and criticism. The old ways were changing. Men and woman were in ceremony together now. In the past they were separated.

It had been a couple of years since his passing, and I was surprised with his appearance in my vision.

I was with a circle of spirit grandmothers in my prayer vision when he arrived and dispersed them upon his entrance.

"Aho grandfather," I said.

"You have to tell him he needs to get on with it and end your waiting. He needs to pass on his four songs and conduct four chanunpa ceremonies to pass on our lineage. It's time to walk with medicine," he said firmly.

The images he placed in my mind were clear - four separate chanunpa ceremonies and he was to pass on four of his personal songs he received from Spirit. It was a transfer of spiritual lineage that went back to this elder grandfather's two teachers, and their teachers, all of whom worked with medicine. He was clear in the images.

"I thought he already passed on his succession," I said telepathically.

"No. It needs to be a formal ceremony," he argued and abruptly left.

I had been conducting ceremony for four years on our land. It felt strange going back to the elder and asking for four ceremonies to formalize and pass the lineage to be his successor, whatever that really meant. I always had the elder's support and he always trusted my visions, but this made me very nervous. The spirits had told him to teach me all he knew and to pass the lineage to be his successor, but neither of us really knew what that meant. Given permission to conduct ceremonies is what I thought it had meant.

I called the elder and asked if I could have some private time with him and he agreed. I remember how nervous I was, stammering and nearly in tears. (challenge) When I had to draw attention to myself, it seemed to be egotistical and not humble, and it caused me great pain. I wanted to help and do what Spirit asked of me but I still did not want to be seen.

After I relayed the message, I asked him to pray on it because I may have misunderstood. I wanted to give him an out and a way to say no to me. But he just laughed.

"Yup, that sounds like him alright, pushing around the grandmothers even in the spirit world," he chuckled. "I will pray on this, but he's right that it needs to be a formal ceremony."

I was relieved to get it off my mind. Now it was on the elder's plate. It didn't take long for the first ceremony. It happened two weeks later. The ceremony brought up many of the memories of the two of us together since we met. We sat alone and smoked the chanunpa together.

The second ceremony happened two weeks after the first. Many of the same memories flooded in and out.

We smoked and after he completed the ceremony he said, "You need to make a feast and invite your family, community, and friends. I need to present you as my successor. They need to know you are the one they need to call for help in spiritual matters. When they know this, they will tell others." (change)

Dumbfounded I asked, "I thought this was all going to be private, just between you and me? I did not see a large group in the ceremonies."

"No, after we have the ceremonies. You will run a feast to feed the people as a giveaway to honor the ancestors of the lineage."

He then proceeded to name the names that he knew of the lineage of teachers before him and I wrote them down to remember.

The elder and I discussed the dates of the last two ceremonies. The next one would be in two weeks and the last one a month later, with the feast and gathering on the day after the final ceremony.

I had to plan a guest list of immediate family, friends, and community. (choice) It was what you call a safe crowd, one that already knew and supported my path of service. The list contained about forty people. The feast was a buffet in a private room at a local restaurant. The cost was about a thousand dollars. (commitment)

I bet the spirit elder who orchestrated this whole thing was having a good laugh at my expense, literally.

The third ceremony that was at the elder's home was slightly different at its completion. The elder took out a cassette tape and recorded four of his songs.

"These songs were all gifted to me by Spirit," he added. He explained when and how he used them. He asked one last thing of me before I left.

"Practice them over and over, but do not use them until I pass. Then they are yours to use."

I wholeheartedly agreed. I have practiced and I know them but as long as he is alive (which to this day I am grateful he still is) they are still his songs.

The final ceremony would be at the elder's home again. My husband and the elder's wife would witness and participate. I brought gifts for him and food to share afterwards.

This ceremony was very traditional. A Pendleton native blanket, the buffalo skull, his drum, rattle, and whistle to call the spirits were laid out on the altar. I was seated to his right. I would be the last to smoke ceremonially. Paul sat in the north direction and the elder's wife sat in the south direction.

The elder with his sacred whistle let the spirits know we were beginning the ceremony. We all sang the traditional chanunpa song as he filled it with the sacred tobacco. Once it was filled, he made many long heartfelt prayers for me and the work I would be doing. He asked all the ancestors of the lineage to assist me moving forward. Then it was passed to the elder's wife. She too made wonderful prayers for me. Then she passed it to Paul. He too said beautiful prayers and asked for the strength to be able to handle whatever this all meant for us. When it was passed to me, I was so emotional I could barely speak.

"Aho grandfathers and teachers, thank you for keeping these ways. Teach me, guide me, and help me to be worthy of this path and lineage. Remind me to work this path in love. Pilamaye (thank you).

This is all I can remember. I am sure I said a few more prayers of gratitude for the elder, his wife and my husband and asked for blessings for them all. But the all of the exact words escape me now.

The elder lit the chanunpa and offered the smoke to the directions. Then blew the smoke towards me. He then passed it around the circle for each person to smoke.

When it finally came to me, four male spirits came forward. I recognized two of them. The elder's teacher and one of his teachers, I had seen before in a picture. The other two must have been the teachers of the generations before. They stood in the west direction facing me with serious faces. They each had an eagle feather in their hand. I smoked deep and offered the smoke to them and returned it to the elder to finish. The elder then stood behind me and sang a song. He placed his hands on my head and blessed me with the lineage stating the names of the teachers.

The spirit grandfathers pointed each of their feathers towards me and then fanned their feathers up and down several times to offer their blessing.

The elder lifted his hands from my head and announced, "The spirit grandfathers have named you to carry on the lineage." He spoke my new name. "You may use this when working with them and Spirit. Your public name will be, *Spirit Singer*. I will introduce you as Spirit Singer tomorrow."

I cannot share my real name as it is sacred and private, known only to my husband, the elder and Spirit.

He gifted me a large tail feather and a paper of authority with the names of the lineage and permission to handle sacred objects. This day would always hold a special place in my heart. The next day at the celebration, the elder gave an eloquent speech about our relationship, our memories together and his kind thoughts about me.

Then he looked directly at my parents announcing, "She is now Spirit Singer. She no longer belongs to you. She belongs to the people."

I will never forget it. They looked so confused. I don't think they really understood, but I did. I was entrusted to help people when Spirit led them to me or I to them.

I made a small speech thanking each person directly for how they supported me on this path. We enjoyed the wonderful banquet meal and I took a small plate of everything and placed it outside on the grass edge of the parking lot. It is a way to give thanks and honor to all ancestors. We call it a *spirit plate*. Hard to believe it has now been over eleven years since that day. It feels like a lifetime ago. Still with gratitude, I commit my life, do the work, offer help, and give service with an understanding of the spirit world, guided by the spirits of the unseen and Spirit.

CHAPTER 17

The Sacred

S acred can be defined in the Merriam-Webster dictionary as "set apart for service or worship, worthy of reverence, relating to religion, holy, sanctified and blessed."

For myself, sacred does not have a religious meaning. Although many people think of the word as relating to a religious object, tool, person, or event, the word to me means a harmonious flow of invisible energy.

It has taken me years with many trials and tribulations, to reach the depth of my understanding. When I was a child, *sacred* meant the Catholic mass, a nun, a priest, a bible, rosary beads, the chalice cup, and the communion host. They were all sacred things that were holy, blessed, and sanctified. The power was in the object, person, or event. This felt true at the time.

Traveling at eighteen, I was exposed to many other religious customs, beliefs, sacred objects, people, and events. In every experience, there were sacred people and their objects who conducted sacred events for others. Different expressions in the beliefs, rules, and customs, but they all were held together for the most part with reverence. It was the divine energy that flowed that brought the sacredness. Some were held in special buildings while others were held in nature settings. I was not looking or searching for a way to leave my childhood Catholicism, but for a way to connect to other people as a bridge of connection through those differences.

It also led me to understand how and why people were different. How we are raised and influenced creates how we respond in life. For example, for me crying was not allowed and anger was swallowed (unacceptable for a little girl). In my service, I came to understand many adult women have learned to swallow both tears and anger but I had to work on releasing my own first before I learned to help.

Today, I would call myself spiritual but not religious. I did follow different doctrines, rules, and customs in every new experience to which I was exposed and invited. I gave my respect to understand them and learn from them. Every path deserves respect whether it resonates with me or not. Each of them can be experiences to open our inner self to connections. The doctrine, objects, and rituals all followed beliefs and customs that come from the spirit within to connect to something greater outside of ourselves. Some call it worship, others call it honor. People have been gathering together and alone since the beginning of time to make this connection.

All teachings and experiences from Santeria, Pagan, Reiki, Hinduism, Buddhism, many of the Christian faiths, many North American, South American, and Central American traditions I learned were similar. Their belief and ceremonies were bridging a gap to the invisible, to communicate, to thank and ask for help and protection.

All the tools I work with; the crystal skulls from the Yucatan, the misha bundle of stones collected from all over the world, the Mullu Khuyas from Peru, several rosary beads, sacred water from special places, buffalo robe, buffalo skull, winged fans, a feather, a drum, a rattle, a whistle, and the bundles of chanunpas, are only sacred if the connection to the divine energy flows through them with intention.

I care for and respect each item and honor its use in the same manner. All are equal. All are used in service for the good of people. But they alone are not sacred for they are just objects I care for. The ritual I use with them does not only define the word sacred. I alone, the person using them, am not the definition of the word sacred.

What I have learned through the years is that all the paths, rituals, customs, beliefs, and objects could not define the word *sacred* to me. In the end, I discovered it was simple. It is when a connection of energy is moving from the divine Spirit through a person, object, ritual, or ceremony that it becomes sacred (wakan). Sacred is a connection of respected energy that is in a harmonious flow of love.

CHAPTER 18

Chanunpa Wakan

The first chanunpa ceremony I experienced as a teenager resonated with me. I was not a cigarette smoker, although I tried smoking a couple of individual times in my early twenties. It was not for me.

From my late teens and into my forties, I traveled and was guided to different elders and invited to ceremonies. I was lucky enough to become part of four lodge communities before building my own. Some religions only allow one doctrine or one way to be followed, this was not for me. I wanted to be exposed to many things so I could understand the world. Even though I have continued to follow the native path for over forty-four years, I continue to be open to all ways.

Though there are many objects, tools, rituals, and customs that I honor and have had healing from, all are equal. But the most profound teaching, observances, and healings that I have received and witnessed have come through the chanunpa.

The English translation used for the Chanunpa Wakan is "the sacred pipe" because it looks like a pipe and it is smoked. Lakota elders have told me that this is incorrect.

The definition I learned means tree, wood or a measure of time day or night (cha), two, twice or two ways (nunpa) and sacred moving energy or to think of as holy (wakan). Sacred energy moving through the two pieces and time is how it was explained to me.

As in the English language, words can have different meanings and pronunciations. Language is complex. How we use words and give them meaning and understanding are subject to differences.

You may ask many Lakota elders, leaders, and medicine men and women, and all will give you a slightly different teaching and personal understanding of the chanunpa and its ceremony. In my experience, there are no English words to describe it. It is not an object though it is physical and you hold it with your hands. For me personally, the chanunpa is understood with the heart.

It is the sacred essence of energy and connection to the divine that is constantly moving and sending each prayer and thought.

The chanunpa is a living unseen force, a being of energy that flows with and through all dimensions of time: past, future, and in the present moment of the breath.

I have smoked with many elders, in many ceremonies, with many tribes, though they may have called this ceremony by a different name in their language. When it is used in a ceremony, it is honored and respected in a traditional way. The wood stem may be made of different woods, shapes, lengths and sizes. The bowls can be made from different stones of various sizes and shapes. But because of my first teaching from a Lakota medicine man and traditional teachings with the ceremony, I use the term Chanunpa Wakan or chanunpa.

The chanunpa has taught me, healed my spirit, given me challenges, deepened the connection to Spirit, and gives meaning to the word *sacred*.

CHAPTER 19

My Life

Praying in ceremony with the chanunpa can be tiring, not just in the physical and emotional sense but in the mental sense as well. When I open to the invisible spirit realm of the past, present, or future, there is a journey I must take and commit to - one that allows my spirit and mental state to shortly escape the physical dimension. It is in these moments the vital energy of my being is raised to an intense level and, in rare times, extremely close to crossing into the death of my body.

This way of praying for others will take a tiny piece of life force from me, and while rest and certain techniques can help re-energize myself, I can never recoup it all.

A lot of the requests come for help for the body, mind, and emotions. Most request for prayers are to help people who are in between worlds and need to cross over. Prayers can also be done after they die to be sure they have completely crossed out of their physical body and are not roaming the earth.

If they have already passed, I will wait four days before conducting the ceremony. It allows the newly deceased to visit the surviving loved ones who are struggling to let them go. I use the chanunpa to open a space, to hold a space for a deceased relative from the light to take the newly deceased home to the spirit world.

In all ceremony I conduct, I connect part of myself to the spirit world. It's like throwing a rope into the sky, lassoing a hoop to anchor myself in the invisible realm and opening the channel inside of me for the information to flow. Some elders call this a hollow bone state. I am not sure if I can humbly use this term for myself, so I will call it a channel of love. If I keep it clean and clear through the daily preparation of prayer and meditation, the information will be easily accessed and understood.

Once connected to the spirit realm, I ground my body to the earth and connect another energetic loop from myself to the person or persons needing assistance. I then release the loop when the ceremony is complete.

If in a chanunpa or purification ceremony one asks a question or needs a dream interpretation, I will relay whatever I hear, see, or feel immediately.

I will tell you the words an elder and a proficient medicine person told me about the path of medicine.

"When one is called to the healing path it is a tough journey. They have to work hard to overcome many things as a human being. Spirit names and calls them before they are born on the earth. To think that another person can teach you to be one who works with medicine is not true. Elders will guide you and show you their way but Spirit does most of the teaching.

No human can make another person a hollow bone or channel. Only Spirit can do that. We have human teachers to share ideas and experiences to help us grow. Each person is able to balance their own individual self, but the minute one gets a little power he automatically thinks he can heal others. They should worry about working on their self and only their self. People want praise for being a healer. They like to hear how great and special they are.

A hollow bone is already a hollow bone when they are born. They have gifts that allow them to see the unseen and work in that world. They have the ability to communicate to all beings on earth and in other dimensions. They work all their life practicing and making this connection become and stay clear. They devote their life to this connection. They give up human desires to serve Spirit. Spirit talks to them in everything physical and non-physical and it is not separate. It is all the time, every day, every minute of their life. They go through trials, hardships and sicknesses to gain a deeper understanding of themselves and how they can help others and keep the hollow bone clear.

Spirit speaks to them directly every day and every moment. Their life looks easy and free from the outside. Yet, in reality, it is hard, lonely, and isolating. They are the last to be honored or remembered once a person is helped. They are forgotten and unappreciated. They spend a lot of time alone in prayer and in communion with nature. They give up financial security to go to where they are needed. Sometimes they give up family to journey to where Spirit leads them.

Spirit flows through them and does all the healing of the spirit, heart, and mind. The healing of the body comes last. Not all illness begins in the body. Not all illnesses are to be healed in the body. Not all who are chosen will follow their journey because it is too hard to worry and care for others. It is a sacrifice of time *and life. It is an unselfish journey, not one that is glamorous or brings fame."*

This is exactly my life now. I was warned about how hard it is and yet I continue in service to the call. It is hard and tiring. It is lonely at times being in isolation to continue to improve and clean the channel. Once a person has been helped, I am forgotten and there is no resulting fame or fortune, nor should there be.

I do it because I know the channel of love is within me. It is in union with everything and I know where the flow comes from. My purpose is to use the connection to pray and send love. I cannot be disconnected from it if I am to service Spirit. My spirit knows my truth. It is most important to me to complete my purpose in this earth life. I see the big picture and my calling won't let me rest. It is my breath of life itself. It is my peace and wholeness. It is hard to put into words because it is a knowing and an all-encompassing energy of love.

I do not get caught up in the ego of self. One may be helped, or one may not. Spirit does the healing or curing and decides what is best for growth. No one would want to work with medicine because it is time consuming. To understand healing, you must go through it yourself before you can help someone else.

My connection to Spirit is one I have built over my entire life. When I was a child I called it God, but now on the path I walk, I use the name of Great Spirit or Spirit because of my personal relationship with the source. I need a lot of personal time and space every day. My husband has obliged me thus far.

I wake up in the morning and go outside to offer a tobacco prayer to all the ancestors of the directions, my helpers, and to Spirit. I offer gratitude for another day of life and open to another day of doing good work and helping others. I sing the sunrise songs to honor the day.

That is the first ritual I do every day, rain or shine. It is something no one sees. It is personal. After breakfast, I sit and pray with a chanunpa.

If someone has gifted me tobacco and asked for prayers or help on a particular issue, I will do another ceremony using the appropriate chanunpa for the issue.

On any given day there can be one ceremony but at times I have done up to four. My work, although private most times, is to speak with the spirit world on behalf of other people. The idea is to open up and ask for help and goodness on the behalf of the situation or person. It is not what I believe to be the best personally. I leave it in the hands and power of the Spirit. I get out of the way of fairness and judgement knowing the outcome will be the best for all concerned. My life is not scripted. It flows and changes every day. My husband and I, from time to time, do make plans but they are loose. He has learned not to get attached to what a day may look like.

Do I spend my whole day in ceremony? In a way, the answer is yes, and in another way the answer is no. When I go for a long walk, I am in ceremony. When I listen to music I am in prayer. When I travel and drive my vehicle I am in prayer. I listen and pay attention to life and nature. My *life* is a prayer ceremony.

One time on a walk, two trees started to squeak, so I stopped and listened. As I looked up at them, there was no wind to speak of in the air. I acknowledged them and waited to understand. The older and bigger one was leaning heavily on the younger smaller one. The younger tree was strong and supported the elder. I put my hands on each of them and thanked them for their message.

My prayer earlier in the day asked how I could deal with my husband's medical diagnosis. He had been diagnosed with a neuro-degenerative disease. How would I be able to physically care for him as time went on? It was the guidance that I had been praying for. It was okay to ask for help and lean on younger, stronger people, if I could not do it myself. It was okay to have the help of a professional caregiver when the time came.

Not all prayers are answered the same way so I have to be mindful of everything for guidance in both the living and unseen world.

When someone calls on the phone, I am in the flow. Sometimes it is as though Spirit is telling me what to do or say. When I go to the grocery store or post office it is the same way. I am called to speak with and or smile at some people. Others I compliment or hold the door open for. I can't tell you how many times complete strangers will walk up to me and tell me their troubles. Spirit gives me just the right words to comfort and uplift them, and I am grateful for that.

If someone needing prayers calls later in the day or if Spirit calls me to get up to pray for someone at night, I do it. Spirit gives me the energy to complete it. Sometimes I may be called to go on our porch in the middle of the night. Animals, like a coyote or owl may call. They could have messages.

I find that nighttime has always been my favorite. It is

quiet and the spirit world is most active. I often nap during the day in case I am called to be up at night.

I talk to Spirit with my mind, heart, and spirit. When I am very quiet, I get feelings, understandings, and a knowing. Sometimes it is with a picture, other times with words. If it is with words, the voice comes from outside of me. The words are not my own and I had no way of knowing they were coming.

To me the terms God/Great Spirit/Source/Spirit are not nouns. They are verbs. It is a mysterious power and flow of energy filled with unconditional love. It encompasses everything. It is a presence yet not a body. It is so unfathomably large it can't be measured. It is the quiet and the storm. It is within everything yet has no form.

For me it is not a human-like man in the sky sitting on a throne. That is not how I understand it or experience it. People should be allowed to believe and experience Creator/God/Great Spirit in the way that allows their own deeper connection to themselves and their life on earth. Who or what we call it, and how we choose to honor it or connect to it, is up to each individual person. If we as humans could feel the verb and not be so invested in the noun of the word there might be less conflict and war in the world over religion.

You might ask, what is your intention when you offer to work with prayer? My intention is for Spirit to direct me to where I need to go. Spirit will guide where the energy needs to go if the person is open to receive it. I have no decision to make. My only intention is to be the open channel with unconditional love. It does what it does. I have learned if the spirit within us is weak, everything else goes downhill until it reaches our physical bodies.

It is a developed connection of awareness to the flow of life that is in and around me all the time. The more time I spend in deep reflection, prayer, and ceremony the more open I become. Once opened, messages can come through even when I am doing mundane tasks, like driving a car or doing laundry.

For over sixty years I have learned and refined my connection to Spirit and the unseen world. For as long as I can remember, I had empathy, compassion, and a desire to help people, animals and all living things.

My primary focus is ceremonial work for which there is never a charge. But the respectful right way is to gift tobacco in gratitude and sometimes people have offered gratitude by gifting something to help me live. I myself have given elders gas cards, grocery cards, brought wood for ceremony, paid for airline flights for travel or bought groceries or Pendleton blankets for the winter, the necessities of life.

I realize now, in the elder stage of life, I must share myself more. I cannot share myself if I am hiding in fear, isolation or not willing to go out into the world and be among the living.

I am being called to step forward out of the isolation to share my stories. In a world that is critical, judging, and ready to create harm, I must step forward. It takes courage and bravery and a deep commitment of purpose to Spirit. I have not been shown what comes after this book so I must trust. My visions have always been correct but they do not come in the timeframe I may expect. Some take years to materialize and some happen very quickly. I have learned to let go of expectations and follow my inner voice and connection to Spirit.

The next chapters are life experiences that deepened my connection to my path of ceremony, medicine and led me to who I am today. It all started with a reluctant trip to Mexico.

Part Two
Trust and Truth

CHAPTER 20

Child's Chanunpa

It was twenty-two years ago as of this writing that my first chanunpa was gifted. I had been learning and following the Native American ceremonial path since I graduated from high school, more than forty-four years ago.

I had seen a small chanunpa in a vision during an initiation vision quest into the White Buffalo Women's Society. I was shown in the vision by a spirit grandmother and grandfather that it was coming. It was very small in the vision and it would be used to pray for the children. Seven weeks later the same small Child's Chanunpa would be gifted to me on a spiritual trip to Mexico.

I had prepared for the initiation ceremony for nine months. I prepared my body through fasting from food and water once a week. It also involved making the necessary traditional articles that a young woman going through a puberty rite would need to make. I was a part of a community that participated in Native American ceremonies in western Massachusetts.

This community had ceremony two weekends a month. I would spend the next three years, Friday through Sunday in ceremony. The singer in the community had previously gone through this initiation ceremony with another community in Texas and now was offering it to the women in our Massachusetts community. Although a few women from our community agreed to prepare for the ceremony, in the end it was only me who would complete it.

The beading of the sacred symbols brought me close to a grandmother spirit called "Two Feathers." She came to me one night while I beaded and sang a song. Later, I found out through the community in Texas it was a woman's song. She sang it over and over until I could sing it myself. It was only melody not words, per say. I remembered the melody and each time she appeared, we sang it together. It made the beading time flow easily. I could hear her voice in my head teaching me about the divine feminine, being a woman, and about my struggles with my mother and within myself being seen, heard, and accepted. I had been an adult for years, yet I still struggled.

The grandmother spirit came many times over the months, especially when I was doubting if I had enough time or money to finish making a shawl, a dress, moccasins, a breast plate of buffalo bones, a deer skin pouch, wrapped prayer feathers, and of course, the four beadings of two different symbols that had to be sewn on the pouch and moccasins.

Before she would appear, I became very relaxed and trance-like, and felt a tingling in my spine. I could see her face clearly as if she was human, while her ghostly body floated above me. She guided my hands in the right way to create the projects. I followed her instructions, and when the time came, I headed to Texas.

The initiation ceremony was hard. The heat during the day was scorching, and the nights were chilly. Swarms of locusts came in, tangled my hair and jumped into my mouth when I prayed. But it was there that I would connect with two women elders and receive an invitation to support my first sun dance ceremony in Texas.

In my vision that day, as I wrote in my book *There's a Whole in the Sky,* an elder male and female spirit came forth, gifted me the small chanunpa, placed it in my hands and told me this was to pray for the children.

The ceremony was completed late in the afternoon the following day. I was given the name "Otter Heart Shining Star" with the help of an elder, who would later invite me to support her for the next few years in the sun dance. I can share my entire name here because it is no longer my name.

Seven weeks after this ceremony, I planned a trip to the Yucatan with a dozen women and a spiritual leader whom I had met two years prior.

I went back and forth on whether to go on this trip, right up until a few days before, because of a nightmare I had of being unsafe on the trip. But I eventually decided to go. This trip was physically hard thanks to the July Mexican heat and having to climb a pyramid in the jungle and days later a large mound of a hill (which by the way I don't like heights) with the other women. A few days into the trip, we engaged a Cuban healer who guided the group for the day, and his family. It was definitely a test for me.

At the top of this mound, the woman leading the trip was going to conduct a chanunpa ceremony. She was a ceremonialist. Over time I got to know that we have walked similar human and spiritual paths and have become spiritual sisters.

It was a bright and sunny day and the wind was blowing through my hair. The ceremony I had been accustomed to many times over the years once again filled me. When it was completed, she began to speak about a small chanunpa, how it was given to her, where it came from and that she was being called to gift it to someone in the group. It was in a bag that was less than a foot long. My head started to spin while feeling a relaxed trance-like state and the tingle of warning. I looked overhead and there was a bird, not a spirit bird but a real one. Others in the group pointed up to it. I felt the significance of it. The Cuban elder said it was a condor, the sacred bird of Central and South America. Others in the group called it an eagle. It did look like an eagle to me but either way it was considered a sacred bird.

The group leader sat down in front of me and gifted the small bag to me. She said I could call her if I had questions or needed teachings. Although I knew how to handle a chanunpa, I had been in many ceremonies with the Lakota elder and had teachings on the chanunpa, I was open to accepting the information she offered, because one can never know enough.

My vision from the women's society initiation was fulfilled. It had now manifested on earth. Nine months later, the Child's Chanunpa was blessed and connected to me. It was then that I would begin to pray for the children.

As I moved forward in life, I came to understand that each chanunpa I would be gifted in the future would have different purposes, needs, and what I call, a personality. This required many tests of trusts for me.

This first one demanded self-reflection to heal issues from my childhood. Feeling abandoned when my brother was born. Not feeling worthy or enough because I was a girl. Feeling alone, not knowing where I belonged. Being misunderstood by my family and the people I encountered. I hid my feelings and strange experiences.

Once I began to smoke the Child's Chanunpa and pray, I met people who asked me to teach children from kindergarten through middle school. I sang social songs and told native stories that taught some valuable lessons. Ones that I was taught. It was then that I developed a program to teach children about animals and respect for the earth and all living things.

I did not teach or feed the wrong representation of Native American caricatures. I talked about things that the native elders taught me. I used their words, not mine. I also shared my personal experiences with animals and what they had taught me. Any stipends that I received went back to helping native elders on the reservations and their families.

Schools, camps, and scouting troops became aware of my program by word of mouth. I had a full-time job, so I didn't want to take the lectures on. In a vision when I was smoking the Child's Chanunpa, Spirit told me that I would do this work for seven years. I did not know how I could since schools are open during the day and I worked during the day. When you are truly meant to do Spirit's work the path is cleared for you.

Within less than nine months, the tech company I worked

for as a supervisor closed its doors and left hundreds of people, including me, out of work. Out of a job and being able to collect unemployment insurance for a year, I accepted the opportunities to lecture full-time. This changed the direction of my life.

Spirit also put a young boy who was home-schooled in my path. He had difficulty expressing himself. His parents brought him to the medicine wheel prayer gathering I conducted.

I prayed for this boy with the Child Chanunpa and was told that a naming ceremony would shift his spirit. His parents supported the idea. In fact, when their other children were born, I had naming ceremonies for them as well.

Still in touch with the Lakota elder and several other elders, I did nothing without permission and their blessing. They knew me, and at one time or another, told me they had seen my path on the road of ceremony and knew Spirit always led me.

I prayed with the Child's Chanunpa for four days before the naming ceremony. I was given his name on the fourth day. Spirit gave me his name and showed me a vision for his life and how he would grow into this new name. The new name would help him become spiritually stronger to handle life. It would help him to accept himself, be patient and come to embrace his gifts from Spirit.

A handful of the family's close relatives came together for the ceremony to celebrate him. I filled the Child's Chanunpa with tobacco and prayers for the boy. I offered the smoke to the directions. I blew smoke over him four times for protection in his life and stated his name. After the ceremony the family had a feast for the friends and relatives in attendance.

It would be the beginning of following and trusting, and taking baby steps with the chanunpa. Praying for children helped me get in touch with the needs, wants, and hurts they experienced and the patterns they used to protect themselves. When I could feel them, I could feel and witness my own unresolved hurts and how to unburden them. Praying for them allowed me to be a child again while seeing through their eyes.

Another story comes to mind. While I did pray for babies and toddlers, I also prayed for teenagers with the Child's Chanunpa.

I offered to pray for a young teenage girl who was the daughter of a woman who had recently become a friend of mine. Her daughter was struggling with rebellion and going down a dangerous road that concerned her mother.

I sat in ceremony for four hours offering prayers for this young girl. I prayed for a life where she could love herself and be happy. She was in an angry place and I prayed for a blessing for her to have the strength to come through this dark time and find the direction that would bring her the most peace and joy. I held that vision for her that day and for many months after. Slowly over time, her mother reported good things were happening for her. Today, she has a beautiful family of her own.

When I first sat with the Child's Chanunpa, I would receive a vision of how to dress it (decorate). Did it need a feather, beading or sage to wrap the stem? Does it want a blanket or animal fur to bundle it? Does it want a skin or leather bag (cante juha) to place it in? It may take up to a year to gather these things.

The chanunpa gave me a song or chant and how to build the altar of animal medicines needed for each of the directions. When I prayed for the first year, the bundle pieces changed as my life changed and I healed. I cannot pray and understand the healing of things if I have not healed those things in me. As humans we struggle because we have egos and want control over everything to feel comfortable in our desires and secure in a false sense of self.

The toughest test would come early on with the Child's Chanunpa when I sat with it before it had been blessed or I smoked. I held each piece, stem and bowl, in my hands. I prayed to Spirit committing that I would care for it and protect it. It was then I was shown in a vision I would leave the community I prayed with in western Massachusetts. I was in shock and disbelief. I had traveled for seventeen years across the country to be in ceremony with elders and now I had found one closer to home.

I couldn't believe I would ever have a reason to leave. But within two months, pressure was being put on me to become a student of the community's leader whom I admired and loved dearly. He was being called to take on students of the path. I knew through my communication with Spirit that he was not my teacher, though I would have loved to have him. Spirit said no. I had teachings of the path for many years with a Lakota elder who told me that Spirit would be my true teacher and would guide me directly. I knew from experience this was true.

It forced me to move on. I did a completion chanunpa ceremony with the community to disconnect.

In my personal experience, the Child's Chanunpa taught, challenged, tested, and healed me until I trusted it completely. It gifted healing that led me one step closer to my true self.

Spirit did find me a temporary home for one year with a community in Connecticut. A friend from my former community invited me to a lecture with another Lakota elder from South Dakota. I would have the opportunity to do purification ceremonies with this Lakota elder for the next year when he visited the community in Connecticut. In fact, he was taught by the same Lakota elder I had first met and learned from years before. I am grateful to that community for giving me a loving, temporary ceremony home.

Being a part of many chanunpa ceremonies is not the same as smoking a chanunpa alone. Spirit was testing and challenging me to learn how to smoke alone, use smaller pinches of tobacco, and take draws of smoke without inhaling the smoke into the lungs. Over the years, as new chanunpas with larger sized bowls and stems were gifted to me, I was in training all over again to learn their needs, purpose, power and how to smoke and handle them with reverence.

I performed naming ceremonies and prayed for all children and the inner child of adults. Spirit led me to know who needed help, especially children who were abused. I also learned to pray for all in the young stages of life. Even for baby animals.

One time a baby robin had fallen out of it nest and died. I found it on the back lawn of the apartment where I lived. I picked it up and I wrapped it in red cloth with sage and cedar, placed a prayer of tobacco in it and tied it with a white string. I took the Child's Chanunpa and smoked it, blessing the wrapped robin with the smoke to release its spirit. Then I buried it. When I finished many birds chirped and sang wildly for several minutes.

I have come to learn throughout the years, I must be empty of ego, and with a clear heart of unconditional love when I pray. My prayer is for the best for all concerned to be answered with a word, or words, or a visionary symbol. In many cases it will be answered by another means, a person, or at another time. The guidance not only comes through when it is being smoked but can come from just sitting with the bundle itself.

The Child's Chanunpa helped me heal and learn to become child-like again and take the time to enjoy and do things I once loved as a child. To bring play and joy back to my life that had become too regimented, responsible, and serious. I was reminded how to have fun again. It was my first lesson in transformation and inner growth. I prayed with the Child's Chanunpa for months before the next one was gifted to me.

CHAPTER 21

Earth Keeper Chanunpa

I had a dream of an Ojibwe elder who gave me teachings about the medicine wheel. He crossed into spirit several years earlier. In the dream, he asked me to spread his teachings and share the prayer gathering ceremony with others. Before following this vision, I contacted his former community to gain permission to share the teachings and have the gathering. I was granted permission and talked at great length over the phone to the new tribal chief who was in charge of the teachings. I stated my intent and shared my dream and calling.

We reviewed the teachings to make sure I indeed knew them and the corresponding ceremony. She gave her blessing but said I would have to dedicate seven years to this task if I did it. There was to be no charge, but a donation bucket was okay to help support native people and others in need.

The first area for holding the ceremony was in a small indoor space in a holistic center. I taught here for about six months. Half a dozen people usually came.

The next space was found through a connection of my best friend. She introduced me to a woman who had land she felt should be used for a special purpose. We connected right away and proceeded to invite friends and anyone whom she thought might need to pray or engage in silence and nature.

With a small group of people, we prepared the land for the prayer gathering. We would have it once a month on a Sunday afternoon rain or shine from May until the end of October. In November we disassembled the space for the land's winter regeneration. The gathering started with about a dozen people. Over the years it grew to about thirty. People were not just from our local area. Friends of friends came through word of mouth.

The woman who owned the land was so gracious to allow us to gather and pray. Those were special days for me.

She called me to her house a couple of months after we began the gatherings. She handed me something wrapped in green wool. It was a chanunpa. She explained she was called to purchase it and gift it to me. Its stem and bowl was larger than the Child's Chanunpa I carried.

A month later, it was blessed and connected to me. I then began to sit in ceremony, smoke it and learn its teachings. Its bundle began to take shape and form. In vision, the stem was shown to be dressed differently and its feather hung in a different manner than the first chanunpa I carried. The bundle asked for more things from the earth for its altar and the song gifted from Spirit was one for the earth and its blessings. It would need a different color leather bag and no beading design. This one called itself the Earth Keeper Chanunpa.

The vision that came when I smoked it in ceremony was to pray for everything the land gives to sustain us. It was used to bless and honor land, homes, land disputes, property issues, and any matters concerning the earth, like clearing the energy of land. This would be one to smoke in ceremony with others.

I needed to smoke it alone for a while, which ended up being a year. Smoking it alone allows me to get comfortable with it, learn its purpose and how it wishes to be used. It becomes an extension and part of my heart energy. This chanunpa was less emotional. It felt more stable and grounded. The Child's Chanunpa brought up many emotions and tears. It helped me revisit my own childhood.

The Earth Keeper brought healing for me to find my home, not necessarily a physical place, but a place within me, where I belonged, to live and be. There was still something inside of me that longed to travel and find something that was missing. I guess it was a yearning for something I could not completely understand. Or perhaps it was a calling but at that time, as self-aware as I was, I still had much to learn.

I began to offer this one in ceremony to our group at the winter closing of the prayer gathering. We would smoke together in gratitude for another completed year, blessing the land and all the critters on it. The more I smoked and worked with it during the year, the more memories from the past were being healed. Just like with the Child's Chanunpa.

During one of the times I smoked, the memories came.

The memory of feeling different and that I did not belong in the family I was raised in. Sometimes feeling I did not even belong on the earth. Maybe I unconsciously wanted to leave. Perhaps that was the reason for having so much illness as a child. At eighteen I began to travel around the country and eventually around the world. I was searching for my place to live and be.

Remembering brought the awareness of feeling at home only

in nature. It brought me comfort. I knew one day when I was older, I would find a way to live a more balanced life and participate in the ceremonies in nature that I had seen in my dreams. I had to accept I was exactly where I needed to be on earth and in the correct family Spirit chose for me, at this point there was no specific state, city, town for me to live.

It was through this memory, my healing came. I realized that I did not have to travel around the country to search for my place to belong. There is nature everywhere and I can connect to it and the earth through my heart and mind. Though I continued to travel and learn, my searching and longing dissipated. It took me more years and the gifting of other chanunpas to accept myself, my purpose, and my gifts.

The Earth Keeper Chanunpa taught me that everywhere I take myself is my home. My search for where I belonged was over. I found through all these memories, I no longer needed to search for a place to live. I could be comfortable everywhere I went because my home was within me. When my searching stopped and I healed that part of me, another chanunpa was gifted to me within two years. It was the third one that would further solidify my journey in ceremony.

CHAPTER 22

Buffalo Chanunpa

A woman who attended the medicine wheel prayer gatherings for a year introduced me to a woman who had a buffalo farm. She heard about the prayer gathering and was interested in having a gathering on her land. When I met her and saw the land, I knew it was special. We walked the land and found the perfect spot. But because of commitments and busy schedules, it was another year before I would see her again.

I had a dream I needed to visit her at her farm. It was important. I saw in my dream that she was crying. The next day I went to visit her. When I arrived, she looked sad and talked about her struggles with another person whom she was having a hard time forgiving. Without even thinking about it, I asked her if she would like to pray with the chanunpa. I could come and sit with her in her home and offer her ceremony. With tears of relief, she agreed.

She invited the woman who had originally introduced us to come too. When the day came, I familiarized them with the ceremony and its teachings. Then we prayed. When she smoked, I sang the forgiveness song. This was a song I learned from the Lakota elder I met in the Connecticut community when he conducted the purification ceremonies. She broke into tears and then comfort came over her face, like she had been unburdened.

At the end of ceremony, I relayed what Spirit had shown me in a vision. Sometimes I divulge the information and other times I keep it to myself, when I sense they are not ready to hear it or it was for me alone to know.

Spirit has spoken to me since I was a child, from the first prayer my mother taught me to recite. It was something I had to learn to trust, to know it was not my own voice or reasoning. When this happened, I would be shown things I could not know. When I failed to relay the message, I would see the people struggle without the information for days or months, but when I relayed the message, it brought them peace and an understanding to the situation.

After the forgiveness ceremony at the buffalo farm, we had a light snack and a cup of tea as the feast. A feast of eating food and drink is always done after ceremony, after offering some of it outside to the spirit world.

The woman said she would like to gift me something. I said the tobacco which she had already gifted was enough. She said she had been holding onto something for a few years and now she knew where it belonged. I have been gifted many things I may need or I can pass on to others. This I thought may be one of those things to pass on, so I gratefully accepted.

She brought out a Mickey Mouse pillowcase and inside it was a buffalo fur-covered chanunpa. I knew for sure it was to be with me. Three years prior, the first Lakota elder from my first vision quest came to western Massachusetts to lecture and conduct a purification ceremony. I had a vision of a buffalo handing me a buffalo fur stem chanunpa. It was much larger than my other stems.

If it had not been for the elder conducting the ceremony seeing and confirming what I had seen at the end of the ceremony, I might have dismissed it was being gifted to me in the physical. I thought it was symbolic like the sacred energy of the path I was on.

"Tatanka (buffalo) is coming to you. He offers you the chanunpa road of the ancestors. He gives his life as you will to help the people live," he said.

"But I already walk the path of the chanunpa," I confirmed.

"This one is to lead people," he thought I understood.

I nodded to him in respect.

As I looked down at the buffalo fur wrapped stem of this chanunpa she was gifting me, my eyes began to mist because I was reminded of my vision in the elder's purification ceremony and his words.

The woman explained the story of how she came to be in possession of it.

"The man that made this was from Arizona. He was contracted to make it for a medicine woman in Arizona and as he was making it, he received a vision that it did not belong with her. It belonged with a woman on the east coast who could work with its medicine and lead ceremonies."

When the woman from the buffalo farm traveled to Arizona and told him she had a buffalo farm on the east coast, he gave it to her and asked her to find the right person for it. She held on to it for a couple of years knowing that she did not smoke or have the knowledge of the ceremony. That was until this moment. She knew it belonged with me. She had never experienced a chanunpa ceremony and was completely moved.

My life was changing quickly. The challenges I faced when I had three chanunpas to care for, each with a different purpose and personality, reminded me of my siblings and how each of us had our own gifts and personalities. I realized that taking care of my siblings at a young age prepared me for the responsibility of the three chanunpas that were now in my care.

This bundle, like the others, asked for certain things to be kept in it, like certain animal medicines, furs, feathers, and altar pieces. Since it was already dressed and decorated, I only needed to make the skin bag, tobacco pouch and wood tamper, and then wrap it in the blanket I saw in vision.

It was blessed and connected to me in a purification ceremony conducted by the elder with his community of whom I spoke of earlier in the book.

After it was blessed, the elder said he was told by the spirits that he needed to teach me to lead purification lodges.

It seemed that the first Lakota elder's words and our vision together in the lodge were coming true. I accepted the elder's teachings and began to lead the purification ceremony with his training. He honored my gifts and life experiences and understandings. When I smoked this chanunpa in ceremony for the first time, it named itself the Buffalo Chanunpa. Within two months the spirits told the elder that I was to prepare for a vision quest on his land out of state.

I prepared for a year. Before I was in the vision quest, he

would begin training me to conduct the vision quest ceremony for others in the community.

I would assist him and train for the first few days on how to put two other people from the community on the hill, each for one night. I would help him complete their ceremony and then I would be placed on the hill for two days and two nights alone. This intense energy of both helping conduct ceremony and being in the ceremony would bring its own form of initiation.

The vision quest ceremony has a purpose. People prepare their body up to one year, by fasting periodically from food and water and praying daily on the question they will be asking for guidance on. The question needs to be a serious one, one that you are committed to following through on. I had been on four vision quests before this one.

On my first quest, the Lakota elder who conducted the ceremony said "Do not ask for help with something that you are not serious about. If you are lucky to get a vision you must be prepared to follow the answer."

One would ask, "Who am I? What are my gifts? What is my purpose? Who am I here to serve or help?" These are big questions and not everyone gets answers or visions. Maybe because the question asked was not specific. Maybe the amount of preparation was not enough. Maybe the question was not ready to be answered at the time. Maybe you were not paying enough attention and you fell asleep during the vision quest to receive a vision.

I considered myself fortunate. Every time I was given a vision, and an animal spirit medicine came in to teach something. Each time I was given some understanding to my question. Four of my questions had already been answered. This time my question would be: how can I be worthy of the calling of Spirit to lead ceremony?

The year of fasting included daily prayer and the making of tobacco-filled prayer ties for the altar where I would be. I would stand and pray to the directional grandfather spirits. At other times, I would sit, listen, and observe. I would go through two rounds of a purification ceremony before being placed on a high hill, alone in nature.

I would be left on this hill inside my altar prayer ties. The elder and community would leave me to face Spirit alone. It is personal. For whatever amount of time, (one to four days) I would fast and stand and pray for a vision to my question. It is not an easy thing. The elements can be harsh, cold, rain, hail, thunder and lightning or burning hot sun. I have been through all those elements. It was never easy. No matter how many times I have been through a ceremony, they are all different.

The day before I was placed on the hill, I was in a support purification ceremony with the other community members. We were praying for an older woman who was on the hill, alone in prayer.

During this ceremony, from the darkness in a vision, I saw four Native American men in the distance on horseback. They had large lances and were charging and chasing something. As they came closer, I could see they were chasing a buffalo. Each horse had a different color painted on it. Black, Red, Yellow, and White, together they were the colors of the four directions.

I felt a rumble on the ground and got a light-headed feeling as they came towards me from the West. The buffalo was running very fast and was way ahead of them. It was heading straight towards me. Part of me wanted to move but the darkened lodged was small and we were knee to knee. No room to move. The only thing I could do was close my eyes as the large charging buffalo approached. I took a deep breath hoping the vision would stop. But the pain in my chest told me otherwise. The visionary horns of this creature had gored my heart. I opened my eyes and saw the four horses stop before me. The riders put their lances down. They were not human faces. They were skeletons. They were dead spirits. They turned their horses around and rode off back to the west direction and disappeared.

I, however, was not alright. The pain in my chest was not okay. I yelled "Mitakuye Oyacin" (all my relations) to get the fire keeper to open the door so I could get out.

I crawled out on my belly in pain. My heart was pounding and I was weak. I tried to take slow breaths. I later told the elder what I had seen and cried. There was only one other time I left a lodge early, and that was during my first time many years ago.

The elder had me lay outside and doctored me with his feathered fan. I recovered slowly.

The pain subsided but I still did not feel right. Later in the evening while training, the elder and I prayed for the older woman on the hill. A storm was brewing. The wind picked up and it was pitch black. We could hear the roll of thunder coming in. The rain began to come down in a torrential downpour, bombarding the tent we had set up at the bottom of the hill. Lightning began to crash and we began a chanunpa ceremony together to protect the quester. When the storm was over, we went up the hill to get closer to her without being seen. We sang four songs to her to give her strength. When we heard her faintly singing back to us, we knew she was okay.

It was then I noticed my chest and head felt better. The elder said the thunder beings of the storm and the vision in the lodge had brought about a symbolic death for me.

"You will no longer be the same person. You are walking into something new," he said.

Then two days later, I was placed on the hill in my own vision quest ceremony. After I completed, the elder interpreted my vision in the final purification ceremony.

"You have been initiated. The buffalo gave you its medicine knowledge and power and your vision gave you the power of the moon and dreamtime. I'd say you had a successful quest. You will be a great leader in the vision quest ceremonies."

By leading chanunpa ceremony and purification ceremony for the elder's community, and assisting with vision quests, I came out of my private shell. I had many teachings and experiences to share from the previous twenty years in ceremony. I was given the opportunity by the elder to lead and teach the community, especially prayer songs and how to prepare for vision quests.

Sometimes there was one who challenged me with conflict. In those times, the elder sat back and let me handle it and learn from the experience. At times I became frustrated and wanted to leave the community. I didn't need this, I told myself. But each time I prayed about it, the answer would be, *"No you're not done yet."*

I am grateful to that person who challenged me. It helped me to stand up for the teachings the elders and their ancestors suffered and died for. It also helped me to stand up for myself and accept my worthiness to lead.

The toughest challenge I remember facing was the hardest test for me. I began to lead every other lodge ceremony and I also led them while elder was away with his wife from the end of May to the end of the September.

The elder led a lodge ceremony before he left for the summer, and I was his lead singer for the ceremony.

At the end of the ceremony, the chanunpa is smoked to complete the ceremony. The fire keeper passed it into the lodge for me to light and offer the smoke to the seven directions, (the West, the North, the East, the South, the Above, the Below and the Center within self) according to protocol.

When it was handed to me inside the lodge, several of the community members were talking and joking including the elder. Obviously, they had forgotten we were still in ceremony. As I took it into my hands, the chanunpa spoke to me, "*Send me back out. Do not smoke me. I am not being honored.*"

Oh no. I had a couple of seconds to decide. Do I listen and act which I knew to be right? Or do I embarrass the community including the elder, by holding up ceremony and having to explain why? This was his community. He was leading ceremony. He should have said something. The chanunpa or his spirit helpers should have spoken to him. Who was I?

I began to shudder and my voice began to stammer, "Aho grandfather." I sent the chanunpa back out to the fire keeper.

Everyone stopped their chatter and laughter and turned to look at me. Since the door was open, I could see all their faces staring at me. I will tell you that I was raised to be a respectful person, especially of my elders and authority figures. Even if elders were incorrect about something, I never disrespected or corrected them. It was not my place or business to be seen or heard.

With a weakened voiced and holding back tears I addressed them.

"Grandfather, I am sorry but the chanunpa told me to send it back out and not to smoke it because people were not honoring it. Everyone was talking," I spoke with tears in my eyes.

It was hard for me to speak those words. I know I am sometimes too serious, but this was ceremony. It needed to be done in a good way. I knew it was the right thing to do, but it was not easy.

"Who is she to disrespect you?" The challenger argued.

The rest of the community was startled and watching intensely, looking to the elder for a response.

The elder looked at them and at me and then responded.

"She is right. We got lazy and were not paying attention. We were talking and disrespecting the chanunpa and that's not right. Good thing she was listening. She has proven she is a leader and protector of ceremony and the chanunpa."

The challenger spoke up again, "But who is she? You're the elder?"

"She is the elder in my place when I am not here. She is the carrier of three chanunpas."

Now up until this point, no one in community knew this fact except him and perhaps his wife. I did not divulge the information as per the elder's request. He told me that it is very unusual and that he only knew of medicine people carrying that many. He didn't want people to feel it was protocol.

But today he spoke it. From that day on, I took on the responsibility. I became a leader in these ceremonies and even though I was continually challenged, I gained the respect of the community and became more confident in using my communication and connection with Spirit.

Once again through the ceremony of smoking alone, memories were revealed to bring about more inner healing I needed from the Buffalo Chanunpa. This was the one that would be used to lead purification and vison quest ceremonies.

After a year of smoking this chanunpa, I heard Spirit's voice.

"It is time to let another help you with your work. You must quit your job and work with ceremony."

But the vision as I smoked brought images of me holding hands with a man, and walking forward together and conducting ceremonies with him supporting. I could not see his face - only the back of his body.

Trusting and relying on someone else was a huge task for me. This healing would only take a year before he entered my life. I had to let go of my fear and allow myself to feel safe with a man who was willing to share my secrets and calling.

As I shared earlier in the book, I went to the sun dance ceremony, held the chanunpa at the sacred tree and offered my flesh and my prayer.

"Spirit if you want this relationship for me to do your work, then put him right in front of me so that I will know. I don't have time to waste."

I wanted to fulfill what Spirit was asking and calling me to do, but at the time I wasn't interested in a relationship and all the commitments. I wanted to be committed only to Spirit.

The Buffalo Chanunpa helped me to heal my unworthiness to lead ceremony. It gave me the strength and trust, to begin a relationship with Paul and quit my job to begin Spirit's work.

Six months after the blessing of the Buffalo Chanunpa, a fourth chanunpa was born.

CHAPTER 23

Crossing Chanunpa

The fourth chanunpa had a different beginning. It had been six months since the Buffalo Chanunpa was blessed and opened. While smoking the Buffalo Chanunpa Wakan one day, I had a vision.

I saw four chanunpa stems. I saw myself working with wood, cutting and sanding, using my father's woodworking tools. I also saw myself praying and singing prayer songs as I worked. The vision progressed until I had made the four stems. There were no bowls to match them - only stems of different lengths and sizes.

I was mechanical and could use tools, but wood working would be a first. In this vision, I could see exactly what I needed to do. I wanted to forget about the vision, but it would not let go of me. All my waking thoughts were about the four stems. I was pestered by Spirit.

Finally giving in, to ease my mind, I bought some cedar wood. I smudged it with sage and cedar smoke. Then I asked my father if he would let me use his tools. Over a couple of months, under my father's watchful eye, I worked, prayed, and sang sacred songs during the creation of the stems.

Each one I made was different in length and design. I did

exactly as I had seen in my vision. I did not know why or who they were for, but I completed them. The hand sanding and making a hole through the center were the hardest and longest tasks. On one of them, I was called to burn black spots up and down the stem on the front and back. Another one looked like a square block and the connecting end that went into the bowl was very skinny. I worked and prayed, and they all took shape and form exactly as in my vison. Now they were complete and my mind was at peace.

Months before, my best friend was called to make two red pipestone bowls without knowing why. She too was led through the chanunpa. She was called to purchase a block of red pipestone, which she had cut into two pieces and had holes drilled into each of them. She filed and formed each of them over the next several months until she completed them both. I was not aware of her calling to do this.

I was praying with the Buffalo Chanunpa and once again a vision came forward.

I saw the faces of three of my friends. In the vision I saw myself giving each of them a stem. Normally the stem and bowl made are together by the same person. The stem needs to fit the bowl exactly for a good fit otherwise it will not smoke correctly.

It felt like only half a vision. No one gifts a stem without a bowl but trusting the vision, I waited until the appropriate time. Of course, Spirit timed it perfectly.

My best friend met me at a bird sanctuary. I was teaching her prayer songs while we were sitting, just the two of us in nature. It was the perfect place for our weekly visits. After we were done practicing, she revealed that she had been working on something that was now complete. She pulled a bowl out of a piece of red cloth. I was surprised. This was not something she had ever done before. I asked her if she knew who it was for. She said she thought so, but added that the person did not carry a chanunpa. We both sat there a few minutes in silence, as I smudged the bowl and held it in my hands. I knew it was for one of the people I had seen in my vision I had made a stem for. I knew exactly which stem was for this person, but would it fit? That I did not know.

She revealed who she thought it was for and I told her that is exactly what I envisioned. Then I shared with her that I had made a stem for this person but I was not sure this bowl would fit. I told her I had made four stems and knew where three of them were going, but the fourth person had not been revealed in my vision.

The following week we gathered together, I with the stem and she with the bowl. Over a shell burning with sage, we decided to see if they would fit together to become a chanunpa. I brought my hand sanding tool in case I needed to shave down some of the wood where the stem connected to the bowl. There was no need. When we placed them together it was a perfect fit. Nothing needed to be adjusted. I did not choose a stem that would fit the bowl. I made the stem and then was shown which stem was for that person before I knew there was a bowl. Soon after, we gifted the stem and bowl together as the chanunpa. I gave the teachings for its use and care.

Unbeknownst to me, my best friend had also made another smaller second bowl of red clay.

I knew one of the stems was for my best friend. It was not

long after that the stem for her chanunpa was unusable and I had a replacement for her, once again fitting perfectly.

The third stem I made was gifted to the third person I saw in my vision. It was the one on which I had burned black spots. She had the bowl that fit it perfectly. Then she gifted it to the right person. I realized more and more that if I listened and was willing to follow, Spirit would lead.

A few months later, I had a dream the last stem I made belonged to me. It was the one that was squarely shaped with the short, skinny connecting piece. It was my least favorite because it was odd looking. I was shown a small red pipestone bowl that was oddly shaped would be its mate.

The dream stayed with me for days.

Less than two weeks later, my best friend called me and asked if we could get together to visit. She came to the condo I was renting.

"I have something to give you. I don't know why or if it's for you or someone else, but here it is."

Again, she handed me the red cloth to open. My body began to tingle and I began to feel light-headed.

"Oh. Yes. It's for me. I have had dreams about this," I confirmed. I excused myself to retrieve the odd shaped stem from the cedar chest.

Amazing, it fit perfectly. No adjustment needed. Both bowl and stem matched in an odd way. Now all that was needed was to begin to build the bundle. I made a leather bag and tobacco pouch and dressed the stem uniquely but plainly. The altar pieces and medicines would only come after it was blessed and connected. Earlier, I wrote about the experience of leaving my body in the purification ceremony to help a friend's spirit, who had died at the exact time this chanunpa was being blessed in ceremony. It was then I understood it was the Crossing Chanunpa.

Up until this point, I had dealt with many lost spirits and their messages, asking them to go to the light of the spirit world, this chanunpa would be used to do so.

The following year I completed another vision quest. My three-day vision quest brought new medicine, a new spirit animal helper and two songs to be used with the Crossing Chanunpa.

The vision also revealed that I would be gifted more chanunpas in the future. I heard the number *seven* but was hoping I heard wrong. I had my hands full with four.

The Crossing Chanunpa Wakan helped me to deal with the spirit world in a deeper way. As I built the bundle with its altar and medicines, I smoked it in ceremony for the first year. Memories returned to me.

I was thirteen in the summer of 1974. I was awake in bed and my great grandmother appeared in ghost-like form. She came to tell me that her heart died. She gave me the vision of her dying in my great grandfather's arms.

She spoke to my mind, "Don't be afraid. I have no pain. Help your mother because she will be very sad. Be kind to your great pepere (grandfather). You will go to the beach on vacation with him. Tell them all I am safe and happy. Je t'aime (I love you)."

"I love you too, memere." I replied in my mind.

She allowed me to go with her spirit only so far because I was tethered to my body by a thin strand of energy. When we approached the tunnel of light, we said our good-byes. She reminded me that I had healing gifts from God and to use them. Then she was gone and I was sent back to my bed with a thud.

The memory faded as I finished the ceremony.

The memory reminded me of my ability to travel to the dead or dying person and see through their eyes. The Crossing Chanunpa would teach me how to cross people dying or who already died on a deeper level. It even gave me a song to sing to help those who were in a coma to let go if they chose.

It gave me a specific ritual to release four places of attachment in the human body. When done properly there can be a clean break for the spirit to release from the body. No spirit wandering. A more defined process than what I used before.

It also challenged me to heal my own fear of dying. Prayers with the Crossing Chanunpa allowed me to see the spirit body clearer and be more comfortable in the spirit world when using the two songs that came on the vision quest. One was a crossing song, and the other was an honoring song.

The final teaching the Crossing Chanunpa gave me was to value my life, to be present in all moments, and find joy in the smallest things because life goes by quickly.

CHAPTER 24

Women's Chanunpa

The fifth chanunpa was gifted to me on the day of my marriage to Paul. We got married in a traditional Native American ceremony by the elder who had trained me in conducting ceremonies for his community.

After the marriage ceremony was over, my husband and I, as in tradition, fed family and friends and had a giveaway (gifting ceremony) to each of the approximately sixty people who attended.

After the ceremony, my parents (with the help of my best friend) gifted my husband and I matching chanunpas. I found it incredible. My father wanted to make us each one but did not know how to make the bowl, so my mother asked my best friend where they could obtain one for each of us. It must have been very difficult for my parents who raised me Catholic to gift me something that was so sacred to me that they did not fully understand. I trust that Spirit orchestrated the whole thing with them. I was touched, but on the other hand, a fifth chanunpa for me to carry was not something I felt I needed or wanted. However, I concluded that if another was gifted to me, there must be a reason and purpose, and more for me to heal.

I sat with it as I did with the others before it was blessed and connected to me. I held it and saw myself praying with a group of women. It would only be used to pray for or with women.

I asked the elder's wife if she would conduct a women's purification ceremony to bless it. She too had conducted ceremony for many years. She suggested that after the ceremony I should fast overnight in the lodge to pray in the darkness and develop a deeper connection with it. This would be the second time I stayed overnight. The first time was before Paul and I were married. It was the process to reflect on the upcoming day and part of the preparation for the wedding ceremony.

A month later, six of us women gathered and prayed in ceremony and it was blessed. With the blessing ceremony complete, I was left alone to fast overnight in the hot and damp lodge.

In the darkness I sat up with legs folded, singing prayer songs and asking for guidance. I lost all sense of time in the darkness.

I was getting pretty tired when the closed door-flap seemed to disappear. It was if I could see to the outside of the lodge at night and see the small glowing coals that once heated the stones for the purification ceremony hours before.

Four older spirit native men sat around the glowing coals. I watched as they conversed and paid no attention to me. I wondered what they were doing. I could see them making some kind of plant medicine over the fire by stirring a wooden or gourd bowl. They were praying and chanting over it, one at a time. I tried to lean closer to hear them from where I sat inside the lodge.

I held the Women's Chanunpa close to me with both of my hands and as I inched closer to hear them, a large great horned owl spirit flew in the doorway. I backed away.

The owl had large round gold eyes and its head turned side to side observing the inside of the lodge and me. It perched itself on the ground blocking the doorway. It began to illuminate itself to the point where I could see it perfectly. It stretched its wings horizontally and began a gentle flap. The owl shifted into an older woman. She had one streak of long white hair on either side of her middle part.

She smiled and communicated, "I am a blood ancestor. I am called, She Who Weeps."

She proceeded to sing a song and said it was the medicine that went with the Woman's Chanunpa.

"Only smoke and pray with this chanunpa with and for women. Let no man touch it. Pray for fertility, marriage, motherhood, and ending all abuses against women," she demanded.

She explained new items would be gifted to me by women and they should be used and kept in the bundle. Over the next year, this would prove to be true.

A cante yuha bag that belonged to a medicine woman, a tobacco pouch from a Cherokee granny, blue corn meal, white clay and a feather that came from a woman on the Hopi reservation were all gifted to me for the bundle.

Through telepathy, She Who Weeps showed me how to build the altar. There would be no animal fetishes, only specific shell and plant-based items. It was different than I had ever seen before. All through the night she gave me instructions and reminded me of her healing song.

I asked about the four elders at the fire that I had seen before she arrived.

I asked her, "Who are the four spirit elders by the fire? Why are they here?"

She said, "They have come to give you a ceremony to use in healing."

"Is it just for women?" I asked.

"Yes," she answered.

Before I could thank her, she changed back into the owl spirit and flew out of the lodge.

I practiced the song she gifted over and over so that I could commit it to memory. It seemed like hours had gone by in the dark. Then once again the door flap illuminated and the four elder men entered the lodge. Two sat to my left facing me and two sat to my right. I was in the back of the lodge facing the doorway and the stone pit.

In the silence, they showed me what was in the bowl they had been stirring near the fire. It was a reddish mixture of red clay and herbs. In a telepathic voice to my mind, they each explained a different part of the potion and how it was used.

They motioned me to lie down, and they proceeded to smear the concoction over my heart, belly and forehead. Once this was complete, they each waved eagle feathers over me, creating a drying effect. The concoction felt stiff like a paste.

They told me to sing the song the owl spirit grandmother taught me.

I sang it internally and felt something from my body rise above me. It was as if sickness, worries, burdens, and stress were being taken out of me. The pulling effect of the paste was drawing something out of me. I held the Woman's Chanunpa tightly over my chest, protecting it from the spirit men. I did not let it go, while all these sensations were happening.

It was then that my mind began to speed up and vison the future, of leading groups of women in and out of ceremonies. This ceremony was to be used to draw out and lift mental, physical, emotional, and spiritual issues.

I asked, "If this is a Woman's Chanunpa, then why are you grandfathers giving me this ceremony and medicine?"

They answered immediately.

"The medicine comes from the earth herself, the feminine. For healing to occur, there needs to be both masculine and feminine present. We represent the masculine of action: the ritual, not the physical man." They spoke together in one voice. As soon as I understood, they disappeared.

The Woman's Chanunpa was helping me with my feminine healing. When I prayed and smoked, many memories from my past came to mind.

These are some of those memories.

At twelve, I went to a Catholic school. We had a short library period after lunch every day to do research for classes or just to take books out for leisure reading.

One particular day, I was at the bookcase alone against the wall and a boy from my class cornered me, grabbed my breast and laughed. I got scared. My immediate reaction was to slap him in the face. He yelled in pain and someone in the library shushed the noise. He quickly ran out of the library and back to class. I was in shock and scared. I told a nun who was my teacher what just happened and she berated me for slapping him .

The next memory came from when I was fourteen. I was sexually assaulted by a man in my family. He roughly touched me under my skirt. It hurt. My face must have shown my horror as he retreated immediately. I pushed him away in silence. I felt shame, guilt, and fear. I buried it to keep his secret. It changed my sense of trust in relationships, especially male. I never felt safe in my body. For years, I felt anxious when I was around men.

At fifteen, I was in high school and entering science class. One boy was standing at the door and as I went to pass him, he grabbed my breast and pinched it. Even though I was in fear, I grabbed him and pushed him against the glass door.

"If you ever touch me again, I will hurt you," I said as I let him go.

I was shaking and began to cry. He laughed. All the boys laughed. I felt shame and guilt for acting out in violence. After that day, I never walked into class without another girl.

I sat and prayed with each of the buried memories that surfaced. I shed many tears during the first year with the Women's Chanunpa. The emotions of fear felt like I was being swept away into an ocean and then drowning in a sea of shame.

The next year would be a test of compassion to forgive myself for suppressing it and the boys and man who assaulted me. It was tough. I decided to voice and release the memories by sharing them with my husband who listened and acted as a witness. I needed to take back my body and my voice to regain the safety and trust I would need to build a healthy relationship and marriage.

CHAPTER 25

Medicine Chanunpa

Two years after receiving the Women's Chanunpa, I prepared to go through another vision quest out of state. The elder who trained me in ceremony would once again conduct the ceremony.

A vision came during the first night.

I was shown another chanunpa. I saw myself holding it. It looked very different from the other five I already carried. The bowl was black pipestone. The stem was rounded with black circles on it, like a porcupine quill or raccoon tail. The vision was very detailed. Several different kinds of bird feathers were tied to the stem. I was told by Spirit that now my real work with medicine, my true calling, would begin.

I was also told that I needed to write a book because I had something to say. I saw myself in the vision writing at the computer.

This was the part of the vision I was not remotely interested in pursuing. In fact, when I came down from the hill and relayed my vision to the elder. I completely forgot about it.

That is until Spirit told the elder in the lodge, who in turn said to me, "Spirit says you need to write a book."

Ugh. I did not want to write a book. What could I possibly write about?

Remembering my first vision quest years ago, a Lakota elder told me, "If you ask for a vision, you need to follow the vision for a good completion. Don't ask for something you're not going to do."

I procrastinated writing my first novel. I hurt my knee getting off a plane traveling to Arkansas for my fourth initiation to become an elder in the Good Medicine Society of teachings and ceremony.

When I arrived home, I could not walk for a month. Having nothing else I could do; I began to write. In a month without rehab the knee got better and the book began to take form. It would take four years to complete my first book of fiction, *There's a Whole in the Sky*.

Not long after I completed the initiation in Arkansas, I was gifted another chanunpa. It was large and had a large bird-shape black pipestone bowl. I knew this was not the one from my vision on my quest. Eventually knowing it was not mine, I sent it to the elder in Arkansas to use in her ceremony.

I would come to understand that it was a test for me. To trust and follow the vision I had received on the vision quest. I was not to be quick accepting any chanunpa but only the one in my vision.

It may take a year or years before a vison completes, even if you are following the signs and paying attention. One must learn patience and trust. Patience is the virtue I work hard to gain every day.

The sixth chanunpa was eventually gifted to me and only after I was disconnected from the elder's community.

The sixth came in two pieces, first the bowl was made by a Blackfoot woman. The bowl was from a black pipestone quarry in Canada near the Blackfoot reservation. Second, the stem was made by a local native man in Winchendon, Massachusetts.

I believe the person who found it and gifted it to me knew of my vision, if memory serves me correctly. Once gifted, I began a closer walk with the spirits and with medicine. Seven feathers from four different birds were called to be placed on the stem. The bundle gathered many more medicines of plants and bird feathers. Three times I asked the elder to bless it and three times we had to change dates. His schedule kept changing.

I got the message. I would bless it myself and connect it to me in the purification lodge on our land over the coming weekend. My husband would build the fire and transfer the stones. I would conduct the ceremony alone in the lodge and then fast overnight in the dark.

Before I entered the lodge, a melody came from the fire as the stones were heating. I swayed to the song and sang aloud to commit it to memory. I knew it was important. I listened and followed as it was planted in my mind.

A thunderstorm came in during the ceremony, with heavy rain and lightning coming very close to the lodge. I was protected. Outside, my husband was doing everything he could to keep the fire going and the stones hot.

In the third round of the ceremony, a visionary large-winged presence entered the lodge. I felt its wing brush against my face as it came from the West and over my shoulder. It made a screeching sound. All I could see in the dark were two gold balls that looked like eyes above and facing me. I sang the new song to this mysterious spirit creature. The golden eyes explained this chanunpa was to be smoked until winter then put away to sleep during winter months. When the first spring thunderstorm of the year happens, it can be smoked and used again. It would be a Medicine Chanunpa, one to make and use medicines in the physical and nonphysical. It would be used for deep healings, ones that were hiding in the spirit. I saw a simple ceremony using red earth paint to use with the song from the fire. Placing the paint in four circles on the face was relayed in the vision. Once it was within my memory, the winged creature departed.

The following year, I began to have unusual symptoms in my body. Light headedness, heart palpitations, racing pulse and a sensation of bugs moving under my skin. My nervous system was on overload.

I was still writing my first novel and it was moving at a snail's pace. I was fatigued and went from doctor to doctor. Blood tests proved nothing. The neurologist did tests and found nothing. The endocrinologist did tests for my hormones, possible perimenopause symptoms, but still found nothing. Finally, I found a naturopathic doctor in western Massachusetts. She did a lot of testing and found I had high levels of heavy metals in my blood and a co-infection of two strains of Lyme disease. It made plausible sense since I had worked for many years in the tech industry in a metal coating department and spent many years in the woods.

I started a detox protocol for the Lyme and a chelation process for the metals. It made me sicker. I called it quits after eight weeks. I could not eat or sleep. My stomach was sick all the time and the dizziness was much worse.

I decided to call the elder and asked if he could conduct a healing ceremony for me. I told him my symptoms and he agreed. I made an appropriate giveaway bundle for the healing and he set the date.

He prayed with his chanunpa, using his eagle fan to bless the smoke over me. Then he used his medicine stone and laid it on my body in two places. It was a simple ceremony but my body responded with a rush of heat and then relaxation. I saw in vision during this healing, he would pass this medicine stone and his wing fan to me when he crossed over.

"You'll be okay. Spirit is just working on you to get you ready," he said.

"Ready? What do I need to get ready for?" I asked.

"That's between you and Spirit."

Three months later, after the healing ceremony and smoking the Medicine Chanunpa daily, I felt much better. Something had shifted.

One day at the end of March, during my prayers, my mind saw a vision of a cabin in the woods on a beautiful lake. I knew where this was because I had been there before when I was called to complete a vision quest with the Women's Chanunpa.

After discussing it with my husband, I decided I would try to book a week at the campground, which was only seventeen miles away. A respite retreat alone sounded like the perfect thing to recuperate both mind and body.

When praying with the Medicine Chanunpa a week later, I saw in vision that it would be another four-day vision quest.

It had to happen fast if I was to get in the campground before it was open to the public. I had only two weeks to prepare the tobacco ties and tobacco filled directional robes. I would have to go the four days and night fasting with very little preparation instead of months or a year. Also from my vision, I was to fill six empty coffee cans with the dirt from our land. There would be no fire outside the cabin.

It was a struggle for me to wrap my head around the vision I was shown. This was different than I had traditionally done in the past. I would run the ceremony myself, with no elder, as is the customary protocol. I would be both the quester and the elder. Still resisting with following through with my vision, I called both the elder granny from Texas and the elder that trained me in ceremony for guidance.

I was hoping for them to both say that I should wait a year, that this was not the way to do it. The elder said he would help if he could but he would be away traveling.

In the end they both said the exact same words, "Do what Spirit has asked and you'll be okay."

I was stressed. I was used to a traditional way to do things with one step leading to the next. My control would have to be released. I was very open to the spirit world, to visions, to receiving and trusting guidance but this was so different. I had to learn to give up my human need to control and to forget everything I thought I knew. All the training and tradition I had learned was out the window.

It felt chaotic. I would soon realize that when it came to this Medicine Chanunpa, I knew nothing. I would have to be a blank slate and surrender my will to complete this ceremony.

I arrived at the campground at the end of April. Instead of placing the altar on the ground, the vision showed me it needed to be placed on the front porch under the roof edge.

The cans of dirt were used to place the direction tobacco prayer robes and for the tobacco ties to be wrapped around them to enclose me inside the altar. The buffalo robe and skull were placed exactly where my vision previewed. I ate my last meal and then went to sleep inside the cabin. I would start the vision quest ceremony in the morning.

At sunrise I filled the Medicine Chanunpa and enclosed myself in the altar. It was cold and chilly by the lake. The porch roof blocked off the sun's rays, making it even colder. I stood and prayed and then sat down to listen and observe throughout the day. When night came, I caught a glimpse of the moon through the pine trees. It was comforting. It was quiet for most of the night until early sunrise when the birds began their morning chatter. By the afternoon, the sky became cloudy and the wind picked up. Squirrels were scurrying in a playful manner, chasing each other in the trees. I continued my prayers and songs while standing and facing each of the directions for hours, and then sitting in silence to listen and observe.

By sunset, the dark clouds billowed over the lake. It looked like a storm was coming in. The weather report before I left had no mention of rain or storms for the week. Several geese and ducks quickly took off in flight together. The wind began to bend the branches of the trees to the West. I could see they were not fighting, but rather were surrendering to the heavy wind. The water on the lake moved in a direct wave of ripples towards me. It was still light enough for me to see it.

I felt a presence over my left shoulder. It was a breath upon my cheek. I could not see anyone. I could only sense the breath.

"Aho grandfather or grandmother," I spoke aloud to greet the presence.

I addressed both because I was not sure if it was a male or female. The presence stayed with me until the moon rose again. Still, I could only see a glimpse of it through the pine trees. My prayers were to ask help for the Medicine Chanunpa's use and purpose and that I could be worthy of being its caretaker/follower. I said this prayer through the night over and over.

In the morning of the third day as the sun began to rise over the lake, I heard a sound of rattles in the distance, coming from the South. A rhythmic beat and then the words came to my mind. Chanting repeatedly, I sang along over and over to commit it to my memory. It was a song to honor the power of the sun. It was not a sunrise song. The words were about the power of the sun and how to ask for its help for vitality in healing. That is what I understood.

I prayed and sang it on and off throughout the third day. The lake was still and the sun's rays reflected off of the water, sparkling like diamonds. At sunset I began to struggle. I was hungry and tired but not thirsty. The breeze off the lake continued to chill me so I wrapped the buffalo robe tightly around me.

I focused on my prayer hoping to shift my hunger. I sang several prayer songs in a row and then I had to sit down because I was feeling light-headed.

In a dream-like state, a song came from outside of me to my mind, but was in my own voice. My voice was being used as the song came through. The melody was simple. It was a song to honor the end of day and the coming of the moon. I sang it over and over. The more I sang the sleepier I became.

Time flew by during the third night. I was no longer hungry but I was very sleepy. I could barely stay awake. The

LORALEE DUBEAU

208

custom is not to fall asleep, to stay awake and be alert during a vision quest.

Once again, I felt a presence over my left shoulder and its breath upon my face.

"Aho, grandfather or grandmother please let me see you. Come and sit with me to smoke," I pleaded.

A male and female face appeared. "Come with us," they spoke.

They puckered their mouths and blew their breath towards me. My eyes felt heavy and the vision began. The seven herbs I was given in the vision quest with the Women's Chanunpa were on the ground in front of me. I recognized all of them. They had me blend them all together. The scene changed. The clay mixture the four spirit grandfathers taught me about in the overnight lodge after the blessing of the Women's Chanunpa were also there. Again, the elder spirits had me mix them in my vision. At last, the winged creature appeared and had me use the red paint on the specific places on my face as I was told when I blessed the Medicine Chanunpa.

Then the scene changed again, and I saw myself lying on the ground and the earth began to beat. I could feel it vibrate through my body. The two elders demanded that I sing my song. I was not sure which one they wanted.

A song arose from my belly with no words. This was a new one. I could feel myself getting lighter almost lifting off the ground. When I looked down, I realized my body was on the ground but my spirit lifted above without being completely detached.

They spoke in unison, "This is your death song. You will sing it to separate from your body when you die. You must be fully present in your separation. Practice it alone and then let go of it until it is time. Even in the unconscious your spirit can sing to separate from your body. Use it for no one but yourself. You have seen three ceremonies of medicine work. We will help your mind get out of the way to conduct them when needed."

They both began another chant and each of them tried my body on. Each of their spirits would enter my body.

The male elder came first and using my voice announced, "I am Wind Rider."

I was scared because I had no control of my thoughts or my physical body. I only sensed a commanding force of wind and a knowing of the exact ritual of red paint needed for healing with him guiding my body.

Then he left and she entered, "I am Many Feathers. I am the soft breath of the songs."

She too used my voice like whispers that grew louder. It was a direct line of communication from the earth to the sky. She knew the exact song for a healing ceremony. She would use me to work with her in the mixture of the seven plant herbs and red clay.

I understood what they asked. But I was still worried about this loss of control of myself. I was used to receiving a vision of guidance and following, but not giving over my body to their spirits for each healing ceremony.

Then a third spirit appeared. This grandfather was hard to look at. He had half of a face. One side looked normal and the other looked melted, like it had been burned in a fire. I tried to avert my eyes. I thought he might be evil or a dark force.

When he entered my vision the other two spirits left.

"I am No Face," he said with dominance.

"Aho grandfather," I replied.

"I am the unseen and the seen. I am the power of lightning

that destroys or gives pity and cleanses. I came to you before. You know me."

He refreshed my mind of the glowing eyes in the purification lodge when I blessed the Medicine Chanunpa. The brush upon my cheek of what I thought was a wing. I nodded in the memory. He embodied the power of cleansing with fire and water.

His power did not enter me but he gave forth a vision of a stone that looked like his face. It was deformed like his. He blew into it and the stone began its medicine song. It had no words. He used a rattle and the song was fast. He was rattling at a frantic pace that was hard to follow. I tried to commit it to memory.

"You will remember when you find me," he said as he pointed to the stone. It was white with a smooth texture, and had a deformed face on one side.

"Where do I find you?" I asked.

"When it's time," he answered. Then he disappeared.

A crow cawed and I awoke from the dream/vision. The sun was up. I recalled the dream and went over every detail. I offered tobacco to the lit sage and cedar burning in the shell as I practiced the songs of the sun, moon rising, my death and the medicine stone of "No Face." To remember them, I sang them in prayer for most of the day.

By sundown the wind picked up again and dark clouds moved across the lake. It began to rain heavily. I was grateful to have covering over my head. The tree branches once again bent with flexibility, reminding me that I too, needed to be flexible to this new way of the Medicine Chanunpa.

The rain continued on and off through the night. Nothing else happened. I made prayers of gratitude for what I had experienced. In the morning I smoked the Medicine

Chanunpa in ceremony and then I broke the ties to my altar and left to break my fast. After a vision quest it is customary to write down your experience in a journal while it is fresh in your mind. Then I disassembled my altar. For the rest of the day and night, I hydrated, ate, and slept. I returned home the following day.

As time went on, I found the stone of *No Face* on a beach in Maine, and the elder spirit and I have reconnected. I have used the songs, red paint, the herbs, and clay mixture in ceremonies to help others. I am no longer resistant to Wind Rider and Many Feathers assisting in ceremony. I have surrendered as part of working with medicine.

I will sing my death song when my spirit is ready to leave my body. I sing it from time to time to remember, to prepare and be at peace with no fear when that time comes. It is a powerful chant.

The Medicine Chanunpa helped me to become another level of ceremonialist. I walked through another door to become a clear and clean channel, releasing personal beliefs, limitations, and protocols. I allow my physical body to be inhabited by spirit guides from the unseen world to send appropriate healing. It took three more years of practice to be able to conduct the ceremonies and keep the channel clear. I would learn to shed my limitations and all protocols to work with the medicines.

I worked with the Medicine Chanunpa for a total of six years before the seventh one was gifted to me. The next one would bring a new set of teachings, and another healing of my spirit and heart. It would help me enter the stage of becoming an elder myself.

CHAPTER 26

White Grandmother Chanunpa

I had been praying with all six chanunpas when the seventh one was gifted. To say which one I sat and prayed with most frequently would be like asking a mother to choose her favorite child. It is not possible. It depends on what I was asked to pray for and what ceremony was needed. Help for children, women, land, purifications, crossing spirits, or medicine work.

The seventh one was gifted a year before I published my second book, *The Honey Pit, Finding the Grandmother's Way*. The novel was a compilation of personal experiences and teachings that I received from native women elders, both alive and in the spirit world.

It also came at a sad time. As I said earlier in the book, I was grieving the loss of my nineteen-year-old furry companion. It was like my child died. He was my shadow right up until the end. I never had the desire to have children but animals always touched my heart. They were vulnerable, uninhibited, and always gave unconditional love.

My cat Sammy was calm and comforting when life was challenging. We were together thirteen years before my husband Paul came along. There was no denying our bond. He sat with me when I prayed and loved to be blessed with the smoke of the chanunpa. When I conducted a group ceremony, he greeted each person and then lay appropriately in the circle with us.

When it was time for him to leave this earth, he made sure to communicate it to me. He had thyroid issues. I gave him medicine daily for his last year despite whatever was going on in my life. He also had a small mass on his pancreas for the last three years of his life, but he never cried in pain. I watched for the signs - lack of eating or drinking, no bowel movements or crying from pain, but he greeted me every day at the door of the bedroom. That is until the last day of his life, when he did not leave his bed and would not eat or drink. I kissed him and knew it was time. I made an appointment with the veterinarian for the next day. I rocked him and held him in my arms and cuddled him the rest of the day and night.

I spoke of my love for him. I rocked him and sang songs to him every day. It was our routine in the morning since he was nine-weeks-old and entered my life. I sang, "You are my Sunshine" and a native prayer lullaby.

The next morning, I did the same routine before we took him for our good-bye. Paul and I went together and they gave us some time with him before putting him to sleep. I coddled him in his favorite blanket and held him in my arms. I still tear up when I think about it. I looked into his eyes and sang the lullaby song. He did not have to search for me because I was right there holding him in my arms next to my heart.

They gave him something to relax him and then I began the crossing song. Then they gave him the shot to give him peace in his body. I held him for a long time kissing him while I cried. The fur on his head was soaked from my tears.

There is one thing I would like to ask of you, dear reader. If you are fortunate enough to be able to witness a pet's crossing, as hard as it may be for you, please be there with them. Let your face be the last thing they see before they close their eyes. Their eyes will search for you in their last moments. They will look to you for comfort. I have seen it many times when helping others cross their pets. Though their body is ready to leave they still need your voice and love so that they can leave peacefully, without fear or panic in a strange place.

I had been grieving for four months when the seventh chanunpa was gifted to me. It was gifted by the same spiritual sister who gifted me the Child's Chanunpa years ago. She gifted this one to me when we met for dinner one night.

She had prayed for guidance where it belonged and knew it was meant to be with me. I accepted believing it was Spirit who orchestrated it all.

This chanunpa was unusual. The bowl was made of white stone with brown veins running through it. The stem was made of very old, hardened wood, shaped in an arc like a native hunting bow.

I blessed it in our lodge during a purification ceremony. I then fasted and spent an overnight alone in the darken lodge wanting to learn its purpose and teachings. Not all information would come in this one night but it was a starting place. It can take at least a year or several to learn its teachings and struggle through the personal challenges that came.

The night in the lodge was warm because it was a hot July evening and the lodge was still heated from the ceremony. As I prayed, a song came forth. The melody came first and I hummed it for a while. Then later a few words to chant. The song came in clear and from outside of myself in my left ear which was usually the case. It was a spirit woman's voice. I sang it over and over to commit it to my memory as I have done in the past. The words spoke of gratitude to a white grandmother, whatever that meant. I sang it on and off through the night.

Through a vision I was shown a few things it wanted for its bundle, a white rabbit skin bag, a white feather, white deerskin tobacco pouch and fetishes for the altar. Also, there needed to be one piece of my medicine tied to its stem. This was minimal compared to the other chanunpa bundles.

Every time I sat and prayed with this one, I cried. My grieving was heavy, missing my cat. There was such a hole in my heart. I prayed daily for thirteen months. I could not speak my cat's name or recall a memory of him without tears. Every amount of sadness from my life in the past had surfaced, even small memories. I found over time much of the sadness was not even connected to his death. Every ounce of sadness I swallowed in my life came forth in loud sobs for those months.

After the first thirteen months, my husband and I went to Roseland Park in Woodstock Connecticut, on a lake close to where my parents live. We visited the park often. We would bring a picnic lunch, take a walk, and then sit with a good book for the afternoon.

However, on this day I was called to take the newer

chanunpa with me. I could not leave the house without it calling to me. My husband brought his flute to play if the park was free from onlookers. He was self-conscious about his amateurish playing.

We made our way to the perfect spot under the pine trees facing the lake. We set up our chairs and had lunch on the only picnic table. Since we were alone, I decided to smoke the chanunpa closer to the edge of the water. I began the ceremony and made my prayers. When I smoked, the tears and sadness were gone for the first time.

There were times I thought it would be called the Grieving Chanunpa because that is all I did with it. But it had never revealed its purpose until this day. Halfway through the ceremony, I became very relaxed and my body began to shiver, lapsing into a vision.

Flying over the water from the west direction, a female spirit approached me. When she got close, I could see the wrinkles on her face and the twinkle in her eyes. Her completely white hair was thin and in a bob style, parted in the middle.

"Aho grandmother, come smoke with me." I offered the chanunpa stem and smoke towards her.

"I am Gladys, the White Grandmother. You know my song. I sang to you in the lodge."

"Yes, I sing it every time I pray with this chanunpa." I replied, remembering the song that came to me when I stayed overnight in the lodge after blessing it.

I must note here that sometimes I speak out loud to the spirits and other times in my head through telepathy. But my action of pointing the stem to her and blowing smoke are done in the physical.

"You ask of its purpose? It is not a grieving chanunpa. It is for you to step into the next phase of medicine, the elder. Embrace your age and end stages of life and pass these teachings to other elders. I have been around you for a long time, waiting, since your first chanunpa. I have been walking this path with you."

I recalled meeting the twelve grandmother spirits in a vision on the initiation vision quest in Texas. It is where I envisioned the Child's Chanunpa.

"Elder women will smoke with you and you will share the teachings, because grandmother prayers are full of wisdom and love. When you smoke this chanunpa alone in ceremony you must pray for elder women, because they carry the heart of the people."

"This is the White Grandmother Chanunpa and the teachings, altar and ceremony will come. Sing the song to honor the grandmother every time."

I nodded in agreement. I finished my smoke and sang her song. Then she disappeared.

I returned to my husband who was sleeping in his chair under the large pine tree. I woke him.

"Good ceremony?" He asked.

"Yes, it was very good," I replied.

I returned to my seat by the water. We were both relaxed and I was a bit sleepy. We were still alone so my husband decided to play his flute. Although he never plays for a long time, today it seemed to go on forever and I loved it.

I looked out on the lake. Ripples from the slight breeze kept my gaze and then I closed my eyes.

I was sucked immediately under the water, deeper and deeper as if the lake was swallowing me. I felt panic because, in reality, I couldn't swim. Someone took my hand and led me into a cave under the surface. There was a circle of elder women, who were from all races. All were in white shawls. The energy was intense. Ancient but gentle. They laid me down in the middle of the circle. I counted twelve of them and they felt familiar, like the ones I saw in my vision quest in Texas. One by one, they took a white starfish, placed it on my heart and said only one word. The first elder held the starfish on my heart and said, "Perseverance."

Each of them did the same except with a different word - honor, respect, generosity, bravery, compassion, sacrifice, fortitude, humility, wisdom, love. The final word was truth. I understood the vision was an initiation by placing them into my heart.

The group laid their starfish in a circle before me. As they lifted each star fish up from the altar, each of their words was imprinted in the sand. Then they blew their breath in unison towards me and a yellow butterfly flew out of my chest.

It was then that I was pulled by an unseen force from the cave and placed above the water, back in my chair. It took many more months of prayer and meditation to understand the new ceremony. I had the song and now the altar for the White Grandmother Chanunpa ceremony. It would take another year practicing the ceremony alone, before women elders would come to be part of the group for which I would share its teachings.

This bundle would encompass the twelve teachings from *The Honey Pit: Finding the White Grandmother's Way* novel and create a ceremony circle of white shawled women elders who came for its teachings and ceremony. The circle would change over the first year until only a small group of dedicated elders continued for four years, until its completion.

Circles of ceremony are meant to change. Some left and

some joined until the main smaller circle became established. Trust is important when in a community or circle. It takes time for a group to solidify and bond, to become a relative instead of a relation.

A relative is not always one of blood, but can be one of heart and unconditional love. A relation for me is being related to everything as a whole on earth. A relative is one with whom you have shared your tears, hopes, dreams, and vision. One who you can completely trust, and have a close heart connection. With a relation is more distant from the heart but still within the circle of life.

The White Grandmother Chanunpa called for women elders to pray for heavy global issues as well as personal ones. When we pray for our personal struggles, we affect change in the world. When we pray for global struggles, we affect change in our self. It is one prayer, one world and one consciousness, because everything in life is in a relationship.

I was challenged with each one of the teachings for the next year before the group was established. I had to learn the teachings and embrace them personally for myself first.

The vision I was shown years ago, was complete. The seven chanunpas I had seen on my vision quest five years ago, that I did not want to believe, was completed. I would work with them to help others as they had helped me.

Why me, would be the question I would ask myself. The answer that came was because I needed them for my personal healing and spiritual growth. I couldn't help anyone if I had not helped myself to understand each's purpose.

A medicine man spoke these words to me when we spent time at a pow wow together.

"You can't help heal what you don't know. To work with medicine is a hard life. You have to heal things in yourself to know how to help others. You will have to go through many hard things in life. But you can't help everyone. Be careful who or what you choose to help because you will take on a little bit of that sickness in you, and give a piece of yourself away to help. Check with the spirits first to make sure you're the one to help. Remember to be holy is not to be perfect because you're a human being first."

Even though Spirit may give me a confirmation to help, it does not mean I have to do it. I still have a choice. If I take a little piece of the illness or issue within me and give a piece of myself away, I have to be sure I am willing to choose to live with accepting the consequence.

It may seem that the seven chanunpas needed me. To care for them, respect them, to dedicate myself to them, to smoke them, to learn their ceremony and purpose, and to communicate with the unseen world. They were like children being birthed into the physical world by Spirit, with me as their caretaker/follower to nurture the qualities they brought.

But I have found in the years that followed, that was not true. *I* did not hold the honor. It was the chanunpas that held it. I was a wounded human though I had a deep connection to Spirit. They were each gifted before or at a time I needed help and healing. They helped me grow and heal my spirit, but I would not completely understand this until number eight was gifted. Yes, there is an eighth chanunpa.

CHAPTER 27

Sun Dance Experience

It was 2017 and I was still conducting ceremony with the White Grandmother Chanunpa and a group of women elders. Every time I prayed with it alone, I saw a vision that I had to return to the sun dance ceremony in Texas. Grandmother Gladys' spirit pestered me each time.

The songs of the dance called me each time I prayed. I was worried because I was hoping the dance was not calling me to commit to dance for four years but to only support it as I had done in the past. Of course, I could always say no, but life can be hard to say no if I am called by Spirit to do something for my growth, experience, and healing.

It had been a few years since I had been to the Lone Star sun dance. I had finished my support for an elder dancer and she had since crossed into spirit. Whenever I prayed with the White Grandmother Chanunpa, I was drawn back in vision to the dance. I contacted one of the chiefs and I asked permission for my husband and I to attend this summer by offering a tobacco gift from each of us.

Since I had kept my connections to the group over the years, I was glad to go back to support the dance. The dance experience would be different this time. Unlike prior years, I could not do the physical work that support requires. Instead, I hoped to offer flower essence remedies and energy work to anyone who needed it. I was older now and washing dishes after mealtimes would be my physical contribution.

It was wonderful to see a few of the old familiar faces and meet new young ones. I was given no reason or understanding of why the grandmother spirit guided me there other than it was important.

In my own ego, I thought I might be called to help a dancer with my prayers, flower essences or energy work might also be offered. Things I could do to help the people.

I shared my vision with the trusted elder in Texas about my being called to the ceremony. She told me as she once did before to "Take it to the tree to understand why you were called. Make a prayer and offer your flesh for an answer."

The sun dance, as a Lakota elders told me, is "The granddaddy of all ceremonies. It is done for the renewal and regeneration of all people and life. It is a large prayer that is carried through sacrifice, sweat, blood, fasting and physical endurance. People who receive a vision to dance may also have a personal reason to dance, like praying for a healing for someone close to them. But the dance is a communal ceremony of prayer for the life of all people and beings on earth, and for the generations to follow."

The people who support the dance will stand outside the circle in a shaded arbor while the dancers dance inside a circle in the hot sun without food and water. Singers and drummers provide the music. Sun dancing is hard on the body, but their prayers and the prayers of the supporters outside the circle help them to endure.

During a short break on the day I arrived, I went to the north gate where one of the chiefs was taking flesh offerings from supporters.

Again, a flesh offering is a tiny piece of skin that is cut from the upper arm. It is placed in a small red cloth as a prayer bundle and tied to the large cottonwood tree. The tree stands in the center of the circle where the dancers dance. I have given several flesh offerings over the years.

These flesh offerings are typically prayers of gratitude and asking help for self or others. I was told by elders they are big prayers, important ones. Most people offer one or two flesh offerings by offering one or two small red swatches of cloth to the chief. I had two of them to gift.

When I was next in line, I approached the chief. He smiled and said "Four."

Once again, I was told I to offer four flesh offerings but I had brought only two swatches of cloth.

He called for four flesh offerings. I did not choose. He chose before I handed him my cloth swatches and I trusted. He place two pieces of flesh in each of them.

I stood in prayer with the chief's chanunpa. I offered my gratitude for the blessings and protection I have received all my life. I offered gratitude for my health. I asked for an understanding of why I was called to attend this year. Finally, I asked for guidance on how I could be of service to people. Since there were four flesh pieces taken, it took a bit longer and I had more time to pray. He took the pieces of flesh from my upper arm in a circle in each of the four directions. When it was completed, I offered a sacred (wrapped in red cloth) package of tobacco in exchange.

Later that night, I learned that the camp I was with would be going into the mystery circle (sacred circle where the dancers dance and connect to Spirit) the next day. The group would dance behind and support a first-year dancer from the camp to give her strength when she broke from the tree. Most dancers are pierced and tied to the sacred cottonwood tree at some point. All supporters in their camp are invited into the circle to stand and dance behind the person needing support. They sing, pray, and dance to give strength to help them break their tied flesh easily and release their prayer, intention, and their reason for dancing.

I have danced inside the circle to support dancers in the camp each sun dance I have attended. The energy is high, sacred, and filled with honor and respect.

To explain further, every day during the dance ceremony supporters from outside the mystery circle are allowed to enter the circle in a reverent way and stand behind but not touch or interfere with a dancer from their camp community who is going to break from the tree because they are in a vision. They are tied to the tree with a long rope that is hooked to a bone that is inserted to each side of their arms, chest, or back. There are many ways this is done but the arms or chest are done most often. It is symbolic of the umbilical cord we have to our mother when we are born is what I have been told.

It is their offering to Spirit while they pray for their personal reason and communal renewal. They dance back and forth tied to the tree. When the dancers pray, they are in vision and when they are ready, they run back from the tree, break free and are caught by sacred helpers in the dance.

This ceremony is definitely misunderstood by some people of other religions. It may seem harsh or animalistic, but in my experience, it is truly sacred to witness. It has been explained to me this way. As humans, our flesh and body is the only thing we truly have to give. It is what we inhabit and live in every day, so the offering of flesh, done only under the sacredness of this ceremony is part of the prayer and gift to Spirit.

My understandings have only come from my experience and observances as a supporter and from elder teachings of the ceremony. I cannot speak from a dancer's point of view because I am not a sacred sun dancer. I am not an authority on the subject. Some dancers have shared their personal vision and experiences over the years but that is private and not my story to share.

The next afternoon when it was time to enter the circle, I followed behind everyone and danced my way from the south gate, to the west gate heading on my way through the north gate to get to the east gate where this young girl was in her vision and dancing tied to the tree.

In the mystery circle, the dancers are offering the only real thing they possess. The mystery circle is where the spirits of the ancestors come to speak. The dance is a place for transformation and a rebirth for the betterment of people and the planet. It is such a sacred space that it touches your soul.

My understanding of the sun dance is that the sun is our spiritual father and the earth is our spiritual mother. The dancers are the children who give of themselves through the sacrifice of fasting, offering flesh, dancing, and praying to re-energize the connection of the earth and sky, integrating the feminine and masculine energy. Feminine energy nourishes the truth in us and masculine energy protects the truth in us. A woman carries the extension of the earth in her body A man carries the sun in his heart. The unity of the sun and the earth is each within us and gives us our life.

As I sang the familiar songs and danced in an almost jog around the circle to get to my place with the camp family, the sun was beating down upon us all. Perspiring from the 110-degree heat, beads of sweat were dripping quickly into my eyes. The sweet smell of cedar and sage smoke was in the air. Long fresh stalks of sage were covering the ground around the base of the sacred cottonwood tree.

While dancing to the north gate, I hit an energetic wall. My feet would not move forward, just up and down and side to side dancing to the heartbeat of the drum.

The supporters from the camp continued on past the north gate toward the east gate and gathered behind the new dancer. I however could go no further. My body could not move. It was like an unknown force was holding me in place. I was being told from the voice outside of me to stay here, to dance, and pray. This made me extremely uncomfortable. I wanted to follow the camp family and stand behind them in support.

An elder once told me, that each time you attend and support a sun dance ceremony, a healing can take place for you in some way. It can open you up for change. Core issues and old patterns need to be dealt with by surrendering and receiving the awareness of the lesson to move forward. As in other past ceremonies I have supported, many lessons were learned and healed, not in the mystery circle, but in working with people in the camp. Mirroring to me and triggering emotions I needed to heal.

When I stopped at the north gate, I stood behind a man I knew for many years. He was a man who had completed his commitment and was a strong sun dancer. He had been dancing for many years. He was offering his prayer by eagle dancing, dancing four days tied to the tree. We had chatted before the ceremony began and he shared with me his reason and personal prayer of why he was dancing again this year. I was honored he shared such a sacred thing with me.

Why did I find myself in support behind him in this moment? My own half-side (husband) was supporting outside the mystery circle in the cedar shaded arbor with the granny, and in prayer watching me. The optics did not feel right. I was judging myself and much anxiety began to fill my mind.

My thoughts for a brief moment began to inflict shame on myself, something I learned to do since I was a child when I was criticized, disciplined or judged for having unbelievable experiences.

What are you doing? Why are you standing here? Why are you not with the others, supporting with the camp family behind the new dancer? What must this look like to the other people watching outside the circle? You are alone and standing behind this one man where everyone can see you. Who do you think you are?

These were the thoughts that ran through my anxious mind. The train was running at full speed and I wanted to jump off.

To say I was uncomfortable with drawing attention to myself seemed very humble but in fact it was the way I understood as a girl, to be invisible is to be safe. Withholding my experiences, emotions, and gifts was the inner wound that I had been trying to release most of my life.

I looked at the tree as the beat of the drum aligned with my heart. The singers of the sacred songs brought a wave of calm to my thoughts and I let them go. The energy was building from the ground and I felt its vibration running through my body as I moved my feet to the heart beat of mother earth.

It is taught that this type of sacred tree is chosen every year because it has heart shaped leaves. It truly reminds the people of the sacrifice from the heart that is made for renewal and healing on both the personal and global levels. The tree is the most beautiful sight. It takes your breath away and makes you shiver in awe.

The beautiful colored spirit robes of tobacco filled prayers waved in the majestic sky, as the breeze began to stir. With the sunshine on my face and wind in my hair, I broke out with a smile of peace. As the wind picked up, a strong commanding voice outside of me and in my left ear shouted, *"Dance hard and sing loud."*

The sacred was communicating. I followed it with a strong will, clear mind, and an open heart to receive whatever blessing, teaching, healing, or understanding I needed.

I danced strong while lifting my feet in time with the sacred drum. The earth was vibrating. I felt her breast effortlessly rise to greet my feet. I could feel and see her life energy rise from the ground. She began to run energy lines in each of the cardinal directions, moving like the spokes of a wheel through each of the dancers and up the tree into the sky.

Although I had seen and felt the energy several times before in prior sun dance ceremonies I had attended and supported, the energy was different this time. It was a stronger pulsation lifting my energy as if I was no longer a body and was floating inches above the ground. I could not feel the soles of my feet. I could barely hear the voices of the singers around the sacred drum across from me in the south gate. So as instructed, I began to dance hard and sing loud to the sacred songs which I had learned by heart over the years of ceremony. The entire north direction encompassed only me and this dancer, which as I recall, was unusual. Usually, the dancers are closer together in the circle. This year there were fewer dancers.

Riding high on the wave of energy from the earth, the tree, and the sky, I could see the energy come back down from the sky, and go through the tree and into the earth, spreading to each dancer and person in the circle.

I began to hear many voices from behind me chanting the sacred songs. Their voices were ethereal in nature. The vibration of the voices was filling a powerful vibrant light in every person in the football-field sized mystery circle.

I felt a tingle on the back of my neck that cascaded down my braided hair and settled in my heart. It was the presence of the spirit world. An ancestor or ancestors were coming through to the earth realm.

Knowing something was about to happen, I focused my eyes, alerted my ears, and opened my heart. I continued to dance strong and seemly without effort. Singing loud, I could hear my voice carrying around the circle along with the ancient spirit voices. I felt an overwhelming need to turn my head over my left shoulder and look behind me to the north gate opening.

It was then in the bright day sun that a white cloud of visionary mist rolled in slowly. It hovered on the top of the cedar boughs directly above the north gate opening.

I was in the presence of the unseen world in the most sacred ceremony. They appeared out of the mist in ghost-like forms, hovering. Hundreds of men and women from days long past. It was then the familiar knowing came to me, and why I was to dance in this exact spot in this very moment. The ancestors were speaking to me in a way that was personal. Perhaps they were bringing the reason of why I was here.

The spirit ancestors sang and danced among all of us. I was not sure if others could see or feel their presence. They floated up to the nest atop the tree where we are taught the wakinyan or thunder beings rest during the ceremony.

As I watched them for a few moments, pictures came to my mind. Four of them hovered in the fork of the tree and were holding a large chanunpa with a dark colored bowl. I had never seen one that large. But this was the spirit world. All things were possible. The other spirits floated behind them in the tree to support them.

I interpreted it as a sign that I would be working more with the ancestor spirits and the chanunpa ceremonies for people. The energy was intense. In my mind I felt it was no epiphany of a vision for I have been conducting chanunpa ceremony for many years.

Then they spoke in a group voice, "Stop hiding. It's time to be seen. Come out of your darkness."

I was not quite sure what they meant but I hoped to eventually understand the message. I made a prayer of gratitude for whatever they were trying to offer me.

I came out of my vision as the dancer in front of me broke from the tree. It was time for me to move and dance back to the south gate, leaving the mystery circle behind.

When I came out of the circle and back to the arbor, the elder granny asked what was going on. Since she reads and feels energy, she knew something was going on. I explained about the ancestor spirits coming in from the north direction and how I could not move from the north gate.

At the end of the week, after the dance was completed, I sat processing my experiences with the granny.

She asked if I understood why I was called to come to the dance. Did what happened in the circle make sense?

As I processed and spoke about my experience, I became very emotional. I started to tear up and soon I began to speak of my concerns about not following the camp family in support in the circle, what the optics may have looked like or drawing attention to myself.

What did it look like to others outside the circle? Did they notice me? Were they judging me? What did people think I was doing behind a man that was not my husband? I could be seen clearly by everyone. Since I did not follow the others, would I appear to be egotistical or disrespectful?

My stomach began to get squeamish. I was embarrassed and felt shame. I started to shake and sob. I told her I still did not know why, but I knew whatever the reason, something was happening. All I wanted to do was cry. Perhaps an unknown healing was taking place. I would accept the vision and continue praying with the chanunpas in ceremony. The words *"Stop hiding. It's time to be seen. Come out of your darkness,"* would take me time to fully understand.

Granny's final words were to pay attention because something definitely was in the midst of change.

She clapped her hands, smiled and said, "Oh goody. I can't wait to see what happens."

But for me I was not as excited. Change is hard and life unravels when it begins to happen.

A year and a half later, part of the vision at the sacred tree manifested. This would begin a dark time for me. A time of depression because the challenges, changes, choices and commitment I would need to make would be of great sacrifice to me personally.

CHAPTER 28

Thunderbird Chanunpa

At the end of September 2018, my husband officially retired from his job in the finance industry. He was having some health issues and a hard time with driving in the dark. He had noticed his mind was not as sharp in the last couple of years. He went through many tests, and after four years of retirement, he received the diagnosis of a neuro-degenerative disease.

In the beginning, I was having a difficult time trying to fit our schedules together since his retirement. He continued to work part-time as a consultant from home a couple of hours a week. His daily routine starts very early. Exercise, breakfast, work at home consulting for an hour, lunch and so on.

My day is filled with a lot of quiet time and differs from day to day, depending if I have clients, ceremony commitments, or if I write and exercise. I am a night owl. On some days I go to bed when he is waking up. I rarely turn the television or the radio on during the day. It is very quiet.

His retirement changed my schedule and stressed me. Seeing him all day, making three meals a day every day, exercising on his schedule, getting up too early for my liking or not getting enough sleep because he was making calls or on the computer early in the morning was not working for me. I was trying to adapt to *his* schedule.

I was invited to dinner by two of my close spiritual friends whom I call sisters and I looked forward to getting out of the house for some *me* time.

One of the ladies asked me if I would pray for her to find where a particular chanunpa belonged. It was one she had rescued and we all smoked in ceremony one time almost four years before. It needed to move on from her to another chanunpa carrier/follower. The memory of the day we had the ceremony on the front porch of my home resurfaced.

I asked her why she wanted *me* to pray on it. I was resistant. I did not want to tell her my experience from that day years ago, as I had put it away in the back of my mind. The day we smoked together, I saw in a vision myself smoking it and conducting ceremony with it. But I dismissed it because she was its keeper and I had enough chanunpas to care for already. I already carried the seven as foretold in one of my vision quests.

We went back and forth and she eventually confided that it told her it needed to be passed on. It was not hers to keep. She asked me to pray about where this chanunpa should go.

I told her I would pray on it for clarity but then I took it one step further.

Very emotional, I asked her again, "Why do you need *me* to pray and get the answer?"

She replied, "Because it told me to give it to you, and that you would know what to do with it."

Her words gave me a confirmation. I shared my vision

and what I had seen years ago. In the vision I was conducting ceremony with it and it spoke that the chanunpa and I were supposed to work together.

When I got home that night, I immediately prayed with the Medicine Chanunpa bundle as it was the one that called to me to be smoked. Each bundle gives me a rush of energy and tingling. Then I see a picture of the bundle and I know it wishes to be smoked in ceremony.

In the quiet time of the smoke, I did indeed see me accepting the new bundle, I saw myself smoking and working with it. In time I would understand its power and use.

My vision showed it would be very demanding and intense. Each chanunpa has brought me challenges, change, and healings. I must bond with it and learn its power, energy, and knowledge. It is safe to say that I have had a lot of challenges, change, and personal inner healing over the years, often at a rapid speed. New challenges can also bring new health issues; some physical, some energetic, and some emotional.

I received this large chanunpa at the beginning of December 2018 and began to build the bundle according to what it wanted and asked for in my visions. I could not imagine what this bundle would bring first: challenge, change or healing? It usually begins with challenges.

It began to speak to me on the very same night I took it home. I was told to pull it out of the leather bag (*cante juha*) and purify it with sage and cedar leaf smoke. Then I was told to hold each piece in my hands, the bowl in one hand and the stem in the other hand. Each was physically large and heavy. I inspected each piece carefully, paying attention to each groove and detail it revealed. Much care and work went into its creation and perfection. I began to see the beauty of its uniqueness. I offered a prayer of gratitude to the native man who made it himself.

As I held each piece and closed my eyes to vision, I felt something slide up my right arm and around my neck. It rested there. In vision I saw and felt a snake. Thank goodness I am not afraid of snakes.

As the snake rested around the back of my neck, my hand that was holding the large black pipestone bowl began to vibrate, as if the stone was a beating heart. I looked deep into the hole where the tobacco is usually placed and I felt myself fall into it. It was there in this blackness of nothing I heard a voice,

"This is the void where everything begins and dies. Everything is born out of this darkness. Everything and nothing exists at the same time."

There were dimly lit faces of people in this darkness with me. It was very peaceful. It felt as if I was both underground and in the cosmos at the same time.

I was only holding the pieces and not smoking and yet it was communicating with me in a vision. It talked about how there were eight steps that I would understand in time. It spoke of the power of North and South native teachings with the eagle and the condor in balance. It explained how the stem wanted to be decorated and the leather bag (cante juha) it came in was not the one for it to be placed in.

Finally, it called for a particular kind of woven blanket that it wanted to be wrapped in. It was not a traditional wool Pendleton blanket. While I received this information, I certainly did not understand it all at this time.

I sat holding each piece for an hour, unaware of the time

that passed. Then I felt movement. The snake began to descend back down my arm into my hand and became the stem again. I asked for a sign of confirmation that snake energy was indeed part of this bundle even if I did not understand it completely. Holding the stem, I heard it speak, "Turn me over." Then the vision ended.

I did as I was told. I turned the stem over and inspected the backside. I had only looked at the front because I was struck by the beauty of the twisted carved wood and inlaid turquoise. But now when I turned it over, there in the grain of the wood, in the middle of the stem, was the side view of a snake's head with one eye. As clear as day, the grain of the wood actually had the entire head and eye of a snake. It gave me a chill up my spine. I was a bit concerned about how this was all going to work.

The same thing happened next time I held the bowl and stem.

The stem became the snake and my mini body fell into the bowl without intention. It just happened. I became comfortable in the darkness of the bowl. The voice in the darkness spoke to me and revealed its needs for the bundle. It showed me specific feathers and where they would be placed on the stem. It showed me what types of fetishes to place in the directions of the altar and it asked to sit with each of my other seven bundles one at a time. It showed me smoking each chanunpa and blessing the large stem and bowl with its smoke. Also, this all needed to be completed in one week, which meant every night for a week, I smoked a different chanunpa and blew its smoke to honor the new one. The vision ended.

It would be an introduction. Each chanunpa had to greet

and honor it. I have never done this before with any of the other seven bundles.

Each night for six nights, I did what was asked. I smoked the Child's Chanunpa the first night and blessed the new stem and bowl with the smoke on the outside of each piece. The large bowl asked the Child's Chanunpa for an offering from its bundle. It specifically showed me it wanted the beaded lighter. I took the lighter from the Child's bundle and placed it in the leather bag with the large bowl and stem. I replaced the lighter in the Child's bundle with another less ornate one.

The second night I smoked and prayed with the Earth Keeper Chanunpa and blessed the new stem and bowl with the smoke. The large stem asked for a bundle of sage from the bundle. I placed it in the leather bag with the large stem and bowl and replaced the sage in the Earth Keeper bundle.

Each night the others in turn would bless the stem and bowl with their smoke and relinquish something from the bundle it had asked for, cedar, a tamper, the leather bag (cante juha), a shell to burn the sage in, and a tobacco pouch. Each item placed in the new large bundle had to be replaced in the other bundles. These exchanges and changes were falling into place but were definitely making me uncomfortable. It was stretching my comfort level to do things I had never done before.

I brought out the Medicine Chanunpa on the seventh night. This bundle is filled with medicines that plants and animals have given to me during vision quests and initiation ceremonies.

As I began to open the Medicine Chanunpa, I was stopped by my spirit helper "No Face." The grandfather said I had to gather the rest of the things for new bundle over the next eight weeks. Only then could I bless the new chanunpa with the Medicine Chanunpa and connect it to me.

In the past, elders taught two ways to open and bless a chanunpa. One way was in the purification ceremony and the second by connecting it to the heart of the person receiving it through the smoke being blown through the stem and bowl by another chanunpa. What I saw in vision was that the Medicine Chanunpa would be used to bless and connect this new one to my heart. I was also shown that all the seven bundles needed to be present on the day of the blessing and that each bundle had to offer a pinch of tobacco from their tobacco pouches to start the new chanunpa's tobacco pouch. Every time I sat with it, I journaled to remember since it was asking for many things.

During this time of sleepless nights, I felt a heaviness of energy, maybe from the changes happening and those still to come. Perhaps the stress of my husband being home all the time, his tremors and health challenges added to the mix. There was sadness inside me but I did not really know where it was coming from. I felt I was in an uncomfortable darkness.

The new chanunpa seemed to be challenging me and asking me again to move beyond things that were traditional and comfortable, changing my understandings to move beyond the knowledge and experience I knew. This had started with the Medicine Chanunpa. Now I was being challenged even further.

Every detail and object the bundle needed was found and gifted except for one thing from South America that I hoped would find its way to me. I was told I did not have to worry about it, it would be given within eight weeks after the chanunpa was blessed.

Many things were revealed over the next eight weeks. I will try to tell them in order the best I can from my journal. The chanunpa began to give me more information as I built the bundle.

The energy of the bundle came from the sacred nation of the thunderbird. It can end or create life, using the power of fire and water, in life and death, and light and dark. The four swirls on the stem were connected to the four winds of the directions. The sixteen turquoise pieces represented the sixteen faces or powers of Spirit. The snake I saw and felt was about shedding, dying and resurrection. It was a primal life force that traveled through the realms of the living and the dead, a rebirth from the ashes and the energy of the directions of the spirit road, from North to the South and from South to North. I did not comprehend it all at the time, but journaled everything I saw and heard.

On one occasion, while sitting with the bowl and stem, a Lakota heyoka's spirit appeared to me. I had met him at a sun dance ceremony years ago. A heyoka is a sacred clown, a medicine man that works in a backwards way. They act out and say things in an opposing way to shift and change energy, though I cannot speak fully on their powers and nature since I am not an authority on the subject. One time to make people chuckle, he danced in the mystery circle with an umbrella in the hot sunshine and said it was raining. It lifted the sun dancers' spirits and shifted their focus to endure the heat.

When I met him, I was participating in a purification ceremony he led for the supporters of the dance. It was run very differently from what I was accustomed. There were songs I had not heard before. It seemed he was running the energy opposite or counterclockwise inside the lodge, at least that is the way it felt within me. It was not bad or anything to be fearful of, but different and unfamiliar to me. It was a very hot purification hotter than any lodge I had been in before or since. There were about forty of us inside the lodge. I sang the prayer songs I knew and listened to the ones he sang alone. I was not sure if they were his personal medicine songs or traditional ones I had not heard before.

At the end of the purification, I gifted him tobacco, stating my gratitude for the ceremony. I proceeded back to camp thinking about the songs he sang.

Later in the evening, the heyoka came into the camp and asked for myself and another man whom I met the year before at my vision quest ceremony to join him at his camp. I had to get the permission of the camp director before I could leave, and since I was going with another person, we both received permission.

We walked to his camp which was on the other side of the arbor circle. He was sitting near a small fire. I don't remember too much of the small talk, only that he was making jokes and being funny. He put sunglasses on and said it was too bright out when, of course, it was dark and the sun had already set for the day. Finally, he got serious.

He pulled out his drum and began to sing a song after offering tobacco and a prayer to the fire. He told us to do the same.

"The song has power. You must feel it and remember.

Always know what you are saying. It's important to feel what you are singing," he said.

He explained the words and meaning and their relation to wakinyan (the thunderbird and thunder beings). He sang it over and over. The song called and honored the wakinyan to a ceremony. I wished I had a paper and pencil to write down the words but we had to train our memory and heart. I am no stranger to prayer songs as I have been learning and collecting them since I was nineteen. I am grateful to all the elders that kept the songs alive and shared them. I understood this was a gift he was giving us although I didn't know why, because I am a woman. A lot of sacred teachings are passed down to men only but somehow there was always an elder that recognized through Spirit to teach me or gift me a song. Did this heyoka know this? Did Spirit or the heyoka's helpers tell him? Why would I need to know it?

The second prayer song he sang was a healing song. Again, he explained the words, but more importantly, the meaning and power of the song. Both of us seemed to catch the songs and sing them verse after verse, over and over. Finally, the heyoka offered tobacco to the fire and told us to do the same. He left us and went into his tent.

I guess it was over. As I lay in my tent I could not sleep, I got out my journal and began to write the words and meanings before I forgot them. Just when I was finished, I heard the call over the loudspeaker for the sun dancers to begin their day with the purification before entering the mystery circle at sunrise. I had been up all night and had no sleep to face the last day.

At the end of the dance and after the feast, I was packing up and the heyoka found me and gifted me a cassette tape.

"Spirit said you're a keeper of songs."

I thanked him and asked him to wait a minute. I struggled through my luggage to find a red cloth wrapped package of tobacco to gift him.

"Pilamayelo, (thank you) grandfather. For your time and teaching the songs, it was an honor to meet you."

Then we went our separate ways. We both attended the sun dance for the next few years. He danced in the mystery circle. We never spoke or interacted again.

I regress to tell you this story so that you may understand the background of this heyoka who appeared in spirit form in my vision. I had heard that he had died a few years earlier so I was confused as to why he would appear to me now. It was many years since our only encounter. Sixteen to be exact. I had learned the two songs by heart and have used them when appropriate.

Now he appears before me (face only) and speaks.

"You need four songs for this bundle. Use the ones I gave you, that you didn't learn," he laughed.

My mind went to the cassette tape. I remember the one thunder being song he taught and the healing song, but I didn't understand there were only two of them. To be truthful the tape he gifted me was marked as heyoka songs, so I never learned them as I am not a heyoka. I have not been initiated as one, nor do I have any desire to be one, so I was confused.

He spoke again "The songs are not for the heyoka dog ceremony. These thunderbird songs bring power to the ceremony. Eight steps on each side of the right and the left. Sixteen powers of Spirit. You will learn them all or die trying. They are what the Thunderbird Chanunpa needs."

"This is the Thunderbird Chanunpa?" I asked.

Just as I was about to ask for more information he was gone.

I put the bowl and stem back in the bundle and proceeded to quickly search through my sacred things. It was now four o'clock in the morning. The noise woke my husband up. Of course, this is not unusual for me. He has adjusted over the years to my nightly spirit visitors, ceremonies and the prayer work I do while he sleeps.

"What are you looking for?" He asked.

"I will tell you in the morning. Go back to sleep."

"Honey, it *is* the morning."

With that he rolled over and went back to sleep for another hour. After looking in a few places I found the cassette and found myself heading to bed.

The next afternoon I listened to the cassette tape with headphones. One of the songs was the original one that he taught years earlier. Great, one down three to go. The next three songs were challenging. I sang them in order. I could remember the words but the melody completely escaped me. This had never happened before. In the past, learning to me was fairly easy. I continued for the next several weeks until it was time to have the blessing ceremony. Each day, I felt a huge wave of heaviness and uneasiness. I was sad and exhausted just trying to get through the day. I was still not sleeping well, only getting three to four hours of broken sleep every night.

Eventually the day came, with all seven bundles seated before me. I opened the eighth bundle and pulled out the large bowl and stem. I laid it on the altar of the Medicine

Chanunpa. Following the vision, I took pinches of tobacco from each of the seven tobacco pouches and placed them in the Thunderbird's Chanunpa's pouch.

I filled the Medicine Chanunpa February 2019 at 11:30 a.m. I prayed and smoked, honoring the directions and blessed the bowl and stem in a sacred way, with the smoke connecting both pieces to my heart. I felt a small jolt of energy, like a skipped heartbeat. When it was complete, I closed up all of the bundles except for the new large one. It was time to smoke it for the first time.

I did not know that the Thunderbird Chanunpa would take me a couple of hours to smoke. It was teaching and showing me things. It asked things of me that were unfamiliar. When I tried to do the ceremony the way I was traditionally taught, things did not work properly. The lit sage flew out of the shell onto the blanket. I quickly picked it up before it burnt a hole in the blanket. The lighter would not light, so I had to use long wooden matches. The altar pieces had skipped around and mixed up the order I had arranged.

I think it took longer because I was resistant to the changes. I was used to following a way and trusting, but now it was asking me to perform the ritual differently. The songs I worked hard to learn needed to be sung in a different order than how I had learned them. Since there was no explanation for conducting the ritual this way, I struggled with it internally. Eventually, as I did what it asked of me, the ceremony flowed better. I was feeling like a novice, who knew nothing, like the teenager who held the chanunpa for the first-time years ago.

It was teaching me how to conduct this ceremony, but not why. I was used to getting information completely and directly with a full understanding that I could comprehend, but not today. In the middle of the long smoke, I heard a loud rumble. I looked at the clock. It was 12:51 p.m. I thought it might have been a truck rumbling down our street, but I knew it felt like more than a truck. Something had hit above me or moved the ground below me.

I heard the voice in my left ear, "Now you know its power."
What the heck did this mean?

The vision I was shown was clear. It was to be smoked once a week and only at night for the time being. It also reminded me of today's date in February was significant. The vision moved on to the day the elder presented me as the successor to his lineage and gave me a new spirit and public name. The vision ended.

When I looked back in my journal to confirm the date of the presentation as a successor, it was the exact date in February. It had been seven years to the day. I turned on the television after I completed the ceremony and the news announced that at 12:51 p.m., a small earthquake was felt in Templeton Massachusetts and that people felt it all the way into Auburn, which is about five miles from where I lived. Could it be the same rumble I felt? Was it all connected? With the experiences I have had in my life, I know better. It was connected. I am not placing any specific meaning to it other than it was connected.

Working with this new ceremony was unfamiliar and challenging. Trying to remember everything was frustrating and evoked a sense of fear that I wouldn't get it right. It took more physical energy from me. Even after I learned all the songs, the melodies continued to escape me during the ceremony. Out of ceremony, I could remember the melodies but in ceremony I would forget. I diligently tried for perfection.

One day in a vision I saw myself writing down the words to the songs on paper, burning sage, blessing the paper and placing it in the bundle. Why? I knew the words. It was the melody I lost. I did what I was shown. I placed the paper in the bundle and never practiced the words again.

The next time I opened the bundle, I looked at the words and the melodies came. I realized I was trying so hard to do it right that I was losing the wonder of the ceremony. I was too much in my head and not enough in my heart.

My dark emotions continued during the next four months. I took the flower essences I previously created for chronic cases. I began with drops for depression, then post-traumatic stress, then for grief and finally anxiety. I knew from experience they would help clear some of the heaviness I felt.

The Thunderbird Chanunpa had me begin to work with snake medicine. Its energy transmutes poisons, and sheds emotions and behaviors. I would learn in vision that the snake is the power from the earth that feeds the thunderbird. It is the fire from lightning of the thunderbird that can kill the snake to feed itself and its remains will be reborn again into a snake. It is a primal energy of rebirth and resurrection.

The bundle also required owl medicine which is the power of death, rebirth, seeing through deception and illusions and working with the night. Both medicines are heavy and dense, much different from the medicines I worked with previously.

Working with the Thunderbird Chanunpa every week would show me something new.

The next time I smoked it and sat in silence, I fell into the dark bowl below me in my mind's eye.

I heard, "There are eight steps down and eight steps up on the stem, leading to the eight-pointed star. You are aware of the sixteen powers of Spirit through the lodge but you will come to know each of them personally."

The memory of the sixteen led me back in time in my vision.

I began my journey meeting a Lakota elder and participating in my first purification ceremony. He did some teaching about the sixteen powers of Spirit that came into the lodge and how the sixteen willows that were used to build the lodge were representative of those powers in the cosmos. If the lodge was built correctly, you could look inside at the top in the center and see all the limbs cross each other in the shape of an eight-pointed star. It is the opening where we connect to the cosmos during ceremony.

The lodge of bent saplings was a complete circle and universe where we sat inside. Just like when we were inside our mother's womb. When the inyans (sacred stones) are heated and painted red with the fire, we put a little green (sage, cedar, sweet grass) on them and pour mni (sacred water) on them to make steam. We breathe it in to cleanse ourselves inside and out to bring back our breath of life. We are cleansed and rebirthed back into the world after every ceremony.

As I came out of the vision, I looked down at the stem of the Thunderbird Chanunpa and made the connection. There are eight sets of turquoise stones. There are sixteen stones laid like footsteps, eight going down and eight coming up the stem.

But what were the steps? That would have to wait until the next ceremony.

Once again in the next ceremony, I entered the darkness inside the bowl. When I looked up, I noticed I was at the bottom of the black bowl but I had not yet touched the ground. I was floating, suspended as if I was in the cosmos.

I asked about the eight steps and a memory came:

I am seven-years-old and my body is developing early. I had been given the talk about my menses and I was horrified. My mother said I needed a bra.

Since my mother did not drive, she turned to my father and said, "It's time we get her a bra. When can you take us shopping?"

My father said, "She doesn't need a bra. She's only seven."

My mother took me aside and told me to put on a sleeveless white jersey shirt. I did as I was told.

"Go and see your father," she commanded.

I was proud. I liked the shirt and it was comfortable and clean.

"Daddy," I called to him.

When I went into the living room and said "Daddy," the look on his face said it all to me. He looked away and shook his head in what I understood was disgust.

He said, "Go and change your shirt. We'll go shopping tomorrow."

I wondered at the time if he didn't like the shirt. Or he didn't like me? It was hard to differentiate between the two.

I felt sadness and was embarrassed. I remember feeling ugly.

That was all I received in the vision, nothing else. Again, I was left with sadness and shame. His look brought up an emotion I clearly did not understand or fully process at that age. Feeling ugly with my body continued for many years. Why was this memory surfacing? I realized I needed to feel it in my body and no longer repress it. I cried. Finally understanding I forgave myself. The look on my father's face was not because my body was ugly but that he agreed with my mother. I needed a bra. I was developing much earlier than other girls my age. Then I forgave him. My painful emotions when buried and not felt and voiced, led me to misunderstand my memory.

The next week, I again asked about the eight steps in my ceremonial prayers. When I again fell into the darkness of the bowl, a memory came forth.

I was twelve. My mother was dieting. She was always dieting, especially after each baby.

"Loralee, you should watch your weight too. You're filling out and you don't want to get fat."

"But I'm not fat," I replied. At least I didn't think I was at the time.

"You don't want to be fat. No man will ever want to marry you and you won't have a family," she argued.

"I don't care, I don't want to get married and have a family." I really did mean it. I was not interested.

"You'll realize someday that's what women do. Get married and have babies."

I felt guilty and angry because I did not want a man or family.

I did not argue further. I swallowed my guilt and my anger. The memory faded.

I was angry and frustrated. Was I fat back then? I did not think so. To cope I swallowed it and walked away. I remember feeling fearful. What if I did gain weight? Would no one love me?

I cried and forgave myself for misunderstanding as a child and holding on to the emotions. Then I forgave my mother for her words that I took personally.

I finished the ceremony with no real answers about the eight steps, only the memories. I realized this was going to become the way answers were revealed, even if I did not know or understand the steps. Memories were to be remembered and worked through.

My daily life was becoming more depressed. I could actually feel myself wanting more and more isolation. Sleep escaped me at night, so I caught a few late morning naps to keep me sane.

The next time I smoked the Thunderbird Chanunpa another memory came.

I was twenty-one. I remember having pain in my chest. I thought it was a heart attack because I was feeling weak and could not breathe. I asked my mother to go with me to the emergency room but she made a face and said no, so I drove myself to the emergency room about seven minutes away.

At first the doctors thought it could have been a gall bladder attack, but after testing they said it could also have been an anxiety attack because I was stressed working two jobs. I never had one before, so I did not know the difference. When I came home, I felt guilty and anxious, like I made a big deal for nothing. The memory faded.

I buried my fear, anxiety and the hurt that my mother did not come with me. I needed her to comfort me. I was scared. As I processed and allowed myself to feel the emotions and cry, I released them. I forgave myself for needing my mother and misunderstanding the event. My father was still at work.

There were no cell phones back then. My youngest siblings were 13 and 11. She did not want to leave them alone. She did not drive. If it was something serious, she could be stranded at the hospital. I knew what I felt and experienced was real, but perhaps I did not understand the whole picture. I cried and allowed the emotions to run their course and forgave her and myself once again for allowing the event to touch me too personally.

The memories and feelings that came left me exhausted that day.

In the next ceremony the ritual changed. When smoking, I was to work with the stem in a certain way bringing the energy down into the bowl before I entered the bowl in my vision.

In the darkness, I was shown the possible future, taking care of my husband in his later years. I was feeling alone, fearful, and I was also feeling sad, depressed, and angry that I would have to change my life to take care of him. How could I possibly do it alone? How could I afford to financially care for him? I was overwhelmed. All I felt was fear. I began to shake and tremble, filling up with tears.

When I began to cry, I came out of the vision. The emotion left me exhausted. It took everything to finish the ceremony and close the bundle.

Within the hour, I had received a call from my best friend telling me that her husband had passed away at the hospital. I had been praying for him for the two days when he was getting tests. He was my friend too, and a really great friend to my husband. Holding my tears back I asked if she wanted me to pick her up or meet her at the hospital. My mind was in a fog trying to hold it together and be strong for her. We agreed we would meet at the hospital, and I would come to do a small ritual to release his spirit from his body.

After I hung up the phone, I ran upstairs to wake my husband and tell him the shocking news. Then I fell to my knees, screaming with my face buried in the bed while I cried so much that I left a large wet stain on the sheets.

My husband rubbed my back and cried too. I gathered myself and the sacred items I needed to take with me. I got dressed and met her within the hour. That night, death was at my front door. I have crossed and done these ceremonies and rituals many times. This one was very close to my heart and saddened me even more to my core. My heart went out to my dear friend for all the emotions she would experience losing her partner and best friend.

During the next weeks, the heaviness would get worse. In eight weeks, two cousins, an aunt and uncle, three close clients and two friends died. Five of them had some ailments, and four of them passed unexpectedly. I was immersed in grief and I worried for my husband's future. I found myself sadder than I ever could remember. Death was in my face. I cried continually for weeks.

The days became long. Feeling overwhelmed, I knew I needed to continue to let this stage go its course no matter how long it would take.

I still conducted community chanunpa ceremonies twice a month. Working with the Buffalo Chanunpa and the White Grandmother's Chanunpa gave me boosts to lift my spirit and emotions compared to the heaviness of the Thunderbird Chanunpa.

The next time I smoked the Thunderbird Chanunpa, I ran my hands down the stem and my vision began.

I found myself inside the stem. I could see the turquoise stones had disappeared and in each of their places was an opening where the stone used to be. I walked up inside the stem on the right side until I got to the top of the mouth piece.

In the darkness I heard the word "sadness." I took a step down and I heard the word "depression." Walking further down the stem I heard the word "grief."

A voice began to speak from inside the dark tunnel of the stem. "You are at the third step, grief."

I could feel the emotional pain. I was grieving for my husband, and the life that would now change for us because of his neuro-degenerative disease that would worsen. Sadness came first, then depression and now, having many deaths around me could I recognize the grief that I had been holding back, the grief of possibly not only losing him to death but also him losing him slowly.

The death of my best friend's husband and my experience of seeing her pain allowed me to get in touch with my own pain I was holding at bay. I cried and stayed with my grief in the darkness.

Eventually the vision receded and I completed the rest of the ceremony.

The grieving continued for the next few months but now that I was aware of it, I was less tense. Was this the only grief or was it also issues of my past. Only time would tell. My daily prayers had begun to change. I asked Spirit to help me with the strength and ability to help my husband and take care of him. I offered my gratitude for our life together.

I must say I did not really look forward to smoking the Thunderbird Chanunpa once a week. I never knew what I would be shown. At least it was beginning to give me guidance on the eight steps.

The first three were sadness, depression and grief. Being inside the stem in vision allowed me to be inside these emotions and experience them deeply.

The next time I smoked the Thunderbird Chanunpa, I ran my hands down over the stem, and again the stones on the stem disappeared and I found myself inside the stem in the dark.

This time in vison, I stepped into the fourth hole. I waited and listened for the word to tell me the fourth step, but instead a memory returned. When I was fourteen, I tried out for the softball team and made the cut. I was excited.

When I returned home to tell my mother she announced, "You will have to quit the team because I just got a job, and I am going back to work. You will have to babysit the kids after school (my four younger siblings were ages four through nine), make dinner, clean the dishes, see the kids do their homework, take their baths and put them to bed."

I remember being crushed. I really wanted this. I worked hard to make the team. I nodded my head in agreement and then went to my room and cried. I was torn between trying not to feel angry and being selfish. My mother was going back to work to help the family. My father was already working two jobs. I had to do my part to help. Tears welled up in my eyes. I did not want to feel this or remember how badly I wanted to play on the team. Am I a bad person because I don't want to babysit and do chores? Am I selfish only thinking of myself? I winced at the thought. As the memory and feeling passed I heard the word, "guilt."

I stayed in the darkness with the word "guilt." Then I heard the voice, "You feel guilt like when you were a teenager. You do not want to babysit again, with your husband. You don't want to have to take care of changing his diapers, feeding him, and bathing him possibly. You feel guilty because you think that makes you a bad person. Once again you will have to sacrifice." Overwhelmed I tried to deny it. But it was true.

Then I felt my feelings turn from guilt to shame. And another memory floated in.

I was fourteen. I had been alone with a trusted relative. He grabbed me and lifted my dress and pulled at my underwear. He sexually assaulted me. I pushed him off me. I was shocked and shamed.

Later that night when my mother got home from work, I wanted to tell her, I wanted to tell somebody. But I didn't. The memory made me so ashamed. Why couldn't I tell someone? Because I didn't think I would be believed, so I stuffed it down deep. I remembered the pain and the tears followed.

How could he? Why would he? Why was I not strong enough to stop him? I wanted to make the memory go away. I sat in my guilt and shame. I allowed myself to feel it and I wanted to die. I cried for my innocence, and I cried for my lost sense of trust. I would never be the same after that moment. I let myself breathe into the painful emotions until they passed.

When I looked up above me, I was below the fifth hole of the stem. The voice in the darkness spoke the word, "shame."

"You are ashamed that you trusted a relative who let you down. Ashamed you feel you have to protect yourself and be on your guard."

I sat and allowed these words of truth to wash over me. It was

257

not comforting. I breathed slowly for a few minutes and came out of the vision.

I sat once again and cried allowing the emotions to be felt and released through forgiveness. I forgave myself for not using my voice to admonish the relative, for not telling anyone of the event and burying my pain. It took me longer to forgive the relative. As in the past, I had to speak about the event with my husband to fully release. For him to be silent witness to the emotions I was experiencing. When I fully forgave my relative, I released my shame and pain it created.

I completed the ceremony and remembered the fourth step of "guilt." And the fifth step, "shame." I certainly didn't enjoy this trip down memory lane or the way it made me feel. Now instead of only feeling sadness, depression, and grief, I would add guilt and shame.

CHAPTER 29

Thunderbird Chanunpa Visions

It was at this time that I took a six-week course on Caregiving. I decided it might be good for me to learn information and caregiving techniques to help ease my stress on future caregiving for my husband.

The next six weeks were eye opening and devastating. Although the class focused more on dementia it also covered other neuro-degenerative diseases. Every week I came home with more information and a sense of doom. The reality I had feared was pretty much on target. I had learned to see through the person's eyes, what their world looked like, from their sight, movement, and body.

It was tearful and yet empowering. The tips and insights were compassionate and helped me deal with the emotions of sadness, depression, grief, guilt, and shame. The women who participated in the class were further down the caregiving road with either their fathers or husbands. They shared a lot of their personal experience. The main focus of the class was how to help the person get through the day with less anxiety, and to give them the best of your time. To do that you must take care of yourself. It is okay to ask for or get outside help, so that you can have a respite to care for yourself. This helped to ease my fear of the road ahead.

In the months after the gifting of the Thunderbird Chanunpa, we began to have issues in our home with our water pipes leaking. It began in the living room. The wall had to be opened to replace a copper pipe. It was an annoyance to have the water turned off for most of the day, but we needed to stop the leak. We had a lot of days waiting for the plumber to come.

Two weeks later another leak started. It was coming from the bathroom wall on the first floor behind the shower. Again, we waited for the plumber for two weeks, having to live with the water turned off. Once again, we had to open part of the wall.

Three weeks later after the second leak was fixed, another leak started in the same pipe higher up in the wall. The wall we fixed had to be opened again. Another month went by before the plumber and his helper could fix the pipe and the wall.

Two weeks after the latest fix, in the same bathroom on the opposite side in the ceiling, another copper pipe began to leak and had to be replaced. The ceiling had to be cut out and removed. It took another month for the plumber to fix the pipe and for the ceiling to be replaced.

Less than two days after the ceiling was replaced and painted, another leak started in the basement. This time it was coming from another copper pipe in the living room wall, the same wall that had already been opened and replaced.

It seemed there was no end. The home was continuingly springing leaks. Was my home taking the energetic hit from all the heavy emotions I was releasing? Eventually we had all the old pipes in the basement replaced with a hefty price tag of ten thousand dollars. All the plumbing issues took an exhausting eight months to resolve. Through this time, I continued with the lessons from the Thunderbird Chanunpa.

The Thunderbird Chanunpa is large and long, not easy to maneuver or smoke alone. It was work and tiresome for me to learn the ceremony and smoke it. The ceremony took much longer to conduct.

The next time I smoked another vision began.

I was suspended in the darkness for a longer time and I wondered why something was not coming through, a vision, memory, a word, or voice. I began to feel impatient. Keeping my mind's eye open and my ears tuned in, all I could hear was my breath heaving in and out. As I slowed my breathing down, I finally relaxed and a memory surfaced.

I was forty-four at the time. My mother was noting that since my father retired, the house was becoming harder and more expensive to maintain.

I asked her if they considered selling. She said they were not ready yet. They had inquired about an elderly apartment and put their name on a waiting list. They expected it would take a year for the apartment to become available.

A couple of months later, my mother asked me to come and visit. When I arrived, my father said nothing and my mother did all the talking.

"I know we said that we would offer the house to you first if we were ever going to sell it, but your sister and her family need

to move. The kids need to have a yard to play in. You don't need the house. You don't have a family. You can live anywhere. Single people don't need houses," she added.

I remember holding back my shock and replied, "It's your house to sell to whoever you want. If she can buy it and wants to live here, that's good for all of you."

But in this darkness of the memory, my anger was so intense that I wanted to scream. Instead, I took a deep breath, exhaled, and cried. The emotion was not because of what I was promised or that my sister would buy the house. It wasn't about the house.

It was because they thought so little of me because I did not have a family. I did not deserve a house, any house. I had to pay a price because I was still single and I did not want to have children. I never wanted their house but her words cut me.

After the tears passed, I heard the word "anger." Anger was the sixth step. I was holding and hiding all this anger that needed to be released. I began to understand that all the steps were emotions I needed to pass through again by remembering the past and completely letting them go. Were they still really stuck inside of me? Did I bury the anger too deep?

I came out of the vision and completed the ceremony. For the next two weeks anger was all around me. Nothing was satisfactory in my life. Contractors, traffic, people at the grocery store, people at the movies, my cat, and my husband. The anger was present and to move it, I walked more and took my flower essences remedy for rage.

I was angered about the past and what happened with the leaking pipes in the present.

I reflected on the leak issues. I have found through experience that what happens around us is a reflection of what is going on inside of us. It was true that the pin holes in the water pipes were old and wearing out on the inside of the walls, so walls and ceiling had to be broke open. On an energetic level, water is about emotion. Leaks and walls being torn down and replaced. Emotions needing to be released inside of me. My internal self-imposed walls needed to be torn down. Once the emotions were released, I could rebuild myself. I cried a lot. I made time in my day to cry alone. It helped release the anger inside of me.

Everything in my life had been in chaos and out of control. I do not do well in chaos. I like calm energy. Prayer was the only calm place for me to be. I prayed and I cried and I forgave myself for taking my mother's words so personally and for burying this anger in my body and mind. She only wanted to help my sister and her family. Besides, I really did not want to buy the house. I forgave my mother for her words that stirred my anger. I forgave myself for taking the episode so personally and burying my emotions. This new chanunpa was bringing deeper challenges. Another breakthrough was about to happen.

Again, praying with the Thunderbird Chanunpa, I entered the darkness. I emptied my mind and relaxed. The memory floated in and relayed the past.

I was about ten-years-old. I was sitting at the dinner table and my mother was yelling. My father was being stern with my younger sibling, admonishing him to eat. My sibling was about four-years-old and was a fussy eater.

It seemed that every dinner at home resulted in tears and yelling. There was no food wasting. My father worked hard to pay for the food. My mother worked hard making the food. We were to eat it and eat it all.

If I put my two cents in, I got scolded and told to mind my own business. My stomach was in knots. Dinner was a stressful time, so much so that I wanted to eat alone in silence outdoors.

The memory brought a restless feeling in the pit of my stomach. My pulse started to race. I hated this memory. I took some deep breaths to allow the feeling to pass through my body. When I relaxed, the voice said, "Anxiety. Anxiety is the seventh step."

I returned from my vision and completed the ceremony. Anxiety was an intense feeling. Hard to breathe and relax. The mind ramps up and perceives the worst. Upon reflection, I perceived the worse. I worried about my husband, about our future together and worried about the house that needed months of fixing. I needed to let go and surrender. I have always been a take-charge girl. Getting things done by relying on my capabilities. Not waiting for or asking others to help. I taught myself to be self-sufficient. I had to rely on contractors to do the work, for them to do it their way, and on their timetable. I had no control over my husband's illness. The anxiety I was experiencing in the present was a continuation from the dinner time of the past. I was sensitive to my sibling's and parents' emotion and that made me anxious.

I breathed and forgave myself for the buried anxiety I held from the past. As a family, we were all doing the best we could at the time.

The steps, sadness, depression, grief, guilt, shame, anger, and anxiety had emerged. I changed my flower essence remedy to anxiety. Almost seven months after beginning this journey, I was moving closer to the eighth step.

Again, I smoked and found myself under the last turquoise stone and the eighth hole in the stem on the right side. I waited again, unsure of what was next and if the eighth step would be revealed.

The memory came in quickly. Four-years-old, telling my mother about my friend Arrow. He was a guide who taught and showed me things. When I tried to talk about it, I was silenced. I was told people would think I was crazy and that it was not true. I did not want to be crazy. That was bad. Was I a bad child? Would I ever be good enough? I was afraid to be crazy. Would they send me away?

I thought I dealt with this already. It was still here inside me. I was still a little girl questioning myself, hiding and silencing myself. Still there was a wound. My heart froze in fear, I became emotional and teared up. Were there any more tears left?

The voice said, "Fear." Look at your fear. All the steps are the primal energy of survival. Emotions are perceived through the misunderstanding of words and situations you were too young to understand. You are living from your primal brain. What you internalize as your story has kept you in the darkness and hidden."

I returned from the vision and completed the ceremony.

Fear is the culprit for our suffering. Fear of not having control of our emotions. Fear of other people in our life. Fear from our own expectations.

Fear was exactly the word I pondered. Fear of change because we get comfortable in our patterns that on the surface seem to serve us. To adapt to change is brutal. If you look at nature, it is in constant flux. This leads us to the biggest fear: death.

Everything in nature including humans, continually shows us birth, stages of change, death, and transformation. But sometimes after loss and death we can't see the transformation, we fight, struggle, deny, and resist the reality. We know it's there. The loss of loved ones and our pets touch us deeply. Yet we don't want to be vulnerable and weak to admit the unbearable pain that death bestows on us. We try to control it, manipulate it, and prevent it but it will not escape us. Yes, I have fears.

I had come to accept death and accepted the belief of transformation of body to spirit. I have seen spirits that were once human all my life. There is life beyond our humanness although not experienced in the same way. What was my fear really about? What did all these memories have in common?

The eight steps on the right side of the stem were sadness, depression, grief, guilt, shame, anger, anxiety, and fear. My path and my memories brought me to this moment and my struggle. I thought I would be done once the eight steps were revealed. But I was not done. I had a nagging feeling I was not going to like where this was going. In fact, I was sure of it. How many more dense emotions did I need to experience?

The next time I smoked the Thunderbird Chanunpa I found some clarity.

When I was smoking and offering the smoke to the seven directions, I found the miniature likeness of my body sucked into the depth and darkness of the bowl. There was smoke all around me. I was standing on the tobacco I had placed inside the bowl moments before. The tobacco was burning and so were my feet. At the same time, I could look up from the inside of the bowl to see my large self, smoking and causing the burning pain in my feet. I was causing my suffering. The smoke inside the bowl was suffocating. I needed to escape the bowl.

I am dying. My little self, tried to climb up the side of the bowl but there was nothing to hold on to. I was in so much pain physically and emotionally and the thought of dying in this bowl was not an option. I knew I was in a vision but the experience and fear that I could not escape added to my torment and panic. The smoke inside the bowl was choking me. Just as I was getting ready for my fate, a set of talons above me grabbed me by the shoulders and flew me out of the burning place. I tried to look up but it was too large. I was dropped into a nest in a large tree. When I looked down, I was reliving my experience at sun dance in 2017. I was seeing myself dancing behind the one dancer and seeing my body glowing as I danced and sang with joy. Reliving the scene of the spirit ancestors entering the dance from the north gate was next.

I saw four of them holding the large chanunpa. They were not smoking it. They were holding it in an offering way. What I understood then, to continue to follow and pray with the chanunpas in 2017 was wrong. They were foretelling me of another larger chanunpa that was coming. It is the Thunderbird Chanunpa. The ancestors sat in the thunderbird nest in the tree when they held it. It came from the thunderbird. They were foretelling about this one, very large chanunpa with a dark bowl. How could I have missed that?

The memory of their voices repeated, "Stop hiding. It's time to be seen. Come out of your darkness."

The scene changed and I was exiting the dance circle. I remembered the thoughts and judgements my mind had been making of myself miserable for not following the others. Worrying about what others might say or think about me.

As soon as I came to the realization, I felt the talons push me out of the nest and the vison ceased.

I completed the ceremony with new awareness. The memories that have come from the dark allowed my emotions and thoughts to surface. That vision was about a large chanunpa in the physical being gifted to me. I thought it was only about continuing my path, not receiving another chanunpa. I did not need or want another one.

The next time I smoked it revealed another vision.

As I smoked and in my mind's eye, my mini body walked down the right side of the eight turquoise stones on the stem. I remembered each step of emotion, sadness, depression, grief, guilt, shame, anger, anxiety, and fear. Then my mini-self jumped into the bowl of darkness.

I floated in the dark abyss in a peaceful and relaxed state. Floating, I sang my death song and rattled to honor the beings in the below world. The large black snake gently slid up the outside of my spine on my skin. Its great head towered above mine.

I was not afraid. It felt comforting, protective, and wildly primal. It reached above me and snatched an egg from the ethers. The egg was luminous and white. It held it over my head. I reached above and as I held on to the egg in the snake's mouth, a large screeching bird came above us and snatched us both. I clung to the egg wondering if the snake had stolen it and the bird was out for revenge. I was thrown into a soft grass-like material, but it was dark. I could see nothing above or below me. I didn't know where the snake had gone. Perhaps the bird ate it.

I waited in the dark for something to happen.

A thunderous roar and the shrill of the bird calling deafened me. The soft ground I sat on quaked and rattled. The soft ground fell away and I felt myself tumble backwards in somersaults, spinning out of control into a black tunnel. I closed my eyes, my body stiffened in fright trying to grab onto anything physical but there was nothing.

"Stop," I screamed in my head.

At last, I came to a stop. I was in a purification ceremony. I was shown the Thunderbird Chanunpa being blessed in the ceremony. The feathers on the stem needed to be removed.

I heard a voice, "It needs to be reborn. Call upon the sixteen powers of Spirit to enter the chanunpa in the purification ceremony." My mind asked why since it had already been blessed and smoked.

The vision proceeded with sixteen supernatural beings looking like trails of smoke that came from above. One by one, each of them entered the bowl of the Thunderbird Chanunpa, traveled up inside the stem and came to rest back in the bowl. It was a magnificent display of empowerment.

I heard their voices. They whispered their names and identified themselves and their powers. I had heard of them from the Lakota elder years ago.

Four were the original higher powers of life. The second four were their companions. The third group of four had lesser powers. The last four had powers related and supportive to Spirit. I could not believe this. I had never experienced or seen them in spirit form, even in vision. They whispered their Lakota names in the darkness.

"Call our names to impart the power from the purification ceremony to the chanunpa. It is time to begin a personal relationship with us. You are at a crossroad. Steps are to be taken to come out of the ashes of the underworld and for you to

rise. Eight sets of steps, eight down the right side and eight up the left side of the stem."

I returned from the vision and completed the ceremony. It asked to be blessed in the next lodge ceremony. The mysterious powers of the spirits made their intent clear. Although I already blessed it, and connected it to me with the Medicine Chanunpa, the blessing in the purification lodge would be a rebirth for the chanunpa and perhaps even myself.

The vision was clear. I was to name and honor each of them. The supernatural spirits would enter, bless, and empower the Thunderbird Chanunpa in the next lodge ceremony.

CHAPTER 30

Thunderbird Lodge

The next lodge ceremony was interesting. Half of the community did not attend. They cancelled with other commitments. It would be a very small purification lodge.

The fire keeper prepared the sacred fire with the amount of grandfather stones that I asked for. Each lodge is different. In my four-day preparation before I conduct the ceremony, I ask and am shown how many stones need to be placed in the fire. These special (inyans) grandfather stones are honored inside the lodge with sweet grass, cedar, sage, tobacco, and sacred water.

The sacred fire took hold quickly in the West and lit all four directions at once. It was beautiful.

Each round is dedicated to one of the four directions. Each time the door flap is closed we are in complete darkness inside the lodge. Prayers are said, songs are sung, and sacred water is poured on the hot stones to create steam that purifies us inside and out, bringing our original breath of life back to balance in our body. The door flap is lifted signifying one round or a door. There are usually four rounds to the ceremony. However, it could be seven rounds for a healing ceremony.

The stones must be used up in the ceremony. There must be no life or heat left in them. If they still have too much heat an extra round must be added to ensure the stones are completely used. This is out of respect for them giving their life so that we can be cleansed and renewed.

In this season, we received a tremendous amount of rain. It felt tropical in nature. There were several short torrential downpours several days each week. Then the sun would quickly reappear. I noticed this summer people in the community had been missing ceremony more often.

I also noticed the land was taking over the ceremony area. Because of all the rain, grass and weeds were now encroaching on the cleared area around the lodge. The altar mound outside the doorway had eroded greatly. The lodge had shifted because the water had shifted the ground. The doorway to the lodge had narrowed and the top of the lodge was closer to the ground. We could barely crawl inside. Was this a sign?

In any case, it would need to be rebuilt next spring. It was interesting how the community had changed this summer. The lives of the remaining community members were changing. In today's ceremony there were only five of us.

Before we began, I carefully hung the Thunderbird Chanunpa over the stone pit inside the lodge. The heated stones and sacred water would create the steam to bless it. The sixteen powers of Spirit would be named and honored in the third round as I was shown in my vision.

It was a clear sunny day with no wind. We entered the

lodge, the door flap was closed, and I began the first round, pouring the sacred water over the stones and heating the lodge evenly. Prayers were made to honor all things that create the ceremony and the elders that kept the ceremony alive. Four traditional songs were sung. Eventually the door flap was opened to release the steam.

After a few minutes the door was closed again by the fire keeper, and I again poured sacred water onto the stones. Personal prayers were spoken by each person in the lodge. Again, four traditional songs were sung and the door flap was opened again,

The rest of the stones were brought in for the third round. The water bucket was refilled and the door was closed once again. The new stones were exceptionally hot. They had been in the fire longer.

In this third round we honored White Buffalo Calf Woman, who brought the sacred ceremonies and the original first Chanunpa Wakan. The third round is considered the healing round. Specific questions could be asked or a dream could be interpreted if asked in the proper way with a tobacco offering.

In this round I offered prayers for the blessing of Thunderbird Chanunpa. As I prayed, a large roar of thunder began outside the lodge. There was no cloud in the sky when we began nor was there a forecast for a storm or rain. It continued the entire round. I sang the four sacred songs gifted by the heyoka for this chanunpa.

The first song was a calling song. People in the lodge began to cry. I heard the sniffles. Later they said they felt a presence or energy for this beautiful song. I spoke the names of each of the powers and offered sacred water to the stones.

"Wi, Skan, Maka, Inyan." I paused. "Hanwi, Tate, Unk, Wakinyan." I paused again. When I spoke the name Wakinyan, (thunderbird or thunder beings), another rumble of thunder rang loud above us. Then it began to rain hard and fast on the lodge. "Tatanka, Tob Tob, Wani, Yumni Wi." I paused again and spoke the remaining four. "Niya, Nagi, Sichun, Yumni."

As I spoke their names, I felt a surge of power and saw small lights enter the lodge from above. The small pinpoint of lights jumped into the bowl then disappeared. I ended the blessing and proceeded to finish with a healing round of prayers.

The door flap opened once again, and steam was released. After a brief pause, the door was again closed. There were more songs and my final prayers for each person in the community. The stones were still not completely used. One in particular was still sizzling. Instead of sending the spirits away at the end of the ceremony, the fourth door was opened, more sacred water filled the bucket, and we closed the door for a fifth round.

The fifth round finished prayers of gratitude for everything in life until the stones had no more life. I sent the spirits back to where they came from, so they could return when I honored them again. The door flap opened for the last time. Since it was raining heavily outside, we smoked the Buffalo Chanunpa inside the lodge and finished offering the four sacred foods, (corn, buffalo, berries, and water) to the fire before putting the fire to sleep.

By the time we exited the lodge the rain had stopped. The fire keeper related an interesting observance. He said the rain poured all around but hardly on the fire and not on the altar where the Buffalo Chanunpa was propped up on the buffalo skull. None of it got wet during the downpour. All that needed protection was protected. I removed the blessed Thunderbird Chanunpa from the lodge and exited.

I did not know what to expect moving forward with the Thunderbird Chanunpa but I knew there was change in the air and I had to be patient, trust, and follow. Please note this particular Chanunpa blessing ceremony was not and will not be a ceremony that is Lakota or any tribal affiliation. This lodge ceremony comes only from my vision from Spirit. It's ceremony and teachings are only for me to use with the Thunderbird Chanunpa and only in this one lodge.

CHAPTER 31

Moving Forward

The day after the purification lodge ceremony, I woke up with incredible pain in my lower back and right hip. It seemed that I had possibly pulled something getting out of the lodge. I remember twisting oddly but I did not feel anything hurt at the time. But the next day I could barely stand, sit, or walk.

I used arnica salve, red willow, and other herbs for inflammation and, of course, iced it. I called my chiropractor to realign my body that I knew was off.

In reflection, I understood that pain is guilt, lower back is fear and my hip is resistance to moving forward. So much change was upon me and with the new blessing of the Thunderbird Chanunpa, more teachings and changes were sure to come.

In the prior month, I recognized there was a real possibility we might need to sell the house and move in the near future. With my husband's retirement and the beginning of health issues it would be difficult physically and financially. The water pipes, walls, and ceilings were fixed and updated with fresh paint. We had updated carpets and flooring in the last couple of years.

I felt sad and guilty that I would have to give up conducting the purification ceremonies if we had no land and moved to an elderly place or apartment. I worried about the community and possibility of lost friendships.

Ceremony was who I was or at least where I found my purpose of service.

A week after the blessing of the Thunderbird Chanunpa, I smoked it. The feather from South America I was waiting for to complete the bundle was gifted to me the day after its blessing, which was no surprise to me. Spirit provides when I trust, so the bundle was complete, for now at least.

It smoked easier than before. Larger drags of smoke came through the stem. A small piece of burning tobacco made its way up the stem and into my mouth. A shock at first, but it was the only one. Making me understand both the bowl and stem were completely open like a hollow bone.

I felt the smoke became easier. But there was more of it. In the darkness I found myself in the stem. Once again, I saw the eight open holes above where the turquoise stones used to be but now on the left side of the stem. As I walked under each of them, one word was revealed.

The bottom ninth one was "joy." Moving up the stem to the tenth was "peace." The eleventh was "passion." The twelfth was "love." The thirteenth was "compassion." The fourteenth was "pleasure." The fifteenth was "gratitude." The last, the sixteenth at the top of the stem was "contentment." When I got to the top of the stem, I heard a loud shrill and two talons grabbed me from the top hole in the stem and pulled me into a bolt of lightning in the dark sky.

There were flashes of light and the sound of thunder all around me.

Next thing I knew, I was struck by lightning in the chest. A putrid burning smell of skin filled the air. It was me. I was zapped. I jolted out of the talons of the bird and I fell downwards.

My body ached. I felt like I was on fire. I wanted to scream but instead only a faint whimper came out of me. Then it got stronger until it became the bird's call. What was happening? I wanted to survive. But I also wanted to be free from the pain.

The fall was gentle. I collapsed in a muck of ashes of the burnt tobacco that had been smoked. Realizing now I was in the bowl, lying in the darkness, I heard the familiar voice.

"Fear will be transformed. Joy is the turning point. The next eight steps of the left side are the balance for the first eight. Accept joy. The sixteen powers are the ones to ask for help. The next months you will begin to know and build a deep relationship with each of them."

"Your understanding of healing must change. True healing can only happen when what is hidden in the dark can be revealed and accepted. Both sides of the steps are inside each human. The goal is not to rid oneself of the heavy steps of sadness, depression, grief, guilt, shame, anger, anxiety, and fear. These emotional steps allow one to be human. They are needed for growth, survival, and awareness. The next eight steps, joy, peace, passion, love, compassion, pleasure, gratitude, and contentment are the balance. Both the right and left sides merge for healing. Calling upon the appropriate power of the sixteen will support the healing and balance."

One by one the names of the sixteen powers lined up with the steps but they were counterclockwise to how I was taught for the purification ceremony. It felt foreign to me but I accepted what I was shown in the teaching. This ceremony was taught for this particular chanunpa only. It is not one recognized by any tribe or tradition that I know of. It was uncomfortable for me to learn. It led me to surrender what I thought I knew to another way that I did not. I would again have to learn to trust. In vision I saw the sixteen power's names and the sixteen emotions connected to them.

The vision ended and I completed the ceremony. These sixteen spiritual powers and the connection to the emotions were not the understandings I had been taught by the Lakota elder. It was not anything that I had referenced or had knowledge of. I did not want to dishonor the teachings from the elder but Spirit and the Thunderbird Chanunpa was a new knowledge that went beyond any tribe or custom I knew.

With this new information of the last eight emotions, I hoped I was going to turn the corner in the teachings to perhaps a lighter energy. The previous eight months were some of the most difficult I have experienced.

The spiritual sister who gifted this chanunpa to me said she rescued it from a Native American man who was going away, which could have meant any number of things. He asked if she understood what this chanunpa was. She said yes in return. The stem has a carved symbol of a thunderbird below all the turquoise stones. It seems to be flying into the bowl. Something I had not paid attention to up to this point. She has a connection to the thunder beings; she had an idea of what the chanunpa carried. It would take me two years of praying with it for *me* to understand its purpose and ceremony. Still, it teaches me. I am grateful that she answered the call to rescue it for she is a special woman who has been the catalyst for manifesting several of my visions from Spirit. I honor her with much gratitude.

CHAPTER 32

A Lighter Side

Every time I prayed in ceremony with the Thunderbird Chanunpa, I became more comfortable with the snake medicine. The four songs I sang brought me into a vision each time. In the next ceremony, another vison came.

I heard a voice whisper. The voice continued as its body stepped towards me out of the darkness in the bowl. An owl came towards me and then stepped behind me and wrapped its wings to cover my eyes. Its feathers were soft.

"I have come to you many times. I gifted you my feather from my living body and you gifted it away out of fear. At sun dance, my feather was gifted to you by a sacred heyoka and you gave it away. The next year, an owl fan from a sun dancer was gifted to you and again you gave it away. You found my dead body when walking on your street and I offered my wings and again you honored me but gifted them to a heyoka. Lastly, I called to you on the road to retrieve me, honor me, bury me, and take my wings. You have prepared them well but you are uncomfortable with them and keep them hidden. The Thunderbird Chanunpa bundle calls for them. You are listening but why are still afraid to use my medicine?"

"Because of the sickness it may bring," I replied.

"It is your medicine. You know how to respect the power. Each time I found my way to you. You understand the darkness of death and the spirit world. You see and deal with the transformation of death and rebirth. You have always had a deep connection to me. You must use me with this chanunpa. My medicine is used to see the hidden and to bring wisdom to the illness and illusions that humans hide from their self. It is time to move to the other side of the steps and balance the dark and the light side by merging them."

The vision ended.

Knowing the next eight steps of emotion that were on the left side started with joy, I wanted to create experiences to bring more joy into my life.

The next time I sat and prayed with the Thunderbird Chanunpa, I prayed for guidance on joy to balance the fear. I needed to be reminded what joy felt like and what used to bring me joy. In my mind the memory began.

Dancing and singing. I loved to dance and sing to the radio, records, and television, twirling around while humming or singing. Whenever I was asked what I wanted to be when I got older, I would reply, "A singer and a teacher."

I had not even been to school yet but I wanted to be a teacher. I don't know how that came to my mind.

Being outside in nature, chasing butterflies, and lifting large stones to observe the ants and insects brought me joy. That was my play time. I loved to swing high into the air on the swing-set hoping to catch the clouds. I loved learning and eventually reading books. I began writing my private thoughts in my hidden diary at age ten. The last joyful thing I was shown was prayer.

Sitting and talking to God by myself. As the memories surfaced, I felt awe and excitement.

I completed the ceremony and pondered my next move with joy. It was simple. I started every day with prayer, talking to Spirit. I listened and sang to music, and I danced to move my body. I took a daily short walk outdoors, read for an hour and journaled my thoughts in the afternoon.

The Thunderbird Chanunpa ceremony was changing in small ways. The way of conducting the ceremony became more relaxed and fluid. The songs came easily. The owl and snake medicine became a part of me.

Heavy rains throughout the summer continued to erode the land where the ceremonial lodge was erected. The land was shifting and so was the lodge. The bent saplings began to shift and widen. I wondered if the land was giving us a sign.

Since the blessing in the lodge ceremony, the Thunderbird Chanunpa was still smoked once week but now it was smoked during the day. This was a harder challenge as I needed windows of opportunity to be alone without my husband, but opportunity arose. Out of the blue my husband joined a bridge league on Wednesday afternoons. This was a perfect time for me to smoke and pray.

The ceremony became more interesting. I began to use the owl wings and when I did, I became its body and could see through its eyes.

I heard the word "Peace. Peace is the helper to anxiety, just as joy is to fear. Peace is the next phase."

I was walking inside the chanunpa but I was not in the stem. I was in the bowl walking in a circle. I heard two loud bird calls. A loud crash of thunder rolled in real time outside my window, but I stayed in vision. I looked above the rim of the bowl and saw an eagle from the north side of the bowl and a condor from the south side of the bowl lock talons above me to begin their swirl of descent. They were spinning around like birds do when they mate. I heard their whooshing sound like a helicopter's propeller blade spinning in the air and creating a great wind. As they fell in a free fall to the ground and disappeared, an enormous bird emerged above me. Its wingspan was huge. I could not see its beak or head but heard its voice.

*"I am the Condor. I represent the heart and the eagle represents the mind. The eagle and I have joined in union to bring the heart and mind power to **Yumni**, the whirlwind. The physical material movement for survival. Descend, die, resurrect, rebuild, rebirth, the essence of change and transformation through love. Movement. This chanunpa unites the native prophecies of the people from the North and South."*

The vision ended.

I realized I had just met Yumni the whirlwind, one of the sixteen beings of power of Spirit. I felt its presence. I was confused as to why it came first. It should have come last as in the purification lodge. I had so many questions. I took a few breaths to relax and then journaled my vision.

Another vision came the next time I smoked the Thunderbird Chanunpa.

Again, I found myself in the darkness of the bowl with the owl assisting me but I was not within its body. The snake appeared and climbed up my spine. For the first time, the snake merged with my body, no longer traveling outside of me. Its head became my head and its eyes became my eyes. The world was cloudy, yet because my eyes were slanted, I could see peripherally. My body began to tingle. My mind began to expand beyond the snake body and beyond myself as human.

*I heard the word, "***Sichun****" the powers of intellect, reasoning, discernment and imagery, or so I was taught. But what I experienced in the vision was that Sichan could be seen as a spark of intelligence, to know what is needed in all moments.*

I saw the condor coming from the South and picking up a dead carcass to feed itself. Then I saw an eagle coming from the North bringing its blessings and feeding from the waters. The eagle was eating what was alive and fresh. The condor ate what was decayed. Each way was important and each bird had a job to do, although they did it in a different way to survive, a primal instinct. One survives off the dead and the other survives off the living. To understand Sichun one must know the spark of balance. In that moment, I felt more than I had words for. Sichun was not the energy of a noun but a verb.

An owl appeared and spoke "I, the owl, will become you. I will help you see the truth of what is needed for the healing. You will change into the snake to help clear the sickness and decay. Then I will release you (the snake) to the earth and you can transform back into the human self."

Then the vision was over.

Each week a new introduction and a new understanding would come. These powers were perceived and experienced personally, but not in the same way as the Lakota elder had shared. I still struggled. His teachings were correct and yet what I was experiencing, though different, was deeply personal and only my perception. In ceremony, I became the owl and then I became the snake. My perception would shift back and forth.

I am not giving a teaching of the sixteen spiritual powers to the reader. I am just relaying my experience. I would have to come to accept the Thunderbird Chanunpa teachings from Spirit.

The next time I smoked the Thunderbird Chanunpa my vision came quicker.

*Tiny blue lights appeared in the darkness and I heard the word "**Nagi**," the ghost. What lives in the shadows. They danced around me touching my skin and giving me goosebumps, a tingling sensation and yet a comforting feeling as well. The energy was exciting. It would happen just before a spirit guide, ancestor, or helper would appear to me. It was not about what they looked like but about the sensation of energy I would feel. That is how I would come to know its power.*

I completed the ceremony and journaled my experience.

The next purification ceremony was scheduled for the following weekend and with it came sadness. Three members of the community had permanently moved out of state. There was a nagging feeling around me that more change was going to happen. I could not shake the grief I was feeling. The heaviness also was felt by my husband.

He too said, "You know hon, I feel a little sad. I think this weekend will be our last lodge ceremony."

I understood what he meant. I too, after the blessing of the Thunderbird Chanunpa, felt a shift and completion.

Early in the morning while my husband took a walk, I smoked the Thunderbird Chanunpa before the few people arrived for the lodge. As in the past I found myself in the dark bowl. My vision began.

I experienced a tingle in my chest and then a warm expansion *of heat. I inhaled slowly and exhaled slowly. Then a voice spoke, "I am **Niya**. I am the breath of spirit within all beings. I am the power that is experienced in the moment between breaths. I am the stillness, awareness and the spark of life in the center of your being. Feel my power."*

I took a breath and held it for a moment. I paid attention to the moment before I exhaled. I caught a glimpse of the spark of my spirit. It is the energy that will move beyond the body. For a brief moment, I felt its power.

I returned from the vision and completed the ceremony. I grasped the stem with both hands and covered both sides of the turquoise stones that ran down the stem. I felt the merger of both the right and the left side of the stem, the human emotions and their balancers. I understood we cannot live as humans without both sides. We do not need to get rid of one dense emotion to become the other lighter emotion. It is a merging and balancing act of combining both.

Joy merges with fear, peace with anxiety, passion with anger, love with shame, compassion with guilt, gratitude with grief, pleasure with depression and contentment with sadness. The sixteen steps I must go through to learn this chanunpa were not eight bad or eight good. An equal balance and merging of each side is what I needed. It was not to be overcome or conquered. It was only to be felt and merged with its opposite.

No need to seek perfection or choose light over dark. Dark is within the light and light is within the dark. Only through my acceptance by revisiting my hidden, dark held emotions and misunderstood perceived memories could the light come forth to merge and balance. My vulnerability would lead me to authenticity.

CHAPTER 33

⎯⎯⎯◆⎯⎯⎯

The Last Purification Lodge

By afternoon our small community came to attend the purification ceremony. I had not been down to the lodge area since I went away to the Cape with two of my close spiritual sisters. The trees that we planted fourteen years ago kept the lodge area hidden and secluded.

We gathered together and saw a devastating sight. With heavy rains the week prior, the lodge had completely collapsed. The ground had flooded and gave way. The saplings broke and came out of the ground. There was no way to fix it. It would have to be rebuilt in the spring.

Together we dismantled the canvas, blankets, and saplings. I offered tobacco as a completion ceremony of gratitude for what the land and the saplings gave to us. After we cleaned the area, I conducted a chanunpa ceremony with the Buffalo Chanunpa. The community was very weepy that day in their prayers. Maybe they all were feeling a sense of the sadness Paul and I were feeling.

I would let Spirit decide if to rebuild the lodge in the spring. I would pay close attention during the winter. I secretly hoped we would rebuild.

The next morning, I sat on the back deck to smoke the Thunderbird Chanunpa. It was a sunny warm day. A blue dragon fly came to greet me from the West as I was filling the chanunpa with the sacred tobacco.

The vision came quickly.

I felt a cool breath on my face inhaling and exhaling. Then I heard the voice, "The Thunderbird Chanunpa has become your purification ceremony. It carries the supernatural powers. They are not physical embodiments but spiritual energies."

*I could see my body riding upon the waves of the ocean. I felt myself pulled to the bottom of the ocean and then up again to ride the waves again, when I heard the voice, "I am **Yumni Wi**, the union of the sea and the earth. I am a circular movement." I was feeling the sensation of being anchored to the earth and then moving out to the sea. I passed through each of them several times as I dove below the sea and rose above the waves. I felt a sense of relief in my body as I discarded all the heavy burdens that I carried.*

My relief ended the vision.

The next two weeks I was in cleaning mode. I began to clean and discard clothes and objects. It was a call to release things I no longer needed. Some things I donated and other things I threw away. Eight bags of donations and half of the boxes in the basement I released. With my husband's help, we moved the furniture around.

It is a habit of mine to shift and change things in the house when I feel the need to lighten energy. I learned this technique from a medicine woman from Texas.

I knew I was intentionally removing all the contractors' energies from my home. I was also shifting the heavy chaos energy to feel lighter for myself, my husband, and the young cat we adopted.

The next time I prayed with the Thunderbird Chanunpa, I offered my gratitude for the projects being completed and my house being cleaner and lighter. Outside in the silence on our back deck, once again I returned to vision and a voice spoke.

*"I am **Wani**, the power of the weather from the four directions. Weathering your inner storms, struggles, lessons, suffering, and pain will lead to thicker, new skin. Acceptance of imperfection will ease your inner storm."*

The wind began to pick up for real around me. I could feel the weather changing. Like the north wind and south wind tangling in a duel.

The voice spoke for the last time during the silence.

"Wani, the weather shifts and changes, adapts, and flows, season to season. Its purpose continues and does what is needed. Wani will help you to weather and share the vulnerable places in yourself."

*In my mind's vision, I became the stem of the chanunpa. I could feel the brush of my fingertips on the turquoise stones down the right side of the stem in the physical. At the same time, I could feel my body had become the stem I was touching. Two separate sensations merged. As I ran my fingers down the right side of the stem the first turquoise stone spoke, "**Sadness,** the next stone, **Depression,** then **Grief,** then **Guilt,** then **Shame,** then **Anger,** then **Anxiety** and finally **Fear.**" Then I ran my fingers up left side of the stones and they spoke, "**Joy,** then **Peace,** then **Passion,** then **Love,** then **Compassion,** then **Pleasure,** then **Gratitude** and finally **Contentment.**" All the stones were named.*

I heard the words, "Now merge." I held both of my hands covering both sides of the stem, overlapping my hands together to cover all the stones on the stem. A power came forth in my body and in my hands that made me shiver. For a brief moment I touched that power as it ran through my body, mind, and spirit. I felt a presence behind me and it flew on my shoulders. Its pressure was heavy. I thought my body would fall forwards and drop the chanunpa. The large talons dug into my skin and sat on my shoulders. The thunderbird honored me with its support. I sang my final closing song for the ceremony and then felt the presence lift and take flight behind me.

The vision ended and I completed the ceremony. The light and dark merged as one. I felt the powers of the thunderbird through the chanunpa. It would help for the next step a week later.

The next time I prayed with the Thunderbird Chanunpa the smoke kept shifting, blowing from North to South and then from South to North, even though there was no physical wind to speak of around me.

The voice spoke, "The ancestors and relationships, healing and wisdom, young adult and elder, North America and South America, and the eagle and the condor." A conversation was being played with the smoke and the wind. I closed my eyes and ran my fingers slowly down the stem as each stone spoke its name as before.

*It was then I heard the word "**Tob Tob**." I felt a soft brush on my left cheek. I saw in my vision a brown bear picking what plants and berries to eat and not to eat. It came from the west direction. Bears I understood are healing energies and full of*

291

wisdom. Knowing when to take rest and knowing when to move, knowing what to eat and what to avoid.

"I am Tob Tob, the power of the bear spirit. I walk using all four paws at a time. I carry courage, love, bravery, and wisdom." I offered smoke to the spirit to acknowledge and thank it. Tob Tob, I could feel, was part of the supernatural power of healing. Then it disappeared.

The vision changed. I saw myself in the distance sitting on the ground holding the Thunderbird Chanunpa within a lodge. The lodge around me began to disintegrate into tiny molecules and they floated inside of me. Then the same thing happened with the chanunpa. It disappeared into molecules appearing as tiny spheres that floated directly into my chest and heart space. I saw my distant body glowing, filling with light. The tingling up my spine, fingers, legs, and my chest began to expand. I was being stretched to accommodate the energy of molecules. The voice explained.

*"You are the Thunderbird Chanunpa and you are the purification lodge. You **are** the ceremony. This chanunpa has been filled with all the powers of the lodge and it is being transferred inside of you. The sacredness of its power in ceremony was always inside of you. It is your calling. It is not about conducting ceremony, but through your heart, song, prayers, and sharing experiences of the sacred you have inside of you. Bring the energy of ceremony. Not all people need or want a ceremony but all people can heal through the energy of the ceremony through song and prayer. Remember you are Spirit Singer to the people." The voice ceased and the vision ended.*

I completed the ceremony in tears. At the time it was nine years ago, I was gifted a name that I only use when I pray alone and a public name that I can share out loud which is "Spirit Singer." I came to understand this name to mean that I could communicate and work with the spirit world and Spirit through prayer and ceremony.

I have been shown through this vision, it is not the physical ceremony but the sacred energy and connection that I carry within me to pray, communicate, and sing to help people. With the community fading, the lodge collapse, my husband's retirement, his health, and my house reconstruction, was this Spirit's plan? Was the thunderbird power deconstructing my life to ash only to rebuild it in another way?

CHAPTER 34

The Next Step

The following week was my birthday. I started the warm autumn day in prayer. My husband was exercising at the local gym. There was a slight gentle breeze in the air.

As the Thunderbird Chanunpa ceremony began, a blue jay flew and sat in a tree in the west direction. It did not make a sound. I continued the ceremony but two of the four medicine songs escaped me. I knew the words but again not the melody. I looked for my trusted cheat sheet of words but still this time the melody was lost. I trusted the songs were not needed or that I needed to experience humility.

As I become one with each chanunpa I carry, it changes me and this one was no different. A little piece of who I am surrenders and makes way for growth, knowledge, and hopefully wisdom. Knowledge is learned and wisdom is to give away. But it takes time for that to happen, sometimes a year or years. A relationship must be built and worked until there is no separation of its power and knowledge, and myself. *It* is the director and healer of its purpose.

By accepting a chanunpa into my life, I am also accepting the responsibility to protect it, keep it safe, and struggle to learn its intention and purpose, while allowing my life to be changed, healed, and eventually used for the good of all people. Only when I have completely learned these things can its power be used to help other people. I cannot help with what I have not experienced. To be honored to carry eight of them is a very humbling experience and tough challenge. The only reason I accept this personal hardship is to be able to help my fellow human beings. It was always what I knew I was put on earth to do, to be of service and help others.

During the ceremony, I sat in the silence. The rattle that I used to go into the silence did not want to be used. The wing that I used as medicine to see, did not want to be removed from its leather bag. A quiet peace came over me while I looked at the blue jay in the tree. Another blue jay joined him. And then another and another, until there were four jays sitting separately in the tree: one high up, one below him, one to the left and one to the right. I was amazed at how quiet they all were. It was very unusual.

A blue jay, as I have learned, is about the right use of power, using and recognizing your own power, or paying attention to power you have allowed another to have over you. I relaxed and closed my eyes since a vision comes more quickly for me in the darkness.

In vision, I felt the wind pick up all around me. The slight breeze had now become gusts of wind. I saw myself as the tree the jays were sitting on. I could feel them sitting on my branches, my arms. I saw the jays working hard to steady themselves against the gusts of winds. It was then they began their unique and distinctive calls. I felt they were warning calls. The calls flooded my mind as I tried to understand. There before me was a large spirit buffalo standing nose to nose with me, rubbing his head on my trunk. He flooded my mind with his voice.

*"I am **Tatanka**. I am the sacred power to achieve completion. The spirit of plenty and all you need that is sacred (wakan). Ceremony is sacred. The sixteen powers are sacred. Life is sacred. Ceremony done over and over the same way makes it ordinary. To keep it sacred it will need to shift and change all the time. Learn to be comfortable with change in ceremony and in life. The sacred can only come when you are open in every moment to give space for it to flow. The sacred needs respect. It is a space outside of the ordinary."*

I now found myself inside the large black bowl standing on a pile of warm ashes from the tobacco I had just smoked. I heard a low rumble and felt the ash begin to move and shift. I lost my balance and fell, lying down on the soft bed of ash. I heard a screeching sound. The dark winged creature entered the top of the bowl and thrust its body upon me. It was heavy and massive. It blocked any possible light. How could it fit in this bowl? I could hardly breathe. I did not fight it, but I was scared because it had power I did not possess. I was under its talons as it pressed on my chest. I thought I would die because I could not breathe. I wanted to fight for my life, but I was so tired. Tired of fighting and resisting things in my life. I felt my body go limp and exhaled the words, "I surrender."

*For what I thought would be my last conscious breath, I heard its feathered voice, "I am **Wakinyan**, the thunderbird, the power to take and give life. What you experienced these months is "**Unk**," the contention of disagreement. You know it well. Unk is needed to remind you of your inner and outer conflicts of misguided beliefs and perceptions. It is the outer you versus society* *and the inner you versus a set of beliefs. This creates struggle and suffering. Your expectation and belief of perfection and fairness are not to be attained. Unk brings an awareness of what is true and what is not. It is the way of balance. It will lead eventually to satisfaction in your life. The heaviness and loss of breath in this bowl is Unk's power to show you the conflicts you hold and to surrender them." The words faded.*

A rumble of thunder charged above my head and woke me from the vision. I opened my eyes. The sky had changed with gray clouds blowing in from the west direction. The jays continued to call but now I could no longer understand their voices. The four birds left the tree together and flew off to the North while the rumble of thunder came closer and louder. I completed the ceremony and went inside the house.

The clouds immediately blew away and the sun returned. There was no rain and no thunderstorm. All had cleared. Wakinyan and Unk, the next powers of Spirit's sixteen had introduced themselves.

I realized the darkness and struggle I had been experiencing this year, was self-imposed. My misinterpreted memories the last months brought back mental, emotional, and even physical pain. My perception became my belief which in turn was not completely the truth. It hurt and I felt wounded, because my expectation of perfection and fairness from others, as well as requiring perfection from myself was misguided. My needs and perception created the thoughts, beliefs, and feelings of the eight heavy emotions within myself. I could not control life, people or even ceremony. It was all symbolic. The Thunderbird Chanunpa was shifting everything around me, the way to conduct ceremony, the loss of the lodge community, and the physical inside of my home. It was also shifting me internally. I had to change my nagging need to do things in only what I was told or believed was the right way. The way elders have taught or modeled what I perceived to be true. I still had much to learn and experience. There were six more powers of Spirit for me to meet. There was no rush. What I went through the last twelve months felt like twelve years.

CHAPTER 35

Changes

C hange had begun to be an integral part of ceremony with the Thunderbird Chanunpa. Sometimes the rattle was used, sometimes not. Sometimes all four sacred songs were sung, sometimes only two or three. Sometimes I found myself in vision in the stem and sometimes in the sacred bowl. Nothing ever was exactly the same. It was disconcerting that there was change every time.

As a ceremonialist for many years, I have experienced that no two ceremonies are ever the same. But the Thunderbird Chanunpa was a different energy than the other seven bundles I carried. It was getting me familiar to unexpected changes and direction.

As I sat on my back deck under the cool cloudy sky, wrapped in my fleece shawl, I offered smoke to the seven directions and then used the rattle and song to descend into a state of deep vision.

*The wind picked up and spun around me until I was lifted and sucked into the bowl. The wind was loud and ferocious I could barely hear its voice. "I am **Tate.** I am the spirit power of the wind. I push and move the wind of the four directions. I* *am the power of change. I cannot be controlled. I can be fierce or gentle. Respect me."*

*When the wind abated, I saw a bright light shining above the rim of the bowl over my head. It grew and grew until I could recognize her. It was the moon. "I am **Hanwi**," she spoke. "I give light and rhythm to the sea and inside you. My power ebbs and flows back and forth. Nothing stands still. It is always changing and moving. I bring inner reflection with my power."*

As the light shined into the bowl I saw a snake slithering on the ground in an s-shape vertical line about five feet in length. It began to make its way horizontally back and forth about three feet wide and five feet long. I noticed as it traveled, the earth was being removed and small stones in the earth were being revealed.

The snake continued until it began to create the shape of a human being. The stones looked exactly like skeleton bones. The snake completed its task, and coiled upon the heart of the human shaped figure.

The voice I heard was clear.

*"We are **Inyan**, the stone nation. We are the bones of the earth. We bring support. We help to hold her together and give her form. We have been here a long time. We hold the knowledge and memories of the ancestors. We gave our power to the earth to make her body."*

I felt the sacrifice Inyan had given to shape, form, and firm the soil. I felt the connection to the internal bones in my own body. Yes, my bones and joints hurt, and I struggled in physical pain at times. But have they not also sacrificed and held my body up no matter what weight I continued to make them carry? I felt appreciation that their power was within me. Staring at the shape outlined in the soil and the skeleton of stones, I recognized myself. It was the same height and width as me. The shape rose up and faced me and spoke.

"I am **Maka**, *your true mother and the earth. Your body is my body. I birthed you and one day you will return your physical body and reunite your dust with me once again. I and you are the sacred and the ordinary. I am ordinary as you walk upon me every day, but I am sacred in the power of my earthquakes and floods. There is power in the unordinary and unexpected. The power of Inyan the stone and Maka, mother earth are stable and unstable. Feel our powers."*

Feeling the sensation and balance of Inyan and Maka within me, I took a long deep breath pulling this teaching within me. The shape of me disappeared. I was alone in the darkened bowl again. I heard the hoot of an owl in my vision. I waited for it to retrieve me and take me on a journey. I looked above me and saw the large opening of the bowl but only a single feather had floated down into the bowl. I followed it until it reached the bottom. It was a large feather. Looking closely, I recognized it. It was one of the three feathers I had placed on the stem of the Thunderbird Chanunpa. I thought it was odd to place this feather there in the first place, but I saw it in a vision in the very beginning.

A lone blue jay sitting in the north direction beckoned me out of the vision.

The next time I opened the bundle to sit in ceremony with the Thunderbird Chanunpa, more changes to the ceremony and bundle were being asked of me. The red cloths that wrapped the bowl and the stem, (the original one that it was placed in by the one who made it) needed to be cut and sewn into two pouches, one to hold the stem and one to hold the bowl.

Before I could sit and smoke, I had to take out the sewing machine and cut and sew the pouches.

It can be hard to explain and understand why I stopped everything to make the pouches in that moment.

When I get a directive (a voice) or a vision (seeing something like in a daydream) it does not stop pestering until I follow and do what I am shown or asked. It is like I cannot focus or am not allowed to focus on anything else until I take care of the request. Through all my years of experience, it works quicker and better for me if I just follow, even if I am not given or shown a reason for what I am told or shown to do. It will always turn out right if I don't struggle or question. And by now, I know when it is something I want to do (ego) or something abstract that comes out of thin air and something I might not want to take the time, energy, or expense to do.

After the pouches were completed, I reopened the bundle and began the ceremony. The ceremony has many moving parts. In this ceremony I was shown to add another pinch of tobacco than what I usually place in the bowl to ask my question or intention.

Up to this point all my intention and prayers were to learn and pay attention to the energy, teachings and how to serve others. Today I had a real question. It came to mind easily as I placed the extra pinch of tobacco.

"Aho grandfathers and grandmothers, I am struggling with knee pain. Help me to see what I cannot see and understand what I do not know, Pilamaye (thank you)."

I began my offerings of smoke to the seven directions and sang a song as I rattled and covered my eyes with the feathered wings.

In my mind's eye, I saw a spark of light immediately, just like a spirit light I see in a darkened purification ceremony. It lasted only a second before I felt myself sucked into a black hole. My body was in pain. Being pushed through this tiny hole brought much pressure to my bones. My knees had sharp pain. I heard the voice.

*"I am **Skan**. I am motion and movement. I am the power of the sky and universe. Feel me inside of you as the motion of living. Feel and know the flow of my motion through your body. It is the life force that connects and moves everything into action."*

I felt and focused on the slow pulse of everything working together to give me life. I teared up and became emotional. The pain in my knee reminded me that I was alive. There was blood and water flowing through my knees and body. Yes, I was alive.

Life to me was heavy. That is what I have believed, experienced, and felt all my life. The sensitivity of feeling another's mental, emotional, and physical pain since childhood led me to be uncomfortable in my body. It led me to want to help people and relieve their pain.

I could see the joy and lightness but I did not live there. I helped others to live there, lifting their burdens and bringing them to the light. But the lightness escaped me. Again, I was sucked out of the dark and found myself sitting at the top of the bowl. The sun was shining on my face. I closed my eyes. I felt its warmth and felt energized.

*A voice above me spoke. "I am **Wi**. I am the power of the sun that nourishes and makes things grow. My power lives in all things. I am your personal power. No growth or life comes without me. I radiate and empower. I am health and light." I could feel a buzz of energy growing inside me. It expanded more and more until I burst open, radiating in sun beams everywhere. The beams were within me and I shined it upon everything.*

A blue jay called and stirred me from the vision. I completed the ceremony. The last of the sixteen, Skan and Wi had made their introductions.

The steps of emotions were revealed and the sixteen powers of Spirit had now all made their first introduction. I would work with them personally for three years, until it was time to use it for others in a group ceremony.

Many changes came within that time. The lodge was never rebuilt. We sold our home and land. We downsized to a small living space with no land, in an elder community. We were led to the right place but I did not go willingly. I did what I thought was best for my husband's future condition, but I struggled emotionally leaving a place where I finally rooted myself to the land.

Change is hard. We get comfortable in the way things are. We find our niche and we stick with it. I have had many changes in my life. Others may say too many. I have had to adapt my life quickly. Maybe because I am older and more settled in my ways that the struggle felt harder this time.

After three years of changes, I realized the Thunderbird Chanunpa helped me to relive dark memories and emotions. The owl helped me to see my illusions and misunderstandings of those memories, which became a powerful healing of surrender, release, and forgiveness. The snake helped with the death of the old energy in me and rebirth a new way of living.

The more I prayed with the Thunderbird Chanunpa the clearer it became. The first eight steps were dense emotions and the second eight steps were the lighter emotions. The sixteen steps are of dark and light energy. They are not separate even though we only see one at a time. They merge. Both are equal and both are needed for growth and healing. Too much of one is not balanced. In darkness we learn what needs to be healed. In the light we can accept the healing. The ceremony evolved over time as the right side of the stem merged with the left side in ceremony. One emotion is never erased. Its opposing energies are merged for balance. The sixteen powers of Spirit became allies to me in this ceremony and brought forth energy for healing in my spirit. They are not physical manifestations but powerful essences, to be honored and respected.

It has helped me, healed me, and taught me how to accept the fluidity of change in my personal life and in ceremony, by letting go of the familiar and all I knew and thought I understood. It would be a clean slate for my life and a new way to work with medicine.

Finally, I can offer or use the Thunderbird Chanunpa in service to others for heavy matters. Praying with and carrying eight sacred bundles would be my new life. I was full. Conducting ceremony for purification lodge and vision quests were no longer what Spirit wanted for me. Praying with the chanunpas would be the only ceremony needed. Life was settled. The struggle was over and my acceptance of this new way and life was comfortable.

I had been through three hard years. It was nice to be doing the work but in a different way. All was good. I settled in and relaxed in our new home, in life with my husband and with the eight sacred bundles.

Spirit must have been laughing at my contentment. Another adjustment would appear less than seven months later, but this time it would be gentler.

CHAPTER 36

Traveling Chanunpa

I was conducting ceremony with the Thunderbird Chanunpa both alone and with groups of people needing help, for the last seven months. It is not one that I pray with daily. I only pray with it for heavy illness of the spirit.

I am called upon to pray with the eight chanunpa for many people in difficult situations. People find me for ceremony and prayers through word of mouth.

It took many years of commitment (forty-three to be exact), sacrifice and practice to develop an understanding. Much fasting, sacrificing of time and in the early years spending my money traveling and gifting to the elders. I missed many family events because of sun dances, vision quests, purification lodges and initiations.

It has never been my wish for this way of life but only something I saw in dreams and visions as a calling to follow. It is one that makes sense and works for my spirit. Elders and leaders were placed in my path as I was led to travel to places alone.

In April of 2021, I was gifted a ninth chanunpa by a woman from our former community. It was passed on from her elderly mother. Both had moved away and left our community in 2019. She had been a student of mine for several years and had completed her teachings with me years before she decided to move South. She holds a special place in my heart, like a daughter.

She contacted me and said she was moving back to New England. Her elderly mother had given her a box of sacred things and told her to take what she wanted and to give the rest to me. Her mother had been in ceremony with me on and off throughout the years.

When the box arrived, I went through it. Often times I am gifted things but I do not always keep them. I pass them on to others who follow the path of ceremony. I would keep a couple of items and gave the rest away. In the bottom of the box were a bowl and a stem. They had never been used. I called the woman to ask if she wanted it and she said no.

I also asked the woman to talk to her mother to make sure that she did intend it to be given away. Maybe she forgot that the bowl and the stem were in the box. The woman asked her mother and confirmed she wanted *me* to have it.

The story that was told to me was that her mother had bought it as a gift for her (the daughter) so she could pray with as a chanunpa. Before I met them, they were following the ceremonial path together, with the same elder that trained me.

But the daughter was gifted a chanunpa by the elder and his wife before her first vision quest, so the woman's mother put it away for twenty-two years and forgot about it.

I felt a pull towards it but I knew I did not need another one. My plate was full. I sat holding each piece for several days in prayerful meditation until I became comfortable with its presence. I asked my brother who had been a former student of mine to pray on this matter too, but the answer became clear to me with Spirit's help.

Not every chanunpa I have been gifted was for me. There have been two I have passed to others because they did not belong with me. There have been four chanunpas and three social pipes (for learning how to pray) I have gifted to students and others who followed the spiritual path.

When I held each piece of this new chanunpa and prayed I could see exactly how it wanted to be decorated on the stem. I saw the simple leather bag and tobacco pouch that needed to be made. I had a feeling of rushing water flowing around me and I became emotional each time I held the pieces in each hand separately. All I could sense was a connection to water.

Often times a chanunpa's bowl is inscribed with the maker's name. I researched him and he was a fifth generation Oglala Sioux chanunpa maker. His name means moving river. I was not surprised but it was a great confirmation to me.

The last time I sat with it in meditation while smoking the Earth Keeper Chanunpa, I asked for a sign or vision to clarify if this chanunpa was meant for me. As soon as I made my prayer, a hawk flew in front of me low to the ground and landed on a sumac tree less than five feet away. Hawks have always been a confirmation messenger for me. I accepted the answer. Though I felt a connection to the bowl and stem over the month, I wanted to make sure. The hawk assured me.

Once I accepted it, I began to build its bundle: the blanket, the small altar pieces, making the tobacco pouch and tamper and the leather bag to place it in. I knew that in time other items would be placed in the bundle.

Four weeks later, using the Medicine Chanunpa during a rainstorm, I blessed the new chanunpa and connected it to me. Immediately I began ceremony with it. I realized that the stem was wide. Much wider than the stems that I carried. It felt symbolic as a reference to me as I am a big woman. It also was shorter but not small like the Child's Chanunpa I carry/follow. It looked like me, short and wide. Perhaps that is why I was very comfortable with it.

The smoke was heavy as I prayed. The bowl, though normal in size, was made flat and was rounded inside. There was no carved funnel inside. A bowl gradually gets smaller as it reaches the bottom. But because this bowl's inside was not funneled, it put out a tremendous amount of smoke. It was overwhelming and at the same time it was teaching me its uniqueness. It also took a much longer time to smoke. The shape of the bowl required the tobacco to be lit numerous times to smoke. It seemed there was no end of smoke to complete the ceremony and yet I had only placed very small pinches of the sacred tobacco inside it.

After smoking a long time, it was after sunset and a vision appeared.

The wind picked up and I felt a presence over my left shoulder. I heard a voice, "I am Big Smoke. It needs a home. It came to you." It is all I heard and then the presence behind me was gone.

The new chanunpa took a long time to clean. The stem would need much attention. Because of the way the bowl was made, the end of the stem that connected to the bowl would collect a lot of burnt tobacco. Not only did the smoking take a long time but the cleaning before closing the bundle took a long time too. I would learn that this would be its way for a while.

The next time I prayed with it was at night. This would become our time to pray together for the next seven months. It would be hard to see in the dark, but the call for ceremony always seemed to be in the window of the full moon. This night as billows of smoke drifted upwards in my relaxed state, the vision began.

In the smoke was a face that kept changing. It morphed into different faces and I could not get a steady picture.

"Aho grandfather, I offer my smoke. Come and smoke with me." I prayed.

The face continued to change like pictures in the clouds. "Listen," *he said.*

The silence of the night began to come alive with the frogs' song. In perfect union they sang back and forth with a continuous rhythm and echo. I felt myself humming along with them. The melody was in my mind but not with words. I sang in union with them. I understood it would become the one used for this bundle.

I was transported to Webster Lake and saw myself sitting on the ground smoking this chanunpa in a particular place. I knew it well for I have been there many times. As I sat there, a frog jumped out of the grass and hopped and plopped itself at the water's edge. Then several frogs came out of the grass and followed. Plunging and jumping in the lake without fear. The last one did not jump in the lake. It sat in front of me. I sang the song I had just learned. When I was done, it jumped in my lap, surprising me. This ended the vision.

In the final smoking, a gurgling sound came from the bowl as I inhaled. It sounded like a bubbling brook. There have been times as the tobacco burns and gets to the bottom of the bowl, there is a crackling, burning sound but this was a gurgle. I paid attention. This would become the new way from then on.

When praying with a new chanunpa, I prayed with it often. A vision or guidance does not happen every time. There are times I only pray in gratitude.

After the last vision of the frogs, I brought frog medicine to the bundle. Now it had its song and medicine. It felt complete.

Big Smoke appeared at the next ceremony.

His face changed back and forth in the smoke, making several faces appear as one again.

"Aho grandfather, welcome," I spoke. I waited with attention.

"This is a Traveling Chanunpa. It brings patience and peace. The original purpose of the love of a mother trying to connect to her daughter is the intention of why it was bought to you. Remember this."

Once again in the vision, I returned to Webster Lake in my special place and found myself in prayer with this chanunpa. I waited to see if the frogs would come as I smoked. I sang the song but none came from the grass.

My vision faded to the past. I was thirty-eight and I going through a divorce from my first short-lived marriage. The date had arrived for me to go to the courthouse. The day before, my mother offered to go with me. I had not asked her. In fact, I did not want her to go with me. I could handle it. I was used to handling things myself. I did not need her support. She kept insisting.

"It will be a tough day. You don't want to be alone to face him," she argued.

Up to that day I had not revealed why I left him. I also kept that hidden. I felt like a failure after leaving him after only three and a half months of marriage. My mother had made a comment when I left him that maybe I was too used to being alone, and not meant to be married. That comment truly hurt me.

But now she was insisting to be there for me. Though I did not want her to come with me to see me sign the papers and witness my failure, I agreed.

The vision continued. She sat in the courtroom and witnessed the dissolution of my marriage. I remember looking out into the galley and seeing her face, I began to tear up in my vision. I was glad she was there. I didn't think I needed her support but I was glad to have it that day. The vision moved on to the afternoon where we shared lunch at a local diner. Now that it was over, I could share the reason why I left him.

"Mom, I never told you the real reason why I left him. I caught him in many lies and he was drinking heavily. He had become emotionally abusive and on the last night before I left it became physical. He threatened to kill me and bury me where no one would find me. I knew I could not stay."

I remember the shock on her face.

"I am proud of you, to be strong enough to leave him. I can't believe it. Your dad and I thought he was a good man."

I remember sharing some things I had been through. It was one of the very few times I did. Then the vision shifted back to Webster Lake.

I looked down through the smoke as it fell and dispersed on the ground. The one lone frog that fell in my lap in the last ceremony's vision was now clinging to the outside of the chanunpa's bowl. I feared that it would be burned from the heat as the tobacco was lit and being smoked. It held on as if it was glued. It did not move or try to jump off.

I was pulled from my vision as the frogs began to sing in the woods around me. I completed the ceremony with more questions than answers. The memory of my mother supporting me at my divorce was a good one. A mother's love trying to connect to her daughter, as Big Smoke reminded me of patience and peace. I was sure a healing was taking place for me. A memory came reminding me of my mother's love, at one of the hardest times in my life.

But I was still confused as to what was meant by a Traveling Chanunpa. I was not sure if I was to travel to places for ceremony or to travel with it every time I went somewhere in the car. I hoped answers would come soon.

It spoke of bringing patience and peace. I certainly could use more patience. The smoking and cleaning of this new one definitely took more effort and patience. I knew the story of it being purchased by a mother for her daughter was important. She purchased it with love to help create a deeper bond with her daughter through ceremony by sharing the native path.

The following week I took the bundle to the Webster Lake before it opened for the season. I went to the exact place I was shown in vision. It was late morning and only one car and boat trailer were in the parking lot. The wind was fairly mild considering I was by the water's edge.

I began my ceremony and sang the frog song in a low voice. As I smoked, prayed, and faced West, I saw a dead frog upside down in the sand of the shore about two feet away from me. Startled, I made a prayer for it and the memory of my vision of the frog clinging to the bottom of my bowl came to my mind. When I completed the ceremony, it felt important for me to bury the frog.

I found a stick and dug a hole in the wet sand. I offered tobacco in the hole, placed the frog in the hole and buried it. I sang the frog song again and thought about the medicine of the frog. They live in water and damp areas of land. They are connected to the rain and the weather. It is also transformative because a frog goes through a metamorphosis and recreates itself. It has creative ability to change from a tadpole to a frog. They are also connected to sound by using their voice near water, as water conducts sound. My voice and its song was to be used with this chanunpa.

In the next ceremony I smoked again during the day.

When I entered the silence there was no vision but a voice in my left ear. I felt Big Smoke's presence but this time I sensed the spirit was coming from the South, instead of the West. The South is the place of warmth and growth and relationships. It is believed by some, that when people die and their spirit crosses into the spirit world, they travel the Milky Way's path back towards the South, returning to where they came from.

His voice spoke, "Use this time to travel back and write your story. Start over and begin again. You now understand the meaning of the "Language of the Sacred." Share your life experience."

I smoked the Traveling Chanunpa every day. In each ceremony, I heard my own voice speaking the words and the memories of experiences to put to page. I knew what to write and would begin the book with new insight. I let go of the one hundred sixty-five pages I had previously written. They were left in the dust. All the work and hours I previously wrote was deleted. No more fear. I would know exactly what I needed to share from start to finish. The Traveling Chanunpa was used to travel back through my life and share my experiences. As the months went on, I became more comfortable with my connection to the Traveling Chanunpa and the completion of this book.

CHAPTER 37

Final Thoughts

I prayed with the Traveling Chanunpa and my thoughts came easily as though I was speaking my life's experiences with others in person. The stops and starts of writing for the last several years had ended.

My words would come through prayer. The memories were recalled on a daily basis. Each day I would pray and set aside time to write. Each day my memories were relayed in text, not as a teaching but as a witness to my life. If no one reads it, that is fine. If no one believes me, that is also fine. I am following Spirit's lead. I am making myself vulnerable and though that has always been tough for me, I am finally at peace with it.

I am coming out of my darkness of hidden experiences and allowing myself to be seen. It is time for me to completely accept who I am and my life's experiences by sharing them. I am no longer hiding in a novel and masked by a character of the imagination. Perhaps it may also be a way for others to find me and ask for help. It is in Spirit's hands. For I serve Spirit and Spirit serves the people.

The Traveling Chanunpa has helped me to work with

frog medicine to balance the emotions in my memories and transform them. It has helped me connect with my voice and the songs I have carried. It has helped me to travel back to my experiences so that I can write them down and share them. I did not choose which ones to write. They were recalled in the order that is written. The memories, though true, are my perception and understanding at the time.

The heart feels the emotion and the mind interprets them. The emotion is made personal and carries an influence. If it is a heavy one it keeps us stuck. If it is a lighter one, it may be less remembered. It seems many heavy ones are easily remembered because they have such a personal charge to them. But all memories create a system of beliefs and interpretations, ones that as children and young adults may be flawed. My memories in my visions needed to be revisited, to see through illusion and feel the emotions, to get to the truth. Words may have been spoken. Actions were done to me, some unintentional and some by wounded people themselves. All were doing their best at the time. Revisiting my feelings helped me to release the memories and emotions, ones that kept me hidden and unable to express.

I have found peace within me. Accepting who I am, knowing where I belong and how I can help the people by serving my connection to Spirit. Today through the Traveling Chanunpa, I can finally feel and accept my mother's love. The healing through the ninth chanunpa has served a purpose.

Sharing my memoire opens another door to serve Spirit and help the people. I am following the vision from the ancestors and Spirit from many years ago. It would take only eight weeks for the first draft of the memoire to be completed, before the long arduous year of the edit phase and publication.

I write the word *medicine* throughout the book. I would like to share my interpretation of the word from my personal experience. Medicine might be understood as a plant, a song, a ceremony, a gifted animal part, fur, or feather that has been shown by a spirit or real-life animal, bird, or insect during a vision. For me, medicine is what brings harmony and balance to the spirit through the selfless intention of love. Medicine is not the object or ceremony. It is a shift in spiritual essence and knowledge completed with intention.

For me, the essence has been a gift that was given through much personal sacrifice. Medicine is a gift of grace, to be able to connect to an essence of the sacred knowledge to help others who need to restore balance and harmony.

Though I use the word medicine and talk about working with medicine, *I* am not a medicine person, shaman, holy person, priestess, healer or any other title of importance. Those titles are to be given to those of specific indigenous cultures. I was not raised or born into any of those lineages. I was lucky enough to meet many special elders and experience many of their spiritual ways.

I am a seer of energy, spirits and the spirit world. I sing and pray on behalf of my relatives and relations. I continue to grow and heal my human flaws of imperfection by bridging the seen and unseen worlds to help those in need. No specific title can or will define me, for a title will create limitation.

These are my experiences. This has made me who I am today, forever changing and evolving until my last breath. It is the collective sum of all I know. I have a purpose and a calling. I choose to help others by serving my connection to the mysterious moving energy of Spirit.

I still consult for flower essence, dream interpretation, and energy readings by phone. Fees from this are given to local charities and elders. Prayers are given freely and chanunpa ceremony when Spirit gives permission.

The *Language of the Sacred*, I understand now, is not about crossing spirits of the dead. It is not about my last sun dance experience. It is not about any one or all the chanunpa bundles that I carry/follow. It is not about any teachings, spiritual path, or way to pray. Yes, all these subjects I have written about in this book are sacred to me.

What is clear to me, the *Language of the Sacred* is about sharing *my* experiences with people. What I do, who I am and how I live. It is what I know. It is the truth of my experiences that has led my life and myself to become *sacred*. All the experiences and all the memories have led to the healings and growth of who I have become as a human being.

The *language* is the manner I used to convey those experiences in my own words. Each person has a truth and understanding of their experiences that can be shared with others. It is what has made us become who we are. We all are *sacred* so our experiences are *sacred*. Sharing and voicing them is the *language of the sacred*. The sacred divine within that makes us who we are.

It does not have to be written down in a book. It is the connection we make to others when we share our journey and embrace who we are even through differences. No holding ourselves back from making a connection to others who may have a different way, path, or experience, for fear of judgement.

Yes, you and I may be judged. But life is about living, in relationship with all things, having experiences and giving it away to help others. Differences of what is sacred and important are a good thing. If we can freely open ourselves to accept our purpose and be fearless enough to express it in the world by being seen, it could leave a small imprint in someone's life and a small legacy of good.

On my fiftieth birthday, my mother wrote me a letter, to note the occasion. It was one that I had forgotten until just recently. I was clearing out boxes filled with old pictures in the basement and found it. I had not read it since that day almost thirteen years ago. I understand now, I could not truly receive her words at that time because I had not completely healed that part but today I can. Though it is personal, I would like to share a part of the letter.

"You always were special because you care and you give all of yourself to everyone. Please don't change. You will be rewarded someday. Being a good person, like you, is harder than being a bad person. A good person suffers more for loving and caring so much for others. Enjoy the good days and tolerate the tough days and you will get along just fine."

I find it no coincidence that I found her words just before I finished the book. I never thought she truly saw me or understood me or my gifts and I accepted that as fact. I was wrong. She saw what I could not completely embrace in myself at the time.

I am good. I am loving and caring. Sometimes I suffer, but mostly I just sacrifice my time and energy. As for change, we know it's impossible not to change. Hopefully my changes will always be for the better. But my purpose will never change until my last breath on earth. I choose to live for all that I can give, to help the spirits, hearts and minds of my fellow human relations and relatives.

Spirit gave me the title for this book eight years ago. It took me years to understand its meaning. Sharing my life's experience in this book as a memoir helped me to open up to express and share my life, and to allow myself to be seen by anyone who reads this book or I meet. I expose my life to the public who may not be of like mind, belief, religion, or spiritual practice.

Open to be seen by all, not only my trusted inner circle of family, friends, ceremonial community, and clients. My last two books presented as novels and works of fiction. I hid behind the characters while threading my life through it.

When I was called to the sacred tree in 2017 asking the ancestors why I was called there and to help me understand the next step for me to both serve Spirit and help people, I heard their voices. It would take me five more years, the gifting of and praying with two more chanunpas to fully understand their words.

To all of you, I offer their words of wisdom to share your own *Language of the Sacred*. You do not need to write a memoire. It can easily be expressed by sharing your experiences and being your authentic self in your daily life. Share your stories, connect with others, and impart your experiences. Life is short. Let's leave a small imprint of our *sacred*.

I challenge you with the words the ancestors have said to me, "**Stop hiding, it's time to be seen. Come out of your darkness.**"

AUTHOR BIOGRAPHY

Loralee Dubeau is the author of *There's a Whole in the Sky*, and *The Honey Pit: Finding the Grandmother's Way*. She is a lecturer and has a private consultation practice for flower essence remedies, dream interpretation, and energy readings.

She is an elder of the Good Medicine Society and follows the ceremonial path. She lives in southern Massachusetts with her husband Paul Samuels.

www.dream-flowerconsultant.com

Printed in the United States
by Baker & Taylor Publisher Services